Love's Argument

Love's Argument

Gender Relations in Shakespeare

by Marianne Novy

The University of North Carolina Press

Chapel Hill and London

Library of Congress Cataloging in Publication Data

Novy, Marianne, 1945–
Love's argument.

Includes index.
1. Shakespeare, William, 1564–1616—Criticism and
interpretation. 2. Love in literature. 3. Marriage in
literature. 4. Sex role in literature. 5. Feminism and
literature   I. Title.
PR3069.L6N6   1984   822.3'3   84-3553
ISBN 0-8078-1608-6

To My Mother,
Dorothy Kern

Contents

Acknowledgments
ix

Chapter One
Introduction: Patriarchy and Mutuality,
Control and Emotion
3

Chapter Two
"An You Smile Not, He's Gagged":
Mutuality in Shakespearean Comedy
21

Chapter Three
Patriarchy and Play in *The Taming of the Shrew*
45

Chapter Four
Giving and Taking in *The Merchant of Venice*
63

Chapter Five
Tragic Women as Actors and Audience
83

Chapter Six
Violence, Love, and Gender in *Romeo and Juliet*
and *Troilus and Cressida*
99

Contents

Chapter Seven
Marriage and Mutuality in *Othello*
125

Chapter Eight
Patriarchy, Mutuality, and Forgiveness in *King Lear*
150

Chapter Nine
Transformed Images of Manhood in the Romances
164

Chapter Ten
Shakespeare's Imagery of Gender and Gender Crossing
188

Notes
203

Index
225

Acknowledgments

Let me begin by thanking all the teachers, students, friends, colleagues, and scholars who have been interested in the questions I pursue here. Especially important to me are those who have since 1976 constituted the Modern Language Association Special Sessions on Marriage and the Family in Shakespeare and Feminist Criticism of Shakespeare. In 1974 the University of Pittsburgh gave me a Faculty Research Grant (Summer Stipend) to study marriage and the family in Elizabethan England. I spent my sabbatical semester in 1980 on a Senior Research Fellowship at the Center for the Humanities at Wesleyan University, where I enjoyed a lively lecture series, under the directorship of Richard Stamelman, entitled, "Marriage and the Ideologies of Love," and the intellectual exchange of the Wesleyan community, especially Coppélia Kahn and Elizabeth Traube, who were Faculty Fellows at the center.

I am particularly grateful to the people who have read and given me detailed comments on the entire manuscript, all of whom also helped me think through earlier versions of various chapters—Carol Thomas Neely, Meredith Skura, Robert Whitman, and Philip Wion. Thanks too to the many other people who improved and eased the writing of those earlier versions and this book by offering generous quantities of suggestions, encouragement, or both: especially Martha Andresen-Thom, Tim Flower, Simon Friedman, Miriam Gilbert, Harriet Gilliam, Gayle Greene, Ray Heffner, Robert Hinman, Coppélia Kahn, Peggy Knapp, William Kupersmith, Marcia Landy, Anita Mallinger, Barbara Mowat, Liane Ellison Norman, Maria

Luisa Nunes, Donald Petesch, Natalie Petesch, Josephine O'Brien Schaefer, William Searle, James Simmonds, Philip Smith, Cynthia Sutherland, and Carolyn Ruth Swift.

Three other people must be thanked separately. Nancy Pollard Brown inspired me (and a generation of other Shakespeare students at Trinity College) with her enthusiasm, interpretive skills, and attention that demanded our best. Diane Janeau (1940–73) was the first consciously feminist Shakespeare critic I met, when we were both graduate students at Yale. Her gifts for dialogue and drawing people out were such that more of this book than I can describe descends from our conversations. David Carrier, my husband, has enriched my life in many ways during the later stages of work on this book. Without him I never would have seen the painting reproduced on the jacket, and much else.

Versions of several chapters have appeared elsewhere, and I am grateful for permission to reprint, with revisions, the following: portions of "Shakespeare and Emotional Distance in the Elizabethan Family," *Theatre Journal* 33, no. 3 (October 1981): 316–26 (from the American Theatre Association); portions of "Demythologizing Shakespeare," *Women's Studies* 9, no. 1 (1981): 17–27; " 'And You Smile Not, He's Gagged': Mutuality in Shakespearean Comedy," *Philological Quarterly* 55 (Spring 1976): 178–94; "Patriarchy and Play in *The Taming of the Shrew*," *English Literary Renaissance* 9 (Spring 1979): 264–80; "Giving, Taking, and the Role of Portia in *The Merchant of Venice*," *Philological Quarterly* 58 (Spring 1979): 137–54; "Sex, Reciprocity, and Self-Sacrifice in *The Merchant of Venice*," in *Human Sexuality in the Middle Ages and the Renaissance*, ed. Douglas Radcliff-Umstead, University of Pittsburgh Publications on the Middle Ages and the Renaissance, vol. 4 (Pittsburgh: Pittsburgh Center for Medieval and Renaissance Studies, 1978), pp. 153–66; "Shakespeare's Female Characters as Actors and Audience," in *The Woman's Part: Feminist Criticism of Shakespeare*, ed. Carolyn Ruth Swift Lenz, Gayle Greene, and Carol Thomas Neely (Urbana: University of Illinois Press, 1980), pp. 256–70 (from the Board of

Trustees of the University of Illinois); and "Patriarchy, Mutuality, and Forgiveness in *King Lear*," *Southern Humanities Review* 13 (Fall 1979): 281–92. Thanks also to the Museo Civico of Turin for permission to reproduce *Il Gioco degli scacchi*, attributed to Sofonisba Anguissola.

Quotations from Shakespeare are taken from *William Shakespeare: The Complete Works*, gen. ed. Alfred Harbage (Baltimore: Penguin Books, 1969).

Love's Argument

Chapter 1

Introduction: Patriarchy and Mutuality, Control and Emotion

Why have Shakespeare's dramatic images of love and power in relations between the sexes fascinated so many diverse audiences? In her Commonplace Book, George Eliot noted a crucial aspect of this fascination: "It is remarkable that Shakespear's women almost always *make love*, in opposition to the conventional notion of what is fitting for women. Yet his pictures of women are belauded."[1] How can they be praised both by standard critics of the mid-nineteenth century and by current feminist critics? Juliet Dusinberre, for example, concludes that "Shakespeare saw men and women as equal in a world which declared them unequal."[2] More to the point here than Victorian writings, why were they also praised implicitly by the heterogeneous audience who made him popular in his own time? The dimension of Shakespeare's appeal that I will explore in this book is that his plays are symbolic transformations of ambivalence about gender relations and about qualities his language sometimes calls the "man" and "woman" within the self.

I suggest that Shakespeare's plays symbolically resolve in the comedies and the romances and act out in the tragedies two related but distinct conflicts—the conflict between mutuality and patriarchy and the conflict between emotion and control. Both conflicts involve the politics of gender: the first, in power relations between the sexes; the second, in the relative value of qualities symbolically associated with each gender. Patriarchy literally means the rule of fathers, and in an extended sense the rule of husbands over wives and men in general over women.[3] Mutuality, by contrast, may be defined, following Erik Erikson, as a "relationship in which partners depend on each other for the development of their respective strengths."[4] While the word itself does not necessarily imply equality or inequality, it implies sharing and companionship, recognition of the activity and subjectivity of both partners. The conflict between emotion and control often explicitly involves metaphors of gender; it also creates difficulty in relations between the sexes.[5] In plays where men try to control women whom they see as irrational, the two conflicts often coalesce.

One of the reasons Shakespeare's plays can have meaning today beyond their status as institutionalized monuments is that these conflicts still have resonance in our society. Patriarchy takes a different form in America in the 1980s than it did in England in the 1600s. Yet the language and action of the plays allow audiences of different times to see recognizable motivations in the characters. Awareness of my own engagement in performances and reading of the plays has led me to historical research about Elizabethan England, where I found evidence of the same conflicts and tensions I see in the plays. It was by no means a monolithic society.

A surprising range of evidence suggests that both patriarchy and mutuality were ideals for marriage in Elizabethan England, whatever everyday behavior was like. Marriage sermons frequently use rhetoric invoking both. For example, Henry Smith, an extremely popular preacher whose sermons were often reprinted, uses many images of partnership and friendship in his *Preparative to Marriage*, published in 1591. Husband and wife are like a pair of oars, a pair of gloves, and even David and Jonathan. He further notes, "Therefore one saith, that marriage doth signify marriage, because a plaifellow is come to make our age merrie, as Isaack and Rebeccah sported together." Yet a few pages later he declares that "the ornament of a woman is silence; and therefore the law was given to the man rather than to the woman, to shewe that he shoulde be the teacher and shee the hearer."[6] Smith is one of a number of puritan preachers of the late sixteenth and early seventeenth century in whom William and Malleville Haller find a similar combination of attitudes: "Everything in the past of these men required them to think of the family as patriarchal, and yet, the more important the family became to them as an institution, the more important became the role they found themselves assigning to women in the life of men."[7] The Hallers emphasize these preachers' praise of marriage as spiritual companionship and their respect for the responsibility and active personal virtues to be shown by women in marriage. While a number of historians have described this combination of patriarchy and mutuality as puritan in origin, more recently Lawrence Stone sees it as present also in Anglican moral theology and Kathleen Davies has shown that it can be found as well in writings about marriage by Catholics such as William Harrington and Richard Whitford.[8]

Such sermons, of whatever theological bent, contain no suggestion that this combination of ideals might involve tension. Other kinds of historical evidence, concerned with practice and not ideals, give a different picture. Most strikingly, there seems to have been increased strain on aristocratic marriages just at the time Shakespeare was writing. Between 1595 and 1620, one-third of the older peers, according to Stone, were estranged or separated from their wives.[9] Was this because, as he suggests in The Crisis of the Aristocracy, 1558–1641, the middle-class belief in equality had risen to the aristocracy and emboldened women to struggle for better treatment?[10] Or was it because, as he suggests in his later Family, Sex, and Marriage in England, 1500–1800, intensified enforcement of patriarchy was reducing women's previous freedom?[11] Whether the situation of Elizabethan women was better or worse than that of their predecessors, tension between patriarchy and companionship existed in the practice of the aristocracy, as it existed without acknowledgment in the sermons. The middle-class controversial literature about women and the diaries discussed by Keith Wrightson suggest similar tensions elsewhere.[12] I am not, however, suggesting explicit Elizabethan awareness of a conflict between patriarchy and mutuality; it is largely the recent development of feminist theory that has made it possible, now that patriarchy need not be taken for granted as a cultural belief, to examine what extends it and what challenges it, to see the ideals that in practice could be harmoniously compromised or could produce an unarticulated sense of tension.[13]

But the plays are theatrical transformations of the social tensions that give them some of their subject matter and their appeal to a divided audience, not examples of Elizabethan social history. Evidence about the typicality in its society of events in a play can help interpret the play only if we take into account the specifics of how the play presents those events; spectators may admire behavior in a play that they would not admire in real life, if the playwright is skillful enough in using their conflicting feelings as well as the conventions of theater.

Using such skill, in his comedies and romances Shakespeare creates images of gender relations that keep elements of both patriarchy and mutuality in suspension. Though the balance may tip in one direction or another, the predominance of playfulness and of festive disguise helps to remove threatening elements in the comedies. Even in *The Taming of the Shrew*, as we shall see in Chapter 3, Petruchio is not only a dominant husband but also a player of games he wants Kate to join. When she finally does, it is partly a matter of beginning to speak the same language; she agrees to follow him in renaming the sun as the moon and elaborates on his greeting of an old man as a young girl. Because Kate and Petruchio share in this game of verbally creating a new world in which anything can be its opposite, we can, if we wish, see game qualities in her long speech on women's duty to their husbands. Petruchio's power as husband coalesces with his power as leader of a game, and we may take as primary whichever definition of Kate's relationship to him we prefer—patriarchal or playful.

In most Shakespearean comedies, as we will see in Chapters 2 and 4, the balance is different. The women may control the games, like Portia or Rosalind. Even those less in command—Viola or Beatrice—escape the trials that Kate undergoes. They and their lovers speak each other's language in most of their encounters, although often through some kind of disguise. Before the characters directly offer and ask love, they ask and yield response to wit and verbal style. In all of these comedies the women are active throughout and the relationships are presented as developing by a mutuality of talking together. Shakespeare even allows them to criticize the limits that their society places on them as women—both by their words and by their competence in the masculine disguise that removes some of these limits. Nevertheless, as Clara Claiborne Park has shown, several of the heroines end their comedies with ritual gestures of submission.[14] Even masculine disguise can be taken as a softening of female assertiveness because it permits us to take anything a woman says or does while in disguise as only part of a role to be discarded. And, as Carolyn Heilbrun has pointed out, we may take the relationships created by some of these couples as allowing the women more freedom only because their condition is still courtship and not marriage.[15] Thus again Shakespeare gives us an ambiguous picture in which both those who emphasize patriarchy and those who emphasize a mutuality that involves female activity can find some elements to please them and, if they wish, take those as the essentials.

Tragic heroines like Juliet, Cordelia, and Desdemona also combine strength and flexibility attractively. Desdemona, for example, bravely chooses Othello and defends her choice before Venice, but she uses the argument that she is acting just as her mother did in following her father. As

Chapter 7 will show, her combination of partnership and deference leaves her vulnerable to Othello's attack. Juliet's attempt to reconcile mutuality and patriarchy also leads to death, as we will see in Chapter 6, because the feud, like war, identifies masculinity with violence.

Later tragedies combine mutuality and patriarchy in a synthesis more clearly destructive from the start. Lady Macbeth and Volumnia accept some social limitations on what women can do directly at the same time as they seek vicarious achievement by encouraging husband and son to the violence they cannot themselves commit. Just as other female characters can be praised for widely diverging reasons, these can be analyzed by feminists as displaying stereotypically feminine qualities—influencing men through traditional roles of wife and mother—although traditionalist critics can describe them as masculine.

The romances dramatize women's vulnerability and familial identity more than do the comedies, but they conclude with more emphatic portrayals of female resilience. However much Hermione, Imogen, Perdita, and Miranda seem familially defined, they all maintain some verbal independence from men. But Leontes still assumes that Paulina, who has converted and punished him and apparently brought his wife back from the dead, will agree to his arrangement of her marriage to Camillo.

Not surprisingly, the comedies emphasize more the negotiation of different social ideals while the tragedies stress more the intrapsychic struggle between emotion and control; the romances link the themes further as they link family ties and family feeling. The chapters that follow will, in general, be weighted accordingly, but both concerns persist throughout Shakespeare's plays. In his treatment of the conflict between emotion and control, as well as that between mutuality and patriarchy, Shakespeare seems to be transforming a conflict of Elizabethan culture. We do not need to accept all of Stone's claims in *Family, Sex, and Marriage* about Elizabethan "psychic numbing" to see in his work, combined with that of other historians as different as Alan Macfarlane and Randolph Trumbach, evidence that there was an ideal personality type valued by many Elizabethans—an ideal that kept feelings of attachment and grief under strict control but was more ready to act out feelings of anger.[16] To borrow Stephen Greenblatt's term, it was a kind of ideal for self-fashioning.[17]

We can see the attempt to transmit this ideal in, for example, letters of advice from aristocratic fathers to sons, which, according to Stone, "normally express a thoroughly pessimistic view of human nature, full of canny and worldly-wise hints about how to conduct personal relations which leave little room for generosity, faith, hope or charity" (FSM, p. 96). We can see it in the sermons that warned parents not to love their children too much, because they might die. Perhaps we can also see it in the frequent separation of children from their parents: upperclass children were sent out to wet nurses and often, around the age of ten, to boarding school; about the same age many middle- and lower-middle class children moved to their master's household to begin work as domestic servants, laborers, and apprentices (pp. 105–14). And we may glimpse the effect of the expression allowed to anger in the "extraordinary amount of casual violence at all levels of society" (p. 93) that Stone finds in the diaries, correspondence, and legal records from the fifteenth to the seventeenth century.

Stone gives largely unexplored hints that patterns and norms of emotional warmth differed according to sex. The parents quoted as sounding distant from children are mostly fathers; furthermore, Stone sees fathers as colder to daughters than to sons, more likely to consider daughters as only a drain on their money. He also provides anecdotes in which women want more emotional involvement in marriage than do men (p. 105). All this suggests that the letters of advice were attempts to initiate sons to the coldness expected of the adult male and that the model of emotional control was primarily a masculine ideal.[18] Because masculinity was more valued than femininity, the

emphasis on control could influence women as well, and
any woman's deviations from it could be seen as signs of
typically feminine weakness. Popular thought often identified women with passion and men with reason, with an
emphasis on the necessary subordination of the first pair
to the second; since women, whether nurses or mothers,
had primary responsibility for child-rearing, they were associated with everyone's first discovery of emotions.[19]
Many documents suggest that Elizabethan men were often
suspicious of women, and this suspicion may very well
coalesce with a conventional masculine ideal of emotional
distance.

In any event, attempts to follow this ideal would lead
both sexes to difficulties in establishing and maintaining
relationships; consequent frustration could fuel the anger
expressed; throughout life one might be influenced by an
emotional dependence that one constantly denied. If emotional distance was an ideal for self-fashioning, it could co-
exist with hatred and with (denied) love.

But even examples of its transmission suggest other
complexities of feeling. If aristocratic fathers told sons not
to trust anyone, perhaps sons provoked the advice by trusting people. If sermons threatened that God might take
away a child whose parents were too fond, some parents
must have grieved intensely for their children. Furthermore, as Alan Macfarlane suggests, Elizabethan society
probably included "some loving parents and some cruel
parents, some people bringing up their children in a rigid
way, others in a relaxed atmosphere, deep attachment between certain husbands and wives, frail emotional bonds
in other cases."[20] The contrasting elements in this mix
would not remain inert; at least some people would notice
the differences and would be affected by them. Probably
Elizabethan England was not so much Stone's "low-affect"
society as one divided within itself about emotion.

The relevance of this conflict, as well as the one between
mutuality and patriarchy, to Shakespeare's original audience may be heightened if we consider that, as Louis

Adrian Montrose has pointed out, "perhaps half the population was under twenty, and that the youthfulness of Shakespeare's society was reflected in the composition of his audience."[21] Most Elizabethan marriages took place between partners in their middle and late twenties—and thus a very high proportion of Shakespeare's audience was delaying marriage, considering its possibility, or negotiating its early stages.[22] A high percentage of the males in the audience had not gained the social status of manhood or were at an age when they were still negotiating their relations to its ideals as well.

If establishing or admitting emotional ties was difficult for many in Shakespeare's audience partly because of their ideals of control and other social restrictions, this ambivalence may have contributed to the appeal of his plays. In the tragedies, the cost of either denying or affirming connections can be mortal; in the comedies and romances, connections mean life rather than death. But in the background of all genres are distances—literal and psychological—between parents and children, and disguises—literal and psychological—that dramatize the difficulties of trusting and understanding as the characters use them to strive for control. Because the tone and construction of the comedies often conceal the importance of this conflict, its most obvious examples are in the tragedies, and I will begin with them.

Coriolanus is the tragic hero whose behavior Shakespeare most explicitly links to child-rearing ideals of emotional distance. His mother tells us: "When yet he was but tender-bodied and the only son of my womb . . . , I, considering how honor would become such a person, that it was no better than picture-like to hang by th' wall, if renown made it not stir, was pleased to let him seek danger where he was like to find fame. To a cruel war I sent him, from whence he returned, his brows bound with oak" (1.3.5–6, 9–14). He tries, as he says, to "stand / As if a man were author of himself / And knew no other kin" (5.3.35–37) to the point of threatening to destroy his own native

Rome and his family along with it, but at his mother's pleas
he finally relents and takes her hand.[23] The ideal of distance proves impossible to maintain and Shakespeare suggests, throughout, the conflict between Coriolanus's emotions and his ideal. Even when he cites the proverbs of
emotional control, it is as part of his mother's earlier
admonitions:

> You were used
> To say extremities was the trier of spirits;
> That common chances common men could bear; . . .
>   . . . You were used to load me
> With precepts that would make invincible
> The heart that conned them.   (4.1.3–5, 9–11)

Coriolanus sounds like Stone's typical aggressive, egocen-
tric aristocrat, molded by cold child-rearing practices; but
Shakespeare, unlike Stone, forces us to see the strength of
the emotional bonds that remain underneath the cultural
ideal. Coriolanus cannot simply keep on killing outside his
family but has to face his feelings toward them. He has to
face the anger behind his distance and the dependence
behind his anger.

King Lear, too, is about conflicts between distance and
emotion in relations between parent and child. Lear cannot freely express his love for Cordelia but must set up his
intended gift as a reward for her performance in a contest
he controls, and then he disowns her for insisting on her
autonomy and not playing her part properly. While his
other daughters treat him cruelly, he strives to control himself and deny his emotional vulnerability, but these attempts break down in his madness. Only Cordelia can save
him, and only briefly. When he dies, torn between realiz-
ing that she is lost forever and straining for a word from
her, it is clear that they are indissolubly bound to each
other. With a similar lack of insight, Gloucester dismisses
Edmund with "He hath been out nine years, and away he
shall again" (1.1.31–32) and then doubts Edgar's love on
the flimsiest of evidence manufactured by Edmund; he un-

derestimates the anger of the one and the love of the other and the impact that both will have on his life. Edgar, his identity disguised, cares for his father in the blindness that his brother helped to cause. When Edgar reveals himself, Gloucester dies of mingled grief and joy, like Lear showing in his death the strength of his connection to his child.

When trust is created in the tragedies, it is a precarious achievement in a perilous world. As Chapter 7 will show, Othello's relationship with Desdemona breaks down in the context of threats analogous to those Stone suggests— distrust resulting from ideals of emotional control. Living down the stereotype of the passionate African and the un-ease of the exile, he is a hero of strong feelings he strives to control. Throughout, the cynical and manipulative world view has its spokesman in Iago. Emotionally detached from his own wife, he can influence Othello partly because of the basic sense of insecurity and distance that makes it difficult for Othello to believe in the initial success of his love and partly because of Othello's ideals of coolness.[24] From the beginning he has denied the presence of "heat" or "young affects" in his love. When his jealousy shows him his passionate attachment to Desdemona, he believes it is alien to his true character and plans to kill her to restore his self-control: "I'll not expostulate with her, lest her body and beauty unprovide my mind again" (4.1.200–202). When he discovers her fidelity, only his own death can restore that control, and his death is equally an attempt to reaffirm their relationship.

In the comedies, the conflicts between emotions and control usually do not require death for their resolution. Thus the distance between parent and child is often presented largely as geographic distance and physical disguise. In *The Comedy of Errors*, Antipholus of Syracuse speaks movingly of his separation from his parents, caused by the romance plot conventions of tempest and shipwreck. Here, and in the romances as well, such externally enforced family separation could dramatize the frequent separation of Elizabethan families by death and standard child-rearing

practices. Feeling separation as rejection probably alter-
nated with feeling it as beyond human control, like tempest and shipwreck. The reticence that the Antipholus
brothers keep in their reunion—they never speak directly
to each other—suggests that the ideal of emotional control may continue its claims even at the happy ending. At
the corresponding point, the Menaechmi twins of Shakespeare's source speak to each other with feeling, and we
might expect even more eloquence at the father-son reunion not found in the source, but we do not get it.[25] This
inarticulacy allows the actors to fill in with gestures, of
course, and the audience with imagination; nevertheless,
one character, the mother, has a long speech of joy at the
resolution and her imagery turns on childbirth:

> Thirty-three years have I but gone in travail
> Of you, my sons; and till this present hour
> My heavy burden ne'er deliverèd.   (5.1.402–4)

The disguises in Shakespeare's comedies can be related
to emotional distance in a number of ways. The self-control that masculine disguise imposes on women is an analogue of the control that the masculine ideal imposes on
men; the disguise suggests, too, that the women may share
in that ideal of control. Rosalind begins *As You Like It* griev-
ing for her banished father, but when she meets him she
does not at once reveal the identity behind her disguise.
"He asked me of what parentage I was. I told him, of as
good as he; so he laughed and let me go" (3.4.33–34). For
all of her warmth, Rosalind maintains some freedom and
distance from her father until the last scene. But unlike
Edgar's analogous delay in revealing himself, this one has
no mortal consequences.

For the lovers in the comedies, disguise can dramatize
the difficulties of establishing emotional connections, although it also fosters such connections by giving less risky
ones time to develop. Rosalind's disguise may express ambivalence about abandoning herself to her love for Orlando; in many of the comedies, the characters' inability to

see through disguise suggests their mixed feelings about forming close ties. Sherman Hawkins has noted the internal obstacles to love in what he calls the comedies of the closed world (*The Comedy of Errors, The Taming of the Shrew, Love's Labor's Lost, Much Ado About Nothing,* and *Twelfth Night*); Orlando's initial inability to speak to Rosalind suggests an internal obstacle in him as well.[26] Proteus, Berowne, Bassanio, Orlando, Claudio, and Orsino all make mistakes about the identity of the women they finally marry. These mistakes, and analogous mistakes made by Phebe and Olivia, are, in part, dramatic images of the postures of emotional distance that can remain even when falling in love; many of these characters are comically self-centered or fascinated with an idealized image—often unattainable—more than with a human being. Often the degree to which the characters grow is open to question, and the conclusion relies primarily on the literal removal of disguise for the sense of overcoming barriers to relationship.

Most of the conversations between comic lovers involve either literal disguise or hostility. Either alternative externalizes such ambivalence as an audience may have about emotional ties. For an audience with a veneer of defenses, Beatrice and Benedick, who begin as mockers of love, consciously cool and rational, or Viola and Rosalind, who in their disguises can never express their love directly, make ideal protagonists; their mockery or concealment of love makes it impossible to dismiss them as pretending to love insincerely. The combination of verbal rapport and concealment in the text permits the audience here, as in the reunions of *The Comedy of Errors,* to fill in with whatever depth they can imagine.

The importance of such disguised conversations in mediating emotional distance becomes more evident if we observe the problems of the problem comedies. There the disguised contact that forms the basis for the final marriages is physical—the bed trick—not verbal, and cannot be played out for the audience. Angelo and Mariana do not meet onstage until the final scene of *Measure for Measure.*

Angelo and Bertram are more clearly split than the heroes of the earlier comedies between the general coldness of their personalities and the sexual drives that trap them into marriages with women for whom they express no personal warmth. The women love, but the couples cannot work out the marriages by themselves; men in authority must impose them.

The romances, like the tragedies, treat difficulties deeper than premarital caution, but present more possibilities for reconciliation. In *The Winter's Tale*, the comparison of control to stone and emotion to flesh—an image Shakespeare has used since the sonnets—becomes part of the visual imagery of the play, as the figure of Hermione moves, in the imagination of the audience offstage and on, from statue to live human being. "Does not the stone rebuke me," Leontes asks, "For being more stone than it?" (5.3.37–38). Its animation is a theatrical parallel for the movement toward feeling for Hermione in Leontes himself. Here, as in most of the other romances, emotional control is less powerful as an ideal than in the tragedies. Leontes' condemnation of Hermione is hard to see as having even a wrong-headed grandeur. We will see in Chapter 9 that the older characters express emotions of familial attachment more readily and the young fall in love more quickly.

Shakespeare's language, as Chapter 10 will show in more detail, often makes explicit gender associations for the conflict between emotion and control. His characters, especially in bereavement, identify expressions of feeling with femininity. Laertes says of his tears for Ophelia's death, "When these are gone, / The woman will be out" (4.7.187–88). When Sebastian thinks his sister Viola is dead, he says, "I am yet so near the manners of my mother that, upon the least occasion more, mine eyes will tell tales of me" (2.1.35–37), and Claudius censures Hamlet's mourning by saying " 'Tis unmanly grief" (1.2.94). When Lear struggles to deny the pain he feels at his daughters' rejection, he cries, "O, how this mother swells up toward my

heart! / Hysterica passio, down, thou climbing sorrow"
(2.4.54–55). Later he prays:

> Touch me with noble anger,
> And let not women's weapons, water drops,
> Stain my man's cheeks.   (2.4.271–73)

This pattern of associations often goes beyond words.
Most of the rejections of children are rejections of daughters by fathers: Leonato and Hero, Old Capulet and Juliet,
Brabantio and Desdemona, Cymbeline and Imogen. Furthermore, fathers' rejections of daughters, like husbands'
rejections of wives, usually result from suspicion of female
sexuality—in one case (Perdita) the daughter is thought to
be conceived adulterously; in the others, the fathers object
to their wishes, real or apparent, to love men other than
their fathers or their fathers' choices. By contrast, neither
mothers nor fathers reject sons because of their sexual behavior. Not only is sexual behavior the most frequent reason given for rejecting daughters and wives, but verbal attacks on a mother's sexuality may suddenly appear in any
threat of rejection from the family, even if the mother herself never appears in the play. Lear says to Regan: "I would
divorce me from thy mother's tomb, / Sepulchring an
adultress" (2.4.126–27), and Isabella to Claudio: "Heaven
shield my mother played my father fair, / For such a
warpèd slip of wilderness / Never issued from his blood"
(3.1.141–43).

In general, attempts at self-control that inhibit relationships are more central to Shakespeare's male characters
than to his female ones. This does not mean that all the
women are warm and compassionate while all the men are
cold and controlled, as the passage from Isabella's tirade
should remind us; but the characters often speak as if such
qualities have each an appropriate sex. Almost all Shakespearean heroes in the tragedies and several in the romances and problem plays distrust both female characters
and qualities in themselves that they consider female. Yet

they do love those characters and possess those qualities. They ultimately find it necessary to express their emotions more than their society's ideals of control permit. They learn, like Lear, that they must weep. Thus the plays implicitly criticize the view that manhood is opposed to feeling. Occasionally the characters themselves hint at different ideals, as Macduff does in his bereavements when he answers "Dispute it like a man" with "I shall do so; / But I must also feel it as a man" (4.3.220–21). And in the romances a few of the men learn to reverse the disparagement of female characteristics and can welcome family reunion with the imagery of childbirth that in *The Comedy of Errors* only a woman could use: Cymbeline says, on finding his children again, "O, what am I? / A mother to the birth of three? Ne'er mother / Rejoiced deliverance more" (5.5.368–70).

→   Although the two sets of oppositions we have been discussing often coalesce, it is important not to collapse them by presuming that important female characters are always unambiguously on the side of emotion. For instance, we can see Rosalind maintaining her disguise and Beatrice insulting Benedick as attempting both emotional control and a relationship of mutuality rather than male dominance. Most of the plays I shall discuss contain material for a reading in terms of both conflicts, though one or the other may predominate. I concentrate here on plays in which love between the sexes is a central issue: the form these conflicts take in the history plays, or in more male-dominated tragedies such as *Julius Caesar*—plays about state power and relationships between men, both loving and hostile—is
→ material for another book.

Norman Rabkin has described many ways in which Shakespeare is an artist of complementarity.[27] I believe Shakespeare's treatment of the two conflicts I have been discussing, and of the relationship between them, shows other ways in which his vision encompasses opposites. The imaginative strength he gives to opposing ideals helped the plays appeal to their first audiences, with all their emotional division, and helps them keep the attention of the divided audiences of today as well.

But another dimension of the plays' power is that the genre of drama is particularly apt for dealing with both of these conflicts. In approaching other literary forms, we confront a text; in approaching drama, we confront human beings in performance. Though stage conventions circumscribe the interaction of audience and actors, nevertheless their simultaneous presence across from each other is an important part of the theatrical experience. It involves the audience directly in confronting human beings who belong to a group defined as other—an experience in some ways rather like that of the social relations of the sexes. Parallels are not simple: from one point of view, the actors act or take initiative, in the conventional role of men, while the audience is passive or responds, in the conventional role of women. But the actors' acts are, by the nature of theater, apart from the larger world; actors are more like women if the audience considers them either trivial or mysterious and itself, like men, the norm. These analogies, however, model actor-audience relations on gender relations of patriarchy; a less hierarchical view would emphasize mutual dependence and the audience's active, intimate involvement in the experience of the theater. I shall show in the next chapter how the comedies, especially, parallel images of mutuality between actor and audience, jester and listener, with that between lovers.

Similarly, the audience must confront the conflict between emotion and control. As I shall discuss in Chapter 5, actors, like women, have been closely associated with the expression of emotion; for the Elizabethan audience especially, the ready expression of emotions, thought to be contagious, was one source of the mysterious and dangerous power actors and women could have—indeed, one reason for the social subordination of both. Again, the more an audience is open to emotion, the more the impact of the play, especially if it is a tragedy. But a necessary limit of the audience's emotion, as of its mutuality with the

actors, is the underlying awareness that the play is a play.[28]
Conflicts about dealing with emotion and with a group
defined as other are thus an inherent part of the theatrical
experience.

If actor/audience relations are something like the social
relations between the sexes, social relations between the
sexes, in turn, are often like the theater in another way—
because societies pattern appropriate behavior for each
gender in roles that are imitated, learned, and played
somewhat as are theatrical roles. As I shall discuss in Chapter 10, the Elizabethan use of boy actors to play women's
parts must have kept this analogy in Shakespeare's mind. A
few critics have argued that Shakespeare was really writing
about boys, not about women, but it is more likely that
here again his imagination seized upon the specificity of
his medium—the Elizabethan stage. Shakespeare was indeed striving for theatrical effectiveness; in the process his
material became both the theater and his society's sexual
arrangements.

Chapter Two

"An You Smile Not, He's Gagged":
Mutuality in Shakespearean Comedy

One of Shakespeare's approximate contemporaries, Sir Nicholas Poyntz, trying to negotiate a marriage with a widow, wrote, "Let me not win her love like a fool, nor spend long time like a boy. As God shall help, I am much troubled to think I must speak to any woman one loving word."[1] Extreme as this attitude sounds, his comparisons are interesting. Spending words on courtship would be reducing his autonomous manhood to the condition of a fool or a boy. In Shakespeare's plays as well, winning love by talking is acting like a fool, not simply because of the irrationality of love but also because the suppliant lover is acting like the Elizabethan court fool or jester; his words show his dependence on a response of acceptance. Wooing speeches and jokes are both attempts to establish relationship. Shakespeare's comedies, as they develop, make the most of this parallel. His lovers act like fools in both senses of the word, and so, in their own way, do the characters that surround them. Indeed, perhaps the irrationality of the comic world is only a detached observer's description of the mutual dependence of its characters.

In the romantic comedies, imagery, structure, and characterization all emphasize the theme of mutual dependence. The characters are defined largely in terms of their relationships, or potential relationships, ranging from love, friendship, kinship, financial exchange, and camaraderie in wit to exploitation and hostility. The population forms a network with various kinds of bonds; those characters initially excluded gradually respond to others and reveal their capacity for connections.

At the culmination of Shakespeare's career in writing romantic comedies, in *Much Ado About Nothing*, *As You Like It*, and *Twelfth Night*, this emphasis on mutual dependence becomes particularly evident. The clowns and fools become professional jesters, more conscious of their wit. Characters like Beatrice, Benedick, Rosalind, and Viola modulate from amateur jester to lover or play both at once.

The lover and the jester both seek mutuality. Both express a need that, as John Macmurray says in his explanation of the concept of mutuality, "can only be satisfied by another person's action. The behavior . . . is therefore incomplete until it meets with a response from the other."[2] As Malvolio says of Feste, "Unless you laugh and minister occasion to him, he is gagged" (1.5.81–82). Similarly, Touchstone complains, "When a man's verses cannot be understood, nor a man's good wit seconded with the forward child, understanding, it strikes a man more dead than a great reckoning in a little room" (3.3.9–12). A jester whom no one ever considers funny can scarcely have a firm identity as a jester. Amateur jesters, while not socially subordinate like the professionals, still emotionally depend on a response—especially if they are in love with one of their listeners. Yet, however risky, the jester's role has its power. Olivia's response to Feste's witty catechizing is a gain for her as well as appreciation for him; she begins to move out of her initial isolation. Providing her with material for response, he permits her to enter into relationship by playing an alert audience to him. Here as in all developing mutuality, persons take on roles that relate them; theatrical imagery is inherent in conceptualizing the process, and drama is a genre particularly appropriate for its exploration.

Shakespeare's most interesting comic lovers develop their relationship by a similar process of interplay in which each encourages the other. In this way they differ notably from most lovers of two previous literary traditions. Classical Roman comedy might end with an assurance of the hero's marriage, but it was usually more a proof of his triumph over others than the culmination of his relationship with his bride; she does not need to appear or speak on stage, and many plays by Plautus and Terence easily dispense with her active participation.[3] Here the conventional contrast between male activity and female passivity becomes so extreme as to give very little importance to the woman's subjective response. In the Petrarchan tradition of love poetry, the situation is more complex; the man may ask for a response, but his poems are concerned with his own subjectivity and not his lady's. Whether the woman is ignored or idealized, the focus is on the man, the initiator; both traditions are patriarchal, although Petrarchan poetry superficially exalts women.

At least one iconological tradition in Shakespeare's time specifically celebrated mutuality in love; classical and Renaissance mythographers pictured a special god, Anteros, as presiding over love in return.[4] He was frequently portrayed with his older brother, Eros; often, as in Ben Jonson's masque *A Challenge at Tilt*, they competed over whether spontaneous love or reciprocal love is stronger. The mutuality imagined here differentiates between the roles of initiative and response. The most interesting relationships in Shakespeare's romantic comedies not only transcend the one-sidedness of the classical comedy and Petrarchan traditions, but they also transcend the clear differentiation between lover and returner of love, or reverse the conventional expectation that the male will be the initiator.

The visual disguise that permits Rosalind and Viola to transcend conventional courtship practice has its verbal correlative in their concealment of feeling; in a more realistic mode, the hostile facades of Beatrice and Benedick maintain an analogous concealment. Much of each play develops the characters' relationships before they directly offer and ask love; instead, they ask and yield response to wit and verbal style. The linguistic mutuality at issue here differs from emotional mutuality but hints at its possibility. By this combination of verbal rapport and concealment, they transcend the simplicity of comic stock characters and encourage the audience not only to a suspension of disbelief but also to a sense of psychological complexity.

→ Mutuality is not equally achieved in all of Shakespeare's romantic comedies, but the failure is sometimes part of the point. In the early *Comedy of Errors* and *Two Gentlemen of Verona*, characters who talk about their concern for relationships at great length often fail to work them out in dialogue. Both comedies make game of this failure. Adriana, who feels she is losing her husband, tries to win him back by saying at length that she is "undividable, incorporate, / . . . better than thy dear self's dearer part" (2.2.121–22)—yet she is actually addressing her husband's twin. In *Two Gentlemen*, Valentine claims:

> Silvia is myself. . . .
> She is my essence, and I leave to be,
> If I be not by her fair influence
> Fostered, illumined, cherished, kept alive.
>
> (3.1.172, 182–84)

But earlier he has missed the transparent message she sends him in the love letter she tells him to write. Valentine's idealism about both love and friendship has the ludicrous result that he offers to give up his Silvia to Proteus to show that he has forgiven Proteus for his attempt to rape her. The satire in Shakespeare's treatment of Valentine's disposal of Silvia has eluded many critics, who have either gasped with horror or tried to explain others' gasps away by presuming uncritical reference to the code of friendship. What has, perhaps, obscured the point most is that neither pair of lovers here talks together enough to assure that the play itself has a standard against which to measure the melodramatic rape attempt and forgiveness.

In *Love's Labor's Lost* the contrast between mutuality and

self-centered or naively idealistic words about love is a
more explicit theme.[5] When the wooing lords Petrarchize
at length, they signally fail to consider the ladies' feelings;
by the end of the play, Berowne's inverted Petrarchan wit is
still not enough to win Rosaline because of a similar failure. She gives a significant reason for the penance she imposes—a year's jesting in a hospital:

> A jest's prosperity lies in the ear
> Of him that hears it, never in the tongue
> Of him that makes it.   (5.2.851–53)

Berowne is to learn to consider mutuality in wit by confronting an audience unlikely to respond because of their
own feelings. By implication, this penance will also teach
him to consider mutuality in love.

In the problem comedies, by contrast, the concluding
marriages are arranged in spite of the relative lack of mutuality between the partners—this is one of their main
problems.[6] In these plays the main example of mutuality is
the officially suspect relationship between Claudio and Juliet; we never see them talk together, and hear the concept
introduced thus:

> Duke So then it seems your most offenseful act
>   Was mutually committed?
> Juliet   Mutually.
> Duke Then was your sin of heavier kind than his.
>   (2.3.26–28)

But before we look, in other chapters, at plays in which
mutuality breaks down, or can be overshadowed by patriarchal elements, let us examine the three plays in which its
achievement is predominant.

Much Ado About Nothing is particularly noteworthy for the ←
contribution of mutuality in wit to the unconventional final relationship of the two main characters. Beatrice's attitude toward Benedick's wit parallels her ambivalent emotional response to him. Her first words to him follow up an
obscure joke of his by saying, "I wonder that you will still

be talking, Signior Benedick. Nobody marks you" (1.1.103–4). She gives him the attention he needs at the same time as she mocks that need. This paradoxical pattern continues as he greets her quick though mocking alertness by calling her Lady Disdain; the insult in her retort is also an acknowledgment of her responsiveness. "Is it possible Disdain should die while she hath such meet food to feed it as Signior Benedick?" (1.1.106–7). The two of them take over the scene for a match of verbal rejections that play on each other's words so carefully as to demonstrate an attentive commitment on both sides of their "merry war."

When the disguised Benedick meets Beatrice at the masked ball, the war escalates as each of them attacks, among other things, the other's wit. Beatrice describes Benedick as "the Prince's jester, a very dull fool" (2.1.122). She finishes with another hit at his need for response. If the conversation is reported to Benedick, she says, "He'll but break a comparison or two on me; which peradventure, not marked or not laughed at, strikes him into melancholy; and then there's a partridge wing saved, for the fool will eat no supper that night" (2.1.131–35). Benedick's subsequent conversations with Claudio and Don Pedro suggest that Beatrice's insults have put him into the same melancholy she predicted would follow a lack of response to his wit.

The ambivalent partnership in which insults show mutual dependence is threatening to break off when Don Pedro and Leonato devise their plot. Each of the wits is to overhear a description of the other in the grip of passionate and unrequited love. Beatrice and Benedick are to imagine each other as wishing to ask for a response of love and prevented by fear of lack of response. "If she should make tender of her love, 'tis very possible he'll scorn it; for the man, (as you know all), hath a contemptible spirit" (2.3.166–68). Believing this description of each other's concealed feelings permits Beatrice and Benedick to love while seeing themselves as responding only in recom-

pense[7]—not as initiating a request for love with its atten-
dant risk of rejection; they feel assured of mutuality in their
love.

In the final scene, Beatrice and Benedick transform an
illusion–belief in each other's lovesickness—into a consciously maintained joke. Love and wit coalesce here as
earlier verbal denial of one accompanied verbal denial of
the other. In a dialogue where the balanced structure of
repartee embodies their equal participation in the relationship, both of them begin by maintaining their own ratio-
nality and reveal their belief in the other's abandonment to
feelings:

> Benedick They swore that you were almost sick for me.
> Beatrice   They swore that you were well-nigh dead for
> me.
> Benedick 'Tis no such matter. Then you do not love me?
> Beatrice   No, truly, but in friendly recompense.
>
> (5.4.80–83)

But the joking quality of the recompense is already beginning to appear, since according to their words there is no
need for recompense. The shared insistence on charging
each other with lovesickness—the shared insistence on
playing the role of the one who responds rationally—becomes plainly a willed pretext and a joke.

> Benedick Come, I will have thee; but, by this light, I take
> thee for pity.
> Beatrice   I would not deny you; but, by this good day, I
> yield upon great persuasion, and partly to save
> your life, for I was told you were in a consump-
> tion.   (5.4.92–96)

For all the wit in the conclusion of Much Ado, the play
suggests a serious point about different kinds of mutuality
in love. One kind of mutuality—in love, or in wit—clearly
differentiates the roles of the partners. The lover is distinguished from the returner of love, Eros from Anteros, and

the jester from the listener. Characters like Beatrice and Benedick, however, are capable of being both listener and wit. In their complexity they are also capable of a more complex and less asymmetrical love relationship, in which a more complete sharing is possible. (This is not to deny that role differentiation between the sexes remains in other aspects of the play's society; Beatrice cannot fight a duel.)

The Petrarchan tradition of love poetry may conceive the role of the lover's partner as beloved rather than as lover in return, and in this emphasis the beloved's feelings, and the lover's need for mutuality, may be not merely shaped by role differentiation but in effect disregarded. Verbally the lover's poems may ask for a response, but they are concerned with his own subjectivity. Petrarchan poetry, Richard Young has suggested, has two basic forms—the blazon or idealizing description of the lady and the intro-spection of the lover, a description of his sufferings.[8] Both kinds of poetry could be written indefinitely without por-traying any interaction between the two parties. Petrarch-ism is a structure of feeling as well as a poetic tradition; if, as, perhaps, Shakespeare discovered in writing sonnets to his master-mistress, Petrarchan love poetry flourishes in the absence of mutuality, a Petrarchizing imagination, such as Orlando displays in his blazon-like poems about Rosa-lind, may make mutuality more difficult. As You Like It plays on this possibility. But Rosalind plays with Petrarchism, too, and eventually the mutuality that she establishes in her sportive conversations with Orlando again serves as a kind of transition to the mutuality of love; the idealization that begins as a threat to mutuality finally supports it in the celebration of the marriage bond.

Although Orlando and Rosalind clearly fall in love at first sight, the play emphasizes the presence of an obstacle in Orlando to developing his love into a relationship. After their first meeting at the wrestling match, Rosalind gives Orlando a chain. He cannot respond to her verbally; he asks in an aside:

Can I not say, "I thank you"? My better parts
Are all thrown down, and that which here stands up
Is but a quintain, a mere lifeless block.   (1.2.230–32)

Rosalind fruitlessly gives him another chance to speak. After her exit and more of his self-questioning, his last cry in the scene suggests the reason for his silence: "But heavenly Rosalind!" (1.2.270). He acts as if he sees her as far above him, and the poems he writes about her show at greater length the image of love as idealization without hope of mutuality. His role is simply to be the devoted servant who spreads her praise: "Heaven would that she these gifts should have, / And I to live and die her slave" (3.2.147–48).

Silvius, similarly, is content to maintain an idealizing worship with very little mutuality from Phebe:

So holy and so perfect is my love,
And I in such a poverty of grace,
That I shall think it a most plenteous crop
To glean the broken ears after the man
That the main harvest reaps.   (3.5.98–102)

It is part of Rosalind's role in the play to mock both of the Petrarchan preoccupations that sharply differentiate and isolate the roles of lover and beloved and thus prevent mutuality. In her disguise as Ganymede she teases Orlando for "deifying the name of Rosalind" (3.2.342) and tries to persuade him that his awe of her is unrealistic. When she catalogs the characteristics of the unhappy lover, she makes them sound ridiculous, and she denies Silvius too the dignity of his adoration. But her mockery is not an isolating monologue such as Jaques might fall into; rather it draws her listeners to participate in the mutuality of conversation. In her disguise, after encouraging Orlando to play straight man in her comic routine about time, she leads him to join in the game of "imagining" that Rosalind is present and attainable, and to see that in that game his love can ask for reciprocation.

> Rosalind But come, now I will be your Rosalind in a more
>   coming-on disposition; and ask me what you
>   will, I will grant it.
> Orlando   Then love me, Rosalind.   (4.1.101–4)

Besides the playful conversations into which Rosalind draws Orlando, there are a number of other examples of mutuality early in *As You Like It*. Involving other bonds than those of romantic love, they are often presented through a verbal ritual in which both partners participate. Orlando and Adam give each other reciprocal praise as ideal master and servant as both of them go off to the Forest of Arden. When the Duke and Orlando recognize each other's "gentleness" (2.7.118) in the forest, Orlando offers a compact that ritualizes their shared ideals and past experiences, and the Duke phrases his courteous acceptance in closely echoing words. When Orlando saves the life of his sleeping brother Oliver, Oliver awakes from his former hostility as well as from his sleep, he tells us later, and reciprocates his brother's love.[9]

With Oliver's quick pursuit of Celia, the play begins its final emphasis on images of mutual love between man and woman. Orlando describes the love of Celia and Oliver in terms that show it as an image of the happiness he wishes. Rosalind's version emphasizes the comical side of their headlong and very physical mutuality:

> your brother and my sister no sooner met but they
> looked; no sooner looked but they loved; no sooner
> loved but they sighed; no sooner sighed but they asked
> one another the reason; no sooner knew the reason but
> they sought the remedy: and in these degrees have they
> made a pair of stairs to marriage, which they will climb
> incontinent, or else be incontinent before marriage:
> they are in the very wrath of love, and they will together;
> clubs cannot part them.   (5.2.31–39)

For all of Rosalind's mockery, the description moves Orlando to more awareness of the inadequacy of a love that is confined to idealization without response: "I can live no longer by thinking" (5.2.48). To his surprise, his companion promises to produce Rosalind, "tomorrow, human as she is" (5.2.64). The adjective is a significant contrast to the celestial words that Orlando used in his earlier praise of her.

In the concluding masque of Hymen, the play finally presents on stage an ideal image of mutual relationship between man and woman. The heavenly imagery reappears in the staged appearance of a god, but the other characters constitute their relationship by their own words—ritual words this time, not the wit of Beatrice and Benedick. The scene's focus is on the mutuality between Rosalind's self-revelation and her father's and Orlando's recognition of her:

Rosalind To you I give myself, for I am yours.
Duke   If there be truth in sight, you are my daughter.
Orlando If there be truth in sight, you are my Rosalind.
                                        (5.4.111–13)

Rosalind's words define her as active giver, as well as passive gift: she does not, as Hymen has implied, wait to be given to Orlando by her father. Now able to respond to her directly, Orlando calls her his, but her next words, while verbally a limitation of her choices, emphasize that the possession is reciprocal: "I'll have no husband, if you be not he" (5.4.117).

The final hymn picks up two of the major kinds of imagery through which characters have pictured their relationships with each other—imagery of food[10] and of religion: "Wedding is great Juno's crown, / O blessed bond of board and bed!" (5.4.135–36). One character speaking of another as food usually reveals a tendency to dominate, as when Touchstone implicitly compares his claim to Audrey to the heathen philosopher's wish to eat a grape. One character speaking of another in religious terms shows some idealization, as when Orlando writes poems about heavenly Rosalind. Rosalind herself characteristically manages to

combine the two types of imagery in her humorous praise
of Orlando as fruit from Jove's tree and of his kisses as "full
of sanctity as the touch of holy bread" (3.4.12–13); perhaps
the extreme of either attitude, domination or idealization,
makes mutual relationship impossible except in the precarious condition of mutual idealization, presented in *Romeo and Juliet*. The ideal that Hymen describes is one of
mutuality; not one partner, but the bond itself, is blessed;
neither partner is objectified, but board and bed are medi-
ators in their relationship. Thus, in the way the play has
modulated the transition out of Orlando's paralyzing image of love as one-sided idealization, it leaves us again with
a kind of mutuality not limited by extreme differentiation
of roles but with a fuller sharing.

While in *As You Like It* the initial internal obstacle to mutuality in love appears to be idealization of the beloved, in
Twelfth Night a more difficult obstacle may be idealization of
one's own feelings. The theme of mutuality in its many
varieties informs this play even more than the other two
we have discussed. To emphasize the development of mutuality in love, the play opens with its lack: several characters who seem particularly content in their apparently
static versions of unrequited love. Olivia is ready to mourn
seven years out of love for her dead brother. Orsino and
Sir Andrew Aguecheek are ineffectually courting her, but
neither one confronts her directly. Orsino's words suggest
a real enjoyment of dramatizing and glorifying his posture
of unrequited lover. As Orsino enjoys reveries of love, Andrew enjoys the revelry with Olivia's uncle, Sir Toby, that
his role as her suitor permits him. Both Orsino and Andrew speak of themselves more than of Olivia; their indulgence in unrequited love, the play suggests, coincides with
self-love. This coincidence is harshly clearer with Malvolio.
As Orsino delights in the verbal prerogatives of courtship
and Andrew in its social prerogatives, Malvolio delights in
his fantasy of the political prerogatives of marriage. Orsino
believes that Olivia must love him in the future, Malvolio
believes that she loves him in the present, and Sir Andrew

can be led to believe anything; all three of them lack consciousness of her subjectivity.

As Beatrice and Benedick and Orlando and the disguised Rosalind begin their relationships with the verbal mutuality of a game, Viola in her page's disguise easily engages Orsino in a confidential conversation and Olivia in a courting game. Like the plotters in Much Ado, she engages them further emotionally by words that lead them to imagine the feelings of others who might love them. Involved in the conversation, they must respond verbally, and that verbal response hints at their response of feeling.

Carrying Orsino's message of love to Olivia, Viola turns conventions to a more urgent and personal description of what it feels like to be denied love; the dialogue has all the energy of her controlled and concealed love for Orsino:

If I did love you in my master's flame,
With such a suff'ring, such a deadly life,
In your denial I would find no sense;
I would not understand it.   (1.5.250–53)

Encouraged by Olivia, she develops an image of herself as wooer demanding response:

              O, you should not rest
Between the elements of air and earth
But you should pity me.   (1.5.260–62)

Olivia sees the personal feeling in the speech, feels a response to the imaginary demand the page has presented, and becomes another version of the unrequited lover, a more insistent one.

The love for Orsino that informs Viola's speeches about love to Olivia underlies even more strongly the subsequent dialogue in which she leads him to imagine himself loved by "some lady, as perhaps there is" (2.4.88). Like Rosalind asking Orlando to imagine that he is speaking to Rosalind, Viola is in part asking Orsino to imagine what is real; this process continues when Orsino objects that no woman's feelings could be as strong as his own and Viola presents her second image of the imaginary lover—her father's daughter who never told her love. Rosalind had to disabuse Orlando of some of his idealization of her so that he could confront her on a more equal level; Viola, by contrast, must work much more on Orsino's idealization of himself by presenting her imaginary sister—and by implication the hypothetical woman who loves him—as equally capable of devotion. In her dialogues with Orsino and Olivia, Viola begins to put them imaginatively in contact with the reality of human feeling as she knows it. But the process brings them all further confusion that she cannot herself resolve.

The resolution in Twelfth Night, like the resolution in As You Like It, receives indirect preparation by the presentation of other kinds of mutuality than love between man and woman. The most idealized of these is the relationship between Sebastian, Viola's twin brother, and Antonio, the sea captain who has saved his life. Sebastian and Antonio are presented in an emblematic mode as ideal friends; the artificial prose of their first appearance adds to the sense of their being characters of a different world than Illyria, where prose is usually relaxed and conversational. Their world is one where kindness invariably brings kindness in return. Sebastian's first expressed concern is to avoid making a bad return to Antonio for saving his life. He would bear his sufferings alone, he says, because "It were a bad recompense for your love to lay any of them on you" (2.1.6–7). Sebastian is painfully conscious of his limitation to words as means to reciprocate, and he acknowledges this as he gives those words: "My kind Antonio, / I can no other answer make but thanks" (3.3.13–14).

Very different kinds of mutuality are the fabric of daily life in Illyria.[11] Feste draws his listeners into joking dialogues that prove their folly and earn him money. Andrew and Toby encourage each other in merrymaking while Toby practices the exploitation that Sebastian so scrupulously tries to avoid. Malvolio's confinement is occasioned

by the pseudo-mutuality of his belief in Olivia's love for
him. The revelry that takes place in his absence involves
another parodic treatment of mutuality in the preparations
for the duel between Sir Andrew and Viola. As Sir Toby
describes each of the reluctant duelists to the other, his
description of their fictitious desire for confrontation is a
parody of the hypothetical demand for love Viola has presented to Olivia and Orsino. In a transfer of emotion from
one plot to the other, the language preparing for the duel
reflects some of the growing urgency and frustration in the
various versions of unrequited love. The fighter that Sir
Toby describes to Viola sounds remarkably like an insistent
suitor, especially if we hear sexual double entendre in his
speeches. Toby advises Viola, "Get you on and give him his
desire" (3.4.231–32). In contrast to the uncompelling suits
of Sir Andrew and Viola/Cesario, Sir Toby conjures up an
image of irresistible demand.

As if by a magic beyond Sir Toby's expectations, the
imaginary fighter takes on life; eager to avenge the youth
he sees as his friend Sebastian, Antonio arrives and breaks
into the duel. In him the imagined hostility finds an em-
bodied answer and the serious, determined demand for a
response enters the Illyrian world. It is his faith in Sebastian's return of his friendship that underlies his reproach to
Viola, who does not remember receiving money from
him. Now Viola guesses that her brother is alive; in the
next scene Sebastian defines himself as able, unlike the
page for whom he is mistaken, to take a male's place in the
play's society by responding to Sir Andrew with a blow and
to Olivia with a promise of marriage.

The progress from hostile confrontation to love, suggested in one form by the duel's preparation for Olivia's
meeting with Sebastian, recurs in a different form several
times in the last act; we may recall as a partial parallel the
movement from hostility to love of Beatrice and Benedick.
Antonio's reappearance to declare his love and expectation of return begins a chain reaction of confrontations in

anger and love. Antonio speaks of his past generosity to Sebastian in almost paternal terms—"His life I gave him" (5.1.74)—before accusing him of ingratitude. Then Olivia's honesty in her first confrontation with Orsino provokes him to bitter reproach. However unjustifiable his anger at a woman who has never pretended to accept his suit, it is nevertheless the most direct emotion he has expressed. Far from the super-civilized music lover of the opening scene, he now dramatizes himself as one who might "like to th'Egyptian thief at point of death, / Kill what I love" (5.1.112–13). In this confusion, flailing around to find the object of his anger, he directs words of violence at Viola as he begins to express affection for her:[12] "I'll sacrifice the lamb that I do love / To spite a raven's heart within a dove" (5.1.124–25). This passage provides at last the opportunity for Viola to speak of her love for Orsino. Her whole-hearted if artful response draws Olivia's reproach and the priest's confirmation that a betrothal has indeed taken place. However confused about the identity of partners to the betrothal, his description emphasizes its mutuality:

A contract of eternal bond of love,
Confirmed by mutual joinder of your hands,
Attested by the holy close of lips,
Strength'ned by interchangement of your rings.
                                        (5.1.150–53)

This gives Orsino in turn occasion to accuse his page of ingratitude, with more of the anger that implies affection.

The entrances of Andrew and Toby wounded give evidence of other kinds of angry confrontation—their fights with Sebastian—and prepare for the play's most emblematic celebration of mutuality, the recognition between Sebastian and Viola. For many lines before Sebastian sees his double, the audience can see both twins on stage. Meanwhile Sebastian's words give verbal emphasis to the theme of relationship; he speaks about kinship and re-union in lines that are relevant to more situations than he intends:

> I am sorry, madam, I have hurt your kinsman;
> But had it been the brother of my blood,
> I must have done no less with wit and safety.
>
> .   .   .   .
>
> Pardon me, sweet one, even for the vows
> We made each other but so late ago.   (5.1.201–3, 206–7)

Character after character has been accused of infidelity; Sebastian is the first speaker to acknowledge directly his own role in past mutual vows in asking for pardon rather than making a reproach. At once his entry provides the answer for all the other reproaches.

Orsino speaks the amazement of all on stage in a metaphysical conceit: "One face, one voice, one habit, and two persons— / A natural perspective that is and is not" (5.1.208–9). The unity in duality remarked by the Duke in the twins here is emblematic for the unity in duality of the relationships that Sebastian first confirms: marriage and friendship. After he speaks to Olivia, his next concern is Antonio, and his words present the loyalty with which Antonio had expected him to answer his devotion. Finally Antonio leads Sebastian to see his twin and introduces the emblem of mutual relationship: "An apple cleft in two is not more twin / Than these two creatures" (5.1.215–16). Rather than emphasizing metaphysical paradox or artistic illusion like the Duke's comparison, Antonio's comes more directly from nature. More than the twins' exact reflection, his words suggest their unity of origin and passage from division to reunion.

Their unity of origin receives further emphasis and resonance in Sebastian's assurance to Viola that he is not an apparition:

> A spirit I am indeed,
> But am in that dimension grossly clad
> Which from the womb I did participate.
> Were you a woman, as the rest goes even,

> I should my tears let fall upon your cheek
> And say, "Thrice welcome, drownèd Viola!"
>
> (5.1.228–33)

While earlier in the play Viola's comparison of the body to a wall (1.2.48) epitomizes the self-enclosure in which most of the characters begin, here Sebastian, in keeping with the celebration of mutuality, describes his body as material for relationship with other people; he has a body by virtue of sharing from birth in the bodily existence of all humanity. Sebastian's vision of achieved reunion continues the emphasis on the body as means of union; momentarily they would be so united that his tears would fall not on his cheeks but on hers. The embrace is only verbally evoked, however, and the artifice involved in describing the body as a means of union through words becomes more obvious when they remember their father's mole. The use of the recognition-scene convention calls attention to itself and to their desire to prolong the stasis in mutual contemplation[13] and to anchor their relationship in as many dimensions of common experience as possible. Bringing the memory of their father into their recognition concludes it with a more serious reminder of the mortality that has been in the background of the whole dialogue. The deaths they feared for each other were illusions, but they remember their father's death as a reality. That shared bereavement—experience of the limits of bodily existence—confirms their mutual recognition, and Viola speaks her own name for the first time as she remembers that her father "died that day when Viola from her birth / Had numb'red thirteen years" (5.1.236–37).

In a way that would be particularly striking to those in the audience familiar with Neoplatonic iconology, the language surrounding the recognition of Sebastian and Viola emphasizes its analogy to the mutual recognition of lovers. Antonio's description of the twins is remarkably close to an image in Plato's *Symposium* where Aristophanes explains the origin of love: every pair of lovers began as a whole but were split "like a sorb apple which is halved for pickling."[14] The twins' description of each other as dead echoes hyperboles about lovers' suffering used elsewhere in this play; their words more specifically literalize the images that Ficino in his *Commentary on Plato's Symposium* applies to mutual love.[15] He describes unrequited love as death and requited love as resurrection, and their evocation of spirits returned or reborn suggests this transition. The completion of Ficino's image of mutual love occurs when the lover "finally recognizes himself in his beloved and no longer doubts that he is loved." Sebastian literally recognizes himself in his sister; his first question when he sees her is "Do I stand there?" (5.1.218).

But in contrast to the usual Neoplatonic role differentiation, through most of the dialogue each emotion or memory one of the twins utters is matched by the other. Sebastian's words on the supposed death of his sister are mirrored by Viola's on the supposed death of her brother. She maintains belief he is a ghost; he maintains belief she is a man. The verbal structure reflects and dramatizes the community of their experience: each has approached death, each has feared the other's death, each has known a father's death, and each is rejoicing in the possibility of reunion. Indeed, their language emphasizes that they go beyond the mutuality between self-revelation and recognition to a further mutuality in which both share both sides of the experience—recognizing and being recognized. This climactic and emblematic brother-sister meeting suggests a vision of mutual relationship between man and woman similar to Rilke's vision in *Letters to a Young Poet*:

> And perhaps the sexes are more related than we think, and the great renewal of the world will perhaps consist in this, that man and maid, freed of all false feeling and aversion, will seek each other not as opposites, but as brother and sister, as neighbors, and will come to-

gether as human beings, in order simply, seriously and patiently to bear in common the difficult generation that is
their burden.[16]

As we move from the more emblematic familial version
of love between man and woman to the version that concludes the most psychologically developed relationship in
the play, the one between Viola and the Duke, the emphasis on mutuality continues. Orsino links the sight of
Sebastian and Viola together with his new grasp of Viola's
love: "If this be so, as yet the glass seems true, / I shall have
share in this most happy wrack" (5.1.257–58). The couple
Sebastian and Viola make is a model for the relationship he
can have with Viola: a sharing rather than the isolating worship he alternately gave and expected from Olivia.[17] This
stress on reciprocity of service becomes more explicit in
his pledge to Viola:

> Your master quits you; and for your service done him,
> So much against the mettle of your sex,
> So far beneath your soft and tender breeding,
> And since you called me master for so long,
> Here is my hand; you shall from this time be
> Your master's mistress.   (5.1.311–16)

For Malvolio, who wished to be his mistress's master,
the promise of mutuality in love is more deceptive—he
cannot get past his self-enclosure. When Feste mocks him
in the passage I quoted in the title of this chapter, he is
presenting the one basis for reciprocal relationship that
Malvolio accepts—revenge.[18] But let us turn from Malvolio
to the concluding words of Twelfth Night for a different perspective on the relevance of mutuality to Shakespearean
comedy. Feste's song to the audience ends with words that
seem to make him spokesman for the play, playwright, and
other actors as well: "But that's all one, our play is done,
/ And we'll strive to please you every day" (5.1.396–97).
Feste thus reminds the audience that the relationship of
mutual dependence is not simply something they have

been watching, but something they are actually participating in.

Muriel Bradbrook has suggested that Elizabethan comedy generally is characterized by "intimate collaboration between actors and audience"[19] and explains further, "When the actor interprets for the audience, and the audience responds, stimulating the actor, the final event belongs exclusively to neither of them."[20] In Shakespearean comedy, I believe, the analogy between this mutuality and the mutuality shown on stage is an important part of the theatrical effect.[21] This is not to suggest that the self-reference is the main point but that the play in performance draws the audience into an embodiment of the experience which is its theme. The more the active roles of both partners in mutual relationship shown on stage have been emphasized, the more the implicit call and compliment to the audience's involvement and imaginative participation.

The most immediate link is between the jester-listener relationship within the plays and the play-audience relationship. For all the limitations sometimes suggested in the jester-listener relationship, nevertheless the plays clearly put it on a continuum with the mutuality between lovers. Malvolio's scorn of Feste's jokes is cognate with his isolation from love. It is more than a coincidence that the plots of so many of these comedies involve happy endings brought about in part because characters respond when they are led to imagine that someone else is dependent on their love; the members of the audience are likewise led to realize the play's dependence on their appreciation, and if they are willing to respond by imaginative belief, they too can enjoy the wish-fulfilling qualities of the ending. For example, as Anne Barton has suggested, the theater audience must use its imagination if it is to turn the "dissimilarity in appearance of the actors playing Viola and Sebastian" into "that marvelous identity hailed so ecstatically by the other characters."[22] From another point of view, the spectators act as partners in their ability to imagine that the characters have the feelings implied by their words and actions (and perhaps to imagine psychological conflicts or growth that makes sense of apparent inconsistency).[23] Indeed, in the epilogue to *As You Like It*, the actor who plays Rosalind explicitly ties the spectators' appreciation of the play to what they know of love from their own lives:[24] "I charge you, O women, for the love you bear to men, to like as much of this play as please you; and I charge you, O men, for the love you bear to women (as I perceive by your simp'ring none of you hates them) that between you and the women the play may please" (Epilogue, 11–16). This teasing implication of the audience, like Feste's final stanza, acknowledges the importance of mutuality in the theatrical experience of Shakespearean romantic comedy, as well as in the world it creates onstage. The festive communion thus invoked completes the play's re-creation of society as a vital process of human outreach and response.

→ But is it also re-creating a society that is a patriarchally ordered structure? At the end Rosalind says to Orlando and her father, "To you I give myself, for I am yours" (5.4.110, 111). When Benedick says to Beatrice, "Peace! I will stop your mouth" (5.4.97), and kisses her, she indeed says nothing more. Are these lines signals that the endings are in fact returns to a hierarchy made more stable by its temporary inversion, as Victor Turner argues happens after rituals of status reversal?[25] Should we take the masculine disguise of Rosalind and Viola, not as a sign of their flexibility beyond the limits of convention, but rather as a bracketing of their assertiveness by labeling it as only part of a role to be discarded, or as a quality so associated with maleness that a character must look male to demonstrate it?[26]

None of these arguments seems to me strong enough to overshadow the emphasis on mutuality in these comedies. Natalie Zemon Davis suggests, counter to Turner, that carnivals and other examples of cross-sex disguise and temporarily prominent female activity could actually keep open "an alternate way of conceiving family structure."[27] Rosalind's silence during the speeches by Orlando, the Duke, and Jaques is hardly sufficient to show that she has given up her vitality of the rest of the play (including the scenes before she takes on her disguise); indeed, she returns, explicitly against custom, to speak the epilogue, thus taking back the presiding position that Jaques and the Duke briefly borrow from her. Even her pledge of herself to Orlando is more active than in the ritual familiar to Shakespeare and his audience—she gives herself, rather than being given by her father.[28]

Similarly, although Beatrice has promised in her soliloquy to tame her wild heart to Benedick's loving hand, she resumes her teasing criticism of him in their final scenes together, and when she says nothing after Benedick's kiss, her silence is matched against Benedick's admission that "man is a giddy thing, and this is my conclusion" (5.4.106–7)—he is finally able to admit his irrationality. When he urges Don Pedro to marry, saying, "There is no staff more reverent than one tipped with horn" (5.4.121–22), in spite of the implied suspicion it is as if he has given up the aspiration to husbandly control that provides Claudio's rationale for rejecting Hero in the other plot.

In these comedies, I am arguing, women's gestures of submission are often balanced by similar gestures from the men. Orlando, especially, seems so willing to subordinate himself that his increased articulacy at the end seems less a defeat for Rosalind than a sign of his growth to a position more worthy of her. In order to argue that the plays end in images of unambiguous male dominance, we must believe that the patriarchal structure of Elizabethan marriage was so powerful as to be incapable of being affected by individuals' behavior. Without denying that structures have considerable power, I believe it is worthwhile to note variations in practice and in presentation.

Conventions of male dominance are relatively marginal in these three plays—more emphasized and implicitly criticized in the subplots, where Claudio can reject Hero or marry her without any room for her choice and Touchstone can order Audrey around. But these, and related conventions of gender difference in attitudes to violence, however marginal, are still part of the plays' worlds. Their status is ambiguous; we can see either patriarchy or mutuality in these plays, as we can see either a rabbit or a duck in the equivocal design discussed by Gombrich and, following him, by Rabkin;[29] and for me, at any rate, patriarchy is harder to see. But patriarchal conventions can hardly be considered marginal in *The Taming of the Shrew*, as we shall see in the next chapter.

Chapter Three

Patriarchy and Play in

The Taming of the Shrew

Some of Shakespeare's recent critics have seen Petruchio's behavior in *The Taming of the Shrew* as an attempt to teach Kate to play, to draw her into his games.[1] Kate's final attitude, they suggest, is less a passive submission than a playful cooperation. Important as this reading is for its insight into the tone and theatrical effectiveness of *The Taming of the Shrew*, it should not dismiss for us the play's treatment of the social order and in particular of patriarchy—the authority of fathers over their families, husbands over wives, and men in general over women. Games, however absorbing and delightful, have some relation to the world outside them; children reenact threatening experiences to gain a sense of greater control over them, and they try out roles that they may use in their adult life.[2] Likewise, the games in *The Taming of the Shrew*, almost always initiated by Petruchio, may have some relation to the patriarchal traditions of the world of *The Shrew* and of its audience. Why this ambiguous coalescence between Petruchio the dominant husband and Petruchio the game-player, between a farce assuming patriarchy and a comedy about playing at patriarchy?[3]

The themes of patriarchy and play both come to the fore in the induction, in which the penniless tinker Christopher Sly is transformed by trickery into a lord and prepared to watch a comedy. This scene introduces a world in which all identify themselves by their place in a social and familial hierarchy; it prepares us for a theatrically self-conscious performance in which those "places" are dramatic roles. As the "real" lord entertains us by showing that Sly can take a completely different place in the social order, the play begins to raise the question of how much that social order is a human construction whose validity is more like that of a game than that of divine or natural law. In the first scene of the inner play, the easy role change between Lucentio and Tranio, a servant clever enough to hide his precise degree of initiative from his master, repeats that question. But the focus of the play is not the apparent changes in social class permitted by changes of clothes; it is Kate's movement away from her original rebellion.[4] Unlike the other two changes, this one superficially endorses the social order, but here too details suggest analogies between the social order and a game.

Analogies between games and such apparently serious institutions as law and war received their first detailed discussion in Johan Huizinga's *Homo Ludens*. One main characteristic he identified in play and in such institutions is the establishment of a separate sphere limited in time and space.[5] Modern psychologists often describe the experience of play in terms of power: it involves the feeling of mastery, the sense of being a cause,[6] the assimilation of reality to the ego.[7] In a different context, these terms could apply to the official prerogatives of the head of the family in a hierarchical society; perhaps it is the power over a limited sphere (the play world or the household) that contributes most to this ambiguous coalescence between Petruchio's possible roles. The sociologists Peter L. Berger and Hansfried Kellner make a similar comparison explicit in their description of the modern nuclear family as a "macrosocially innocuous 'play area'".[8]

> It is here that the individual will seek power, intelligibility, and quite literally, a name—the apparent power to fashion a world, however Lilliputian, that will reflect his own being: a world that, seemingly having been shaped by himself and thus unlike those other worlds

that insist on shaping him, is translucently intelligible to him (or so he thinks); a world in which, consequently, he is *somebody*—perhaps even, within its charmed circle, its lord and master.[9]

The comparison between play and household power is particularly relevant to *The Taming of the Shrew* because Petruchio and the other characters play games—separable units of play—in a literal sense. Roger Caillois enumerates four basic types of games; two of his categories, *agon* (competition) and mimicry (pretense) are clearly present.[10] In all of Petruchio's scenes with Kate until the last, ambiguous one, his words and actions involve some kind of pretense. For a period of time in each, Petruchio behaves according to "the fiction, the sentiment of 'as if,'"[11] which in mimicry takes the place of rules. In his first meeting with Kate and their only scene alone together, he invents an imaginary Kate and an imaginary society that values her: "Hearing thy mildness praised in every town, / Thy virtues spoke of, and thy beauty sounded" (2.1.191–92). He is using language with regard not to its truth value but to her response. This use of language is appropriate to a game; as Caillois suggests, "Games generally attain their goal only when they stimulate an echo of complicity."[12] As game player and as wooer, Petruchio needs her response.

What Kate does is to initiate another kind of game—the only game in the play that she begins—a competition of puns. In language markedly earthier than Petruchio's overtures, Kate introduces animal imagery and first brings out the sexual meanings in his retorts, even while verbally rejecting him.

Kate	Asses are made to bear, and so are you.
Petruchio	Women are made to bear, and so are you.
Kate	No such jade as you, if me you mean.

(2.1.201–3)

Petruchio joins in this game with gusto. He seems undeterred—even encouraged—when she calls him a fool, and indeed there is often a hint of invitation in the lines where she makes the charge.

Kate   If I be waspish best beware my sting.
Petruchio My remedy is then to pluck it out.
Kate   Ay, if the fool could find it where it lies.
                                                    (2.1.212–14)

After a few more rounds, he changes back to the original game—although with the variation that now his praise of her social merit is contrasted with her reputation.

'Twas told me you were rough and coy and sullen,
And now I find report a very liar,
For thou art pleasant, gamesome, passing courteous,
But slow in speech, yet sweet as springtime flowers.
                                                    (2.1.245–48)

Repeatedly Petruchio manipulates the language of social convention and roles for his own purpose—his relationship with Kate. The way he talks about society proves him independent of its actual judgments and ready to reverse its expectations drastically. The one word that describes both a social virtue and Kate's current behavior—gamesome—describes his attitude here as well. Caillois identifies in play a polarity between "frolicsome and impulsive exuberance" and "arbitrary, imperative, and purposely tedious conventions."[13] We might see Kate's enjoyment of this battle as a kind of wild exuberance, but "gamesome" may also apply to the ability to perform in a highly conventional civilization that she will show later. Petruchio, by contrast, seems to be using the language of the higher pole in the spirit of the lower. "Go, fool" (2.1.259), replies Kate to his praise, and she again moves the conversation down to earth; but this time the wordplay very quickly comes out just where Petruchio wants it:

Petruchio Am I not wise?
Kate   Yes, keep you warm.

Petruchio Marry, so I mean, sweet Katherine, in thy bed.
(2.1.267–69)

And when the others return, she is quiet as he gives the explanatory fiction that, like the end of the play, makes crucial the private mutuality between husband and wife:

If she and I be pleased, what's that to you?
'Tis bargained 'twixt us twain, being alone,
That she shall still be curst in company.   (2.1.305–7)

From now on, Petruchio's games will have the endorsement of the husband's rights over his wife. Yet, to the extent that Petruchio's power depends on a public belief in patriarchy for its legitimation, he behaves paradoxically when he violates the conventions of the social order. He plays the role of the "symbolic fool, who seems to have originated somewhere outside society and its normal laws and duties."[14] In a not unfamiliar anomaly, the man in a position of relative social power laughs at the conventions of the society that gives him that power, while the woman subordinated by her society worries about its judgment of her. As she repeats the charge of folly, her concern for public opinion becomes explicit in the face of his provocation.[15]

I told you, I, he was a frantic fool,
Hiding his bitter jests in blunt behavior. . . .
Now must the world point at poor Katherine
And say, "Lo, there is mad Petruchio's wife,
If it would please him come and marry her."
(3.2.12–13, 18–20)

Petruchio's sabotage of wedding ritual concludes when he takes Kate away from the banquet while playing the role of the defender who will, he says, "buckler thee against a million" (3.2.235). He insists:

I will be master of what is mine own.
She is my goods, my chattels; she is my house,

My household stuff, my field, my barn,
My horse, my ox, my ass, my anything. (3.2.225–28)

This speech again shows the coalescence of the role of player and patriarch, for the terms in which he declares ownership—the objects into which he transforms her—are extravagant enough to be a parody of patriarchal attitudes. The climactic phrase—"my anything"—declares the infinite malleability of identity within his world. Whether this hyperbole is play or domestic tyranny, his pretense of defending Kate from the attacks of the wedding guests is a more obvious invention. Like his earlier invention of a private bargain between Kate and himself, it seems intended ultimately to create such a bargain.

The suggestions of companionship in the play motif receive a challenge from the animal imagery here and elsewhere. In the title, *taming* identifies the hierarchy of husband over wife in marriage with the hierarchy of humanity over animals. Furthermore, several curious passages associate marriage with beasts of burden—usually the grotesquely described worn-out horse. For enough money, according to Grumio, Petruchio would marry "an old trot with ne'er a tooth in her head, though she have as many diseases as two and fifty horses" (1.2.77–79). Biondello enjoys enumerating the ailments of the horse Petruchio rides to his wedding, and Grumio makes a comic routine of the couple's falls from the horse on the trip back. These passages make comic emblems for an unattractive picture of marriage. The farcical tone, however, distances the threat. Since the passages are extravagant to the point of parody, the workhorse image becomes part of a larger game.

But other images of animals and many of the more explicit comparisons between animals and people are directly in the world of play—the aristocratic world of the hunt. In the induction, the lord's pride and concern for his hunting dogs remind us that domesticated animals attain a different status in the social order; they can benefit from human care and contribute to human enjoyment. Their position changes from an abstract subordination to an active and mutual (if unequal) relation. Play and mutuality may be goals of taming. (In Saint-Exupéry's *The Little Prince,* an anthropomorphic fox uses taming as a metaphor for the establishment of a relationship.[16]) Petruchio's falcon-taming involves more hierarchy and coercion, but it also involves a wish for play and mutuality. As the means of Petruchio's taming move from denials of food and sleep to denials of the trappings of fashion, the farce that depends on the audience's withholding sympathy (and can therefore verge on brutality) modulates to a higher level of comedy. In the most important scene for the play theme in *The Shrew,* as we shall see, the medium is the even more sophisticated one of language.

Both clothing and language are important concerns in the other plots as well, and there too they can be material for play, but the effect is more obvious and more superficial. The lord makes a game of costuming Christopher Sly for his rise in the social hierarchy: Tranio's masquerade as his master Lucentio provides obvious enjoyment for the servant. When his former master Vincentio appears in Padua, Tranio refuses to recognize him, saying, "Why sir, what 'cerns it you if I wear pearl and gold? I thank my good father, I am able to maintain it" (5.1.64–66). Petruchio, by contrast, is not interested in using clothes as signs of a playful or serious rise in the social hierarchy. Instead, his choice of clothes for the roles he plays dramatizes his independence of the concern for status usually coded by Elizabethan clothing.[17] Instead of dressing up for his wedding, he wears the most grotesque old clothes he can find—in their lumpish disproportion, he may be literally dressing like a fool.[18] He pretends to offer Kate new clothes, as he pretends to offer her the food and sleep that are also conventional symbols of regeneration used parodically in the induction. His subsequent reversals have more function than frustrating her; like the fool's costume, they act out his scorn for convention and his preference for internal rather than external values:

> To me she's married, not unto my clothes.
> Could I repair what she will wear in me
> As I can change these poor accoutrements,
> 'Twere well for Kate and better for myself.   (3.2.113–16)

>   'tis the mind that makes the body rich;
> And as the sun breaks through the darkest clouds
> So honor peereth in the meanest habit.   (4.3.169–71)

Kate, by contrast, is still concerned about fashion; she protests, "This doth fit the time, / And gentlewomen wear such caps as these" (4.3.69–70). When she accuses him, "Belike you mean to make a puppet of me" (4.3.103), he pretends to think she is talking to the tailor; and this pseudo-misunderstanding raises the question of which rules are more restricting, Petruchio's or the anonymous judgments of fashion and other social conventions. Thus, although characters in all plots play games with clothing, Petruchio's games challenge rather than pay tribute to the social order in other matters than the subordination of women.

Language, like clothing, is a medium for the games in both marriage plots. We have discussed its use in the pun battles and imaginative fictions of Kate's first scene with Petruchio; several later scenes explicitly turn on questions of translation, naming, and meaning. Disguised as a tutor, Lucentio uses the pretense of Latin translation to convey his identity and intentions to Bianca. She adapts to this mode of translation easily; equivocation comes naturally to her, and she uses the trick not only to disguise his intentions from the other suitors but also to keep Lucentio himself in doubt. Petruchio's games create a private language between him and Kate slowly but more effectively. Infuriated by his criticism of the new cap, she wants to use language to express her feelings regardless of his reactions:

> Your betters have endured me say my mind,
> And if you cannot, best you stop your ears.
> My tongue will tell the anger of my heart

Or else my heart, concealing it, will break,
And rather than it shall, I will be free
Even to the uttermost, as I please, in words.   (4.3.75–80)

Petruchio's game of pretending to misunderstand her—he
responds to her outburst with "Why, thou sayst true. It is a
paltry cap" (4.3.81)—shows her that self-expression unac-
knowledged by a hearer is not enough.

Up to this point, the games Petruchio has begun have
been played more on Katherine than with her. Typically,
they have been pretenses that the emotional situation she
experiences is far different than she feels it is. On their way
back to her father's house, he finally begins a language
game that turns on redefining the external world, and perhaps this different focus for redefinition makes it possible
for her to join in and begin creating a new world and a
new society between the two of them. He claims that the
moon is shining, not the sun, and refuses to continue the
trip unless she agrees; she consents to his bargain:

Forward, I pray, since we have come so far,
And be it moon or sun or what you please.
An if you please to call it a rush-candle,
Henceforth I vow it shall be so for me.   (4.5.12–15)

She replaces a language determined by the external world
as she sees it alone with another determined by her relationship with Petruchio: "What you will have it named,
even that it is, / And so it shall be still for Katherine"
(4.5.21–22). Here, with comic literalness, the play dramatizes the point Berger and Kellner make that "the recon-
struction of the world in marriage occurs principally in the
course of conversation. . . . The implicit problem of this
conversation is how to match two individual definitions of
reality."[19]

Their use of language and their relationship are now becoming the kind of game that Petruchio has intended:
"Thus the bowl should run, / And not unluckily against the
bias" (4.5.24–25). In spite of the ambiguity of this image,

now Kate seems more like a partner in the game rather than an object used in it. She participates with wit and detachment, agreeing that "the moon changes even as your mind" (4.5.20).

In the background is the traditional association of the moon with the transforming imagination, and perhaps also a self-conscious parody of stage conventions of description. Since, as the mechanicals in *A Midsummer Night's Dream* knew, it was impossible literally to bring in moonshine, the Elizabethan audience depended on the dialogue for indications of whether a scene was set in day or night. They must have frequently watched a nighttime scene in literal sunlight and used their imaginations. By accepting similar conventions, Kate is following Petruchio in defining their relationship as an enclosed sphere where imagination can re-create the universe. At first it seems that it will be only Petruchio's imagination, but the entry of a stranger—Vincentio—heightens the possibilities of the game.

Vincentio, as an old man, represents the class at the top of the social order within a patriarchal society, but when he is with Katherine and Petruchio his identity is temporarily within their power. Petruchio gives Kate her cue by transforming him into a sonneteer's dream of a lady:

> Such war of white and red within her cheeks!
> What stars do spangle heaven with such beauty
> As those two eyes become that heavenly face?
>
> (4.5.30–32)

While her acceptance of Petruchio's renaming began as accommodation, here Kate shows her own creative imagination at work. She further confuses the patriarch by emphasizing the "lovely maid's" youth and role in the familial order that her imagination is temporarily subverting:

> Happy the parents of so fair a child,
> Happier the man whom favorable stars
> Allots thee for his lovely bedfellow.   (4.5.38–40)

It is as if in the new world of the game, ordinary social identities and inequalities are arbitrary and unimportant, because other identities can so easily be assigned—anything can be its opposite. Categories of day and night, young and old, male and female, lose their strict boundaries. Petruchio, who so often refers to his father, in this scene alone swears by himself as "my mother's son" (4.5.6).

When Petruchio returns them to the ordinary world, where Vincentio is "a man, old, wrinkled, faded, withered" (4.5.42)—epithets perhaps in their own way a subversion of patriarchy on the youth-oriented comic stage—Kate triumphantly apologizes, with another inside joke:

Pardon, old father, my mistaking eyes
That have been so bedazzled with the sun
That everything I look on seemeth green.   (4.5.44–46)

Petruchio is leading the dialogue, but Kate clearly plays an active role in what he calls "our first merriment" (4.5.75). Faced with irrational demands, she has experienced the benefits of seeing them as part of a game and playing along. It will soon become apparent that her education in folly has taught her how to live with relative comfort in a patriarchal culture, and this coincidence implies a certain detachment about that culture's assumptions.

As part of the structural emphasis on patriarchy, The Taming of the Shrew concludes with three scenes in which characters ask pardon of father or husband. We have discussed the ambiguity of the tribute in the first; in the second, Lucentio's apology at the same time announces his marriage to Bianca and his own true identity and saves his father from jail. By the end of the scene, the two fathers, Vincentio and Baptista, are still grumbling at the deception and insubordination, but young love has found its way. In his bliss Lucentio hardly notices the discontent of his father and father-in-law after his ritual apology, and Katherine and Petruchio turn it into entertainment; Petruchio wins Kate over to a further independence of social convention by drawing a kiss from her on the street. Thus the tribute to patriarchy is ambiguous here too, and these precedents hint at a continued ambiguity in the end.

Fathers are clearly important in The Shrew. The word "father" appears fifty-four times—more often than in any other Shakespeare play except *King Lear* and *Henry VI, Part III*.[20] Lucentio, Tranio, and Petruchio all introduce themselves as suitors with reference to their fathers and identify themselves by patronymic at other times in the play.[21] But Tranio and Lucentio are eager to introduce a counterfeit Vincentio as the father who will legitimate the wedding, and throughout the play the younger characters' words about tradition, loyalty, and hierarchy in general, as well as patriarchy, are frequently in pursuit of their own ends.[22] This is a familiar ploy in comic societies; Ann Whitefield's use of it in Shaw's *Man and Superman* receives a more explicit gloss.[23] In the opening speech after the induction, Lucentio proclaims his gratitude to his father and his intent to study virtue and moral philosophy; his servant Tranio, who can bandy classical allusions with the best, advises him to follow his own pleasure and "study what you most affect" (1.1.40). In their next conversation the two are already plotting how to win Bianca. Following his advice to his master, Tranio too can use the rhetoric of loyalty to his own advantage. He provides the hint for Lucentio's idea of disguising himself as a schoolteacher and Tranio as Lucentio, and then accepts the role with great protestations of dutifulness: "I am content to be Lucentio / Because so well I love Lucentio" (1.1.213–14). Lucentio's peculiar mode of Latin translation exemplifies not only a purposeful use of tradition but also the predominance of patriarchal images on the microscopic level: the Ovidian passage ends "*Priami regia celsa senis.*" When Lucentio translates the last two words "that we might beguile the old pantaloon" (3.1.35–36), *senis*, at least, is being translated literally. Bianca too can use the language of tradition for her own advantage to play up to Baptista and discomfit Katherine. Although we have seen her ability to do what she likes with Latin, furthermore, she refuses Hortensio's analogous attempt to woo her by writing new words for the musical scale. Her reason? "Old fashions please me best" (3.1.78).

Thus profession of traditional values in *The Shrew* repeatedly turns out to be pretext, and it is against this background that we must see the last scene. At the wedding banquet, sexual wordplay like that in Katherine's first scene with Petruchio spices the dialogue, but each set of puns concludes with a reaffirmation of sexual and social roles. Meanwhile the imagery again turns to sport, much of it sport in which animals and human beings collaborate. Petruchio and Hortensio cheer on the duel of insults between their wives, crying "To her, Kate!" and "To her, widow!" (5.2.33–34). Bianca resentfully asks Petruchio, "Am I your bird? I mean to shift my bush" (5.2.46), and leaves the room. Tranio, after comparing himself to a "greyhound, / Which runs himself and catches for his master" (5.2.52–53), leads the others in returning to the attack on Petruchio for reversed hierarchy in his marriage: "'Tis thought your deer does hold you at a bay" (5.2.56). After his delight in playing a role at the top, Tranio has returned to his original adjustment to a lower place; he pleases his master by using words of hierarchy against others.

The wedding guests speak of their insults as jests and appropriately it is through a game that Katherine and Petruchio finally justify their marriage. Proposing a wager for the most obedient wife, Petruchio speaks like the sportsman proud of the creature he has trained, even as he protests her superiority:

> Twenty crowns!
> I'll venture so much of my hawk or hound,
> But twenty times so much upon my wife.   (5.2.71–73)

When the other wives refuse to come when called, they are refusing to play; Bianca sends word "That she is busy" (5.2.83), and the Widow says Hortensio has "some goodly jest in hand" (5.2.94). Katherine, as we know, has now learned to play her husband's games, and after appearing at his command she brings in the recalcitrant wives. At his word—"Off with the bauble," (5.2.127)—her cap becomes a fool's toy. The other women are still scornful of folly, and their anticomic language undercuts their position on the comic stage.

> Widow   Lord, let me never have a cause to sigh
>   Till I be brought to such a silly pass.
> Bianca   Fie, what a foolish duty call you this?
> Lucentio I would your duty were as foolish too.
>   The wisdom of your duty, fair Bianca,
>   Hath cost me a hundred crowns since supper-
>   time.
> Bianca   The more fool you for laying on my duty.
>   (5.2.128–34)

Bianca's scorn for folly has modulated into a scorn for duty, although she has earlier spoken of duty to appear self-righteous before her sister—"So well I know my duty to my elders" (2.1.7). As in her Latin translation, she uses the word to mean whatever she wants, but not something her husband can rely on.

When Petruchio gives Kate her cue for her final speech, the Widow is still objecting from a spoilsport position: "Come, come, you're mocking" (5.2.137). Kate, however, talks on—and on. It is, of course, the longest speech in the play and should hold the onstage audience rapt. There is no need to hear Kate speaking ironically to consider the speech more as a performance than as an expression of sincere belief; against the background of many other incidents in the play, it should be clear that sincerity is seldom so much in question as social ability in the tribute to traditional values. With the flexibility of the comic hero, Kate has found a new and more tenable social role, and she plays it with energy and aplomb.[24] Instead of her earlier colloquial and often bitter language, she now speaks eloquently in a higher style[25] and dwells on the language of patriarchy: the husband is "thy lord, thy king, thy governor" (5.2.143).

She has found a way of using language that reconciles her to her society. Following a long tradition of conventional wisdom about marriage, she sees woman's place in the home and man's in the outer world. Elizabeth Janeway has shown that this tradition serves a mythological function much more than it accurately defines social history;[26] and it is surely not for its factual value that Kate gives her audience—onstage and off—this idealized picture of marriage.[27] Rather, the speech serves as a reassurance to them that Kate now uses language as a common code reinforcing its society's beliefs about its members' spheres.[28] Within her society's worldview, however, she elaborates on that language to give an explanation of her society's expectations of women: The husband is

> one that cares for thee
> And for thy maintenance; commits his body
> To painful labor both by sea and land,
> To watch the night in storms, the day in cold,
> Whilst thou li'st warm at home, secure and safe;
> And craves no other tribute at thy hands
> But love, fair looks, and true obedience.   (5.2.152–58)

She speaks of marriage as an affectionate contract[29]—a relationship in which both partners have a role to play. Assuming men's greater physical strength, she contrasts the roles in a hierarchical way, but the roles also relate husbands and wives to each other in mutual need and interdependence. The language of her performance reconciles patriarchy and mutuality.

Meanwhile, Kate preaches some of the virtues traditionally praised and fostered in women—peace, service, love, obedience, flexibility, and the sense of one's own limitations—and reconciles them with self-assertion; she holds the center stage while preaching humility. Thus her speech, like the quite different apologies she and Lucentio make to Vincentio, has a tone of triumph. Her energetic resilience helps distance the threatening elements of compulsion in Petruchio's past behavior. When she concludes by offering to place her hands below her husband's foot in a hierarchical gesture of submission, his answer sounds less like an acceptance of tribute than praise for a successful performance in a game: "Why, there's a wench! Come on and kiss me, Kate" (5.2.185). Indeed, the series of games and game images that has led up to this speech makes it possible to see her improvisation very much as a game. How different is an ingenious creation of a culturally sanctioned role from an elaborate masquerade? Since socialization is a process of learning roles, a sharp distinction between play and social reality seems difficult to maintain even offstage,[30] and here we are dealing with the conclusion of a game within a play within a game within a play. If hierarchical societies perpetuate their structures by the roles each new generation learns to play, Kate's performance is a dramatically heightened version of the kind of compromise that keeps such a society going and can at best afford its members a sense of enjoyment and creativity within strict limits.

Kate's new command of socially approved language corresponds to a new command of social convention; she is no longer ashamed to kiss her husband in public and can still draw Vincentio's patriarchal approval: "'Tis a good hearing when children are toward" (5.2.187). With social praise surrounding wife and husband for the order in their marriage, Petruchio is free to leave the banquet saying frankly, "Come, Kate, we'll to bed" (5.2.189).

Before he leaves, however, he sets up another hierarchy different from the marital hierarchy that has been the foundation of Kate's language:

> We three are married, but you two are sped.
> 'Twas I won the wager, though you hit the white,
> And being a winner, God give you good night.
>
> (5.1.190–92)

In most other Shakespearean comedies the final scenes are filled with reconciliations; here distinctions prevail, and these distinctions heighten the sense of privacy, of a separate, limited world, about the marriage of Kate and Petruchio. When Kate reprimands the other wives, she confirms her uniqueness as the only Shakespearean comic heroine without a female friend at any point in the play. For all the patriarchal approval, the character distribution gives her and Petruchio exclusive dependence on each other; it presents their marriage as a private world, a joke that the rest of the characters miss, a game that excludes all but the two of them.

This image of privacy in marriage has a parallel in the architectural history of Shakespeare's time. From 1570 on, many English people rebuilt their houses to produce more rooms—most notably, a private bedroom for the married couple.[31] Perhaps the spread of the ideal of privacy was related to changing beliefs about the relations between husband and wife among Shakespeare's contemporaries. Shakespeare shared his audience with Protestant preachers who, as I noted in the Introduction, were glorifying marriage more than had their pre-Reformation predecessors, and could imply ideals of both patriarchy and partnership—even of play—in the same sermon. The more the husband-wife relationship was private, the more couples could negotiate it on a variety of different terms without threatening assumptions of male dominance in the society at large.

Modern sociologists can, as we have seen, describe marriage as a play sphere with "mutuality of adjustment" and discuss the advantages for the husband of the role of lord and master without mentioning the disadvantages for his wife;[32] similarly, The Taming of the Shrew combines patterns of patriarchy and companionship that members of its society may also have been combining. What is the role of play in this combination? Or, to rephrase an earlier question, what is the relationship between patriarchy per se and patriarchy as played by Petruchio?

To answer this question, we should first note that patriarchy itself rests on an ambiguity of values. The ideology of female subordination assumes the general superiority of men in physical strength; yet patriarchy in its strictest sense also involves the subordination of the young to the old, and here physical strength yields to order, tradition, and experience. In dramatizing the relation of man to woman, The Shrew may assume patriarchy, but in dramatizing the relation of youth to age, it gives lip service to patriarchy and victory to youth—to Petruchio, who cuffs the priest at his wedding.[33] But Petruchio's challenge to this aspect of patriarchy is not simply brute force: it is the energy of his words and imagination—his play—that verbally transforms old Vincentio into a young woman and back again with the utmost show of respect. Thus Petruchio's games combine the attractions of the rhetoric of order and the energy of disorder while removing the dangers of both poles. Analogously, the game element in Katherine's characterization both removes the threat from her earlier aggression and adds vitality to her final defense of order.

In summary, the ambiguous combination of patriarchy and play in The Taming of the Shrew helps it appeal to spectators who are divided among and within themselves in their attitudes toward marriage. In a time of social transition when Renaissance England felt conflict not only between contrasting images of marriage but also between nostalgia for an older order and a new awareness of individuality, inner passions, and outer chaos,[34] the game element in The Shrew sets up a protected space where imagination permits the enjoyment of both energy and form, while the dangers of violence, tyranny, deadening submission, and resentment magically disappear. The game context permits Petruchio and Katherine to modulate from antagonists to co-creators of a new world to ruler and subject, and encourages the spectators to see as most important whichever pair of roles they choose and consider the others as "only a game."

Yet it may be significant that the mutuality between the main characters in Shakespeare's later romantic comedies —whatever other gender differences persist—never differentiates their roles to insist on the man as leader of the game. In The Merchant of Venice another kind of role difference is at issue—the difference between giving and taking.

Chapter Four

Giving and Taking in

The Merchant of Venice

Many critics describe *The Merchant of Venice* as contrasting taking to giving, Shylock to Portia and Antonio.[1] A few have begun to note that the play also contrasts two kinds of giving, and that neither Portia nor Antonio is uncritically portrayed as an ideal of perfect generosity. Antonio's attempt at total self-sacrifice is different from Portia's willingness to give and take while setting limits.[2] Antonio's words in the trial scene suggest a rivalry between himself and Portia.[3] I believe that the personal rivalry dramatizes a struggle between two types of giving which was a central issue in the historical, religious, and psychological conflicts of Renaissance Europe. As a further sign of the centrality of this conflict in *The Merchant*, not only is Bassanio at the pivot of the personal rivalry between Antonio and Portia, but he also mediates between them in his mode of giving and moves his closest alliance from Antonio to Portia during the play. If these types of giving are rivals, it is Portia's that wins; Antonio cannot maintain the attitude of self-sacrifice all the time, and his depression, as well as his antagonism to Shylock, casts doubt on the attractiveness of his attempts. Thus I would argue that *The Merchant of Venice* implies a criticism of the ideal of self-denial in favor of the more comprehensive attitude of Portia, who is not only more assertive than Antonio but also more accepting of sexuality.

In this reading, Antonio's anti-Semitism is closely related to the denial and projection required by his attempt at total self-sacrifice. The play's outsiders by race and sex, Shylock and Portia, are paralleled as well as contrasted. Portia's echoes of Shylock in the final ring episode cohere with the self-assertion she has shown throughout, as well as with Shakespeare's use and revaluation of his culture's association of both women and Jews with the flesh.

Both W. H. Auden and C. L. Barber make some interesting connections between *The Merchant* and the socioeconomic changes of its time, and these, with related psychological and religious changes, are the best context in which to see the oppositions within the play.[4] The traditional ethic of Shakespeare's society was still that of the medieval theologians who found it sinful both to lend money for personal profit rather than out of generosity and to have sexual relations for pleasure rather than for procreation. On usury, Aquinas, for example, had said, "To take usury from any man is simply evil, because we ought to treat every man as our neighbour and brother."[5] And summing up the thought of many other theologians, Saint Raymond said, "One ought to lend to one's needy neighbor only for God and principally from charity."[6] In Elizabethan England the condemnation of usury was repeated both by caricaturing dramatists and also by such preachers as Henry Smith, Miles Mosse, Roger Fenton, Nicholas Sanders, Philip Caesar, and Gerard Malynes.[7] On sex, Aquinas had said, "The end, however, which nature intends in copulation is offspring to be procreated and educated, and that this good might be sought it has put delight in copulation, as Augustine says, *Marriage and Concupiscence*, 1.8. Whoever, therefore, uses copulation for the delight which is in it, not referring the intention to the end intended by nature, acts against nature."[8] Various medieval theologians made various accommodations to mixed motives, but in general both money-lending and sex were supposed to be for the benefit of others more than for oneself. Actual behavior, of course, fell short of these ideals, but in the Middle Ages the feudal socioeconomic system supported them, while in the Renaissance socioeconomic changes pulled in the opposite direction.

Although some of our pictures of the community life from which the Elizabethans were emerging may be oversimplified, nevertheless it seems clear that they experienced an increasing individualism, acquisitiveness, and competitiveness. Of course, Shakespeare's audience did not make a sharp break with the past and give up the ideals of charity and self-sacrifice. Rather, their very retention of traditional ideals added to their sense of inner conflict. The need to define charity so that it could be combined with greater self-consciousness and a changing socioeconomic system led many theologians, both Protestant and Catholic, to new formulations; the struggle between communal and individualistic social systems had its analogue in psychic struggle.[9] The Merchant of Venice provides a dramatic reflection of these struggles, and in its resolution of them, as apparently in history, the role of the outsider is particularly important.

Value systems that emphasize self-sacrificial giving—like the Christianity still honored in the world of The Merchant and its audience—often differentiate sharply between the community of those who give and the outsider, who has what they consider the uncivilized habit of taking and uncivilized anger at the excluding community. But of course those within the community are also taking from each other—and from those outside—although they may not admit it. Thus they may project their own acquisitiveness—and all the aggressions they cannot acknowledge—onto the outsider and persecute him or her as a scapegoat. Here Shakespeare draws on the Elizabethan theater's frequent identification of Venice with acquisitiveness to suggest its paradoxical similarity to Shylock, the outsider it calls a devil.[10]

There are many kinds of outsiders in The Merchant of Venice. Not only Shylock, but also most of Portia's suitors are ethnic outsiders to Venice. Although a citizen of Venice,

Antonio as well can be seen as a psychological outsider.[11] Portia, as a woman, is different in a more obvious sense, although in Belmont the proper metaphor for the limitation on her actions is confinement rather than exclusion, and in Venice she passes for a Roman male. Insofar as her society is structured in patriarchal terms, it justifies its subordination of her by beliefs similar to those that justify its subordination of Shylock. Women and Jews could be seen as symbolic of absolute otherness—alien, mysterious, uncivilized, unredeemed. In this tradition, femaleness and Jewishness as qualities in themselves were associated with the flesh, not the spirit, and therefore with impulses toward sexuality, aggression, and acquisitiveness.[12]

However, as the Introduction to this book has suggested, the attitude toward women in Shakespeare's society was not simply patriarchal, nor is it in this play. Nor could the attitude toward sexuality, aggression, or acquisitiveness have been monolithic. I believe that The Merchant of Venice likewise shows a divided attitude toward these qualities and distinguishes among their manifestations. Portia's active capacity for mutuality integrates and transforms associations of women with the flesh. Her self-assertion promises energies to sustain a more realistic love and community. In her betrothal speech to Bassanio, she explicitly denies the egoism of the isolated self, but suggests that her loving marriage to Bassanio multiplies her wishes for what she can share with him.

> Though for myself alone
> I would not be ambitious in my wish
> To wish myself much better, yet for you
> I would be trebled twenty times myself,
> A thousand times more fair, ten thousand times more
>   rich.   (3.2.150–54)

Shylock, however, both speaks for and suffers from the most threatening possibilities of self-assertion. He is portrayed as one who is ambitious for himself alone.

Shylock's main role is to speak for the aggressive and

acquisitive motives that his society follows but does not admit. His powerful appeal to human commonality that begins "Hath not a Jew eyes?" (3.1.51) makes its climactic point "And if you wrong us, shall we not revenge? If we are like you in the rest, we will resemble you in that" (3.1.57–59). In his first scene with Antonio and Bassanio he explains his anger at being treated like a dog, as if they might remember their own anger at being insulted and understand him. But insofar as his audience considers anger one of the seven deadly sins, his defense fails; it plays into the tendency to project anger onto an outsider and becomes a justification for further exclusion.

While his hostility and acquisitiveness are most evidently what his society fears in him, he suggests other qualities important in the transition to the Renaissance. When he tells about Jacob's breeding of spotted sheep by sympathetic magic, Shylock emphasizes the potency of Jacob's cleverness: "Mark what Jacob did . . . the skillful shepherd" (1.3.73, 80). By contrast, Antonio, the spokesman for his society's traditional values, denies Jacob's power and emphasizes his risk—using, of course, the same word that applies to his own attempts to make money:

> This was a venture, sir, that Jacob served for,
> A thing not in his power to bring to pass,
> But swayed and fashioned by the hand of heaven.
> (1.3.87–89)

What Shylock stresses and Antonio denies is precisely the element of individual mastery that became more important in the Renaissance; such mastery correlates with the humorous vitality of Shylock's speech, which, as Sigurd Burckhardt has pointed out, contrasts with the somberness and ineffectiveness of Antonio's.[13] On the other hand, Antonio's emphasis on the uncertainty of Jacob's ventures corresponds to the fact that the scholastic analysis of usury distinguished it from other more lawful forms of moneymaking, like Antonio's, by its lack of risk.[14]

Although he profits financially from the new acquisitive

society, Antonio cannot admit that he is anything but a giver, whether to Bassanio or to his other debtors.[15] At the start, he says to Bassanio, "My purse, my person, my extremest means / Lie all unlocked to your occasions" (1.1.138–39). Suggesting a coalescence with classical Roman ideals of generosity, Bassanio describes him to Portia as

> The best-conditioned and unwearied spirit
> In doing courtesies, and one in whom
> The ancient Roman honor more appears
> Than any that draws breath in Italy.   (3.2.293–96)

Courtesy and honor demand a minimizing of the giver's own needs and risks; Antonio plays down the danger of taking Shylock's bond and refuses to accept Bassanio's promise of a speedy return from Belmont. Thus his generosity denies a need for mutuality and tends toward an attitude of combined self-effacement and self-sufficiency. (As policy he lends money without taking interest.) When the wreck of his ships entitles Shylock to claim a pound of his flesh, according to their contract, Antonio plays the role of one who endures and gives all for the love of his friend; he is following an ideal of self-sacrifice and imitation of Christ.[16] Benjamin Nelson has suggested that this, as well as his general willingness to lend money without taking interest, links Antonio closely with predominant medieval ethical emphases. He would have been viewed critically by such reformers as Luther, who said, "Standing surety is a work that is too lofty for a man; it is unseemly, for it is presumptuous and an invasion of God's rights."[17] The weakness of his language and his opening complaint of a sadness whose cause he does not know suggest other grounds for viewing him critically, and, in general, using a psychological perspective.

Many contemporary critics have seen homosexual feelings in Antonio's love for Bassanio.[18] But it is important to note that Shakespeare's language can go much further in suggesting sexual undertones between men than Antonio's does. The sonnets play with far more witty double entendre than do Antonio's serious and asexual words. Antonio is one of the most reluctant punsters among Shakespeare's major characters and also one of the least given to talking about sex in any way.[19] If we think of how Shakespeare's men usually talk about women among themselves—Benedick and Claudio, Oliver and Orlando, Romeo and Mercutio, Berowne and his fellows—it is remarkable that Antonio refers to Portia only at the beginning of the conversation: "What lady is the same / To whom you swore a secret pilgrimage," (1.1.119–20) and at the end as "fair Portia" (1.1.182). Nor does Antonio make punning references to male sexuality like those at the end of Sonnet 20:

> But since she pricked thee out for women's pleasure,
> Mine be thy love, and thy love's use their treasure.

Antonio typically presents himself as completely asexual, as if following an ideal of celibacy; he behaves like the altruists described by Anna Freud who have given up to another person, with whom they identify, the right to have their instincts gratified.[20] Nevertheless, there is one point at which Antonio finds it impossible to maintain his attitude of total self-sacrifice; the wreck of his ships finally forces him to make a request of Bassanio. Even then he tries not to ask it directly: "My bond to the Jew is forfeit. And since in paying it, it is impossible I should live, all debts are cleared between you and I if I might but see you at my death. Notwithstanding, use your pleasure. If your love do not persuade you to come, let not my letter" (3.2.317–22). For all Antonio's self-effacing posture, this wording makes Bassanio's appearance a test of his love.[21] In spite of his intent, Antonio expresses a need for a mutuality of relationship in which he can receive as well as give. And it is interesting that this is also a point where sexual double entendre may lurk in Antonio's language. Bassanio has just betrothed himself to Portia, and in that context "use your pleasure" sounds a little more like the end of Sonnet 20.[22]

But if in general Antonio denies or sublimates his own sexuality and instead supports Bassanio's pursuit of Portia, he also denies the acquisitiveness inherent in being a merchant and instead attacks Shylock, the double who shares and exaggerates his mercantile profession and marginal social status. Even in this respect, however, he generally presents himself as self-denying, patiently holding in check his hostility to Shylock everywhere but in the scene where he arranges the loan. In his verbal attack on Shylock there, his speech takes on unusual energy; this is the one scene in which Antonio does not speak about being sad. His temporary recovery resembles the relief from a sense of powerlessness and depression that modern psychologists have often found to be one function of anti-Semitic outbursts.[23]

Subject to the conflicting forces of Antonio and Portia, Bassanio mediates between them in his attitude toward giving. His giving is responsive rather than self-sacrificing; impoverished as he is, he is quite willing to take as well, but the juxtaposition of the two men ultimately emphasizes Bassanio's frivolity as well as Antonio's somberness. With Antonio's help, he can indulge in inviting his friends and even Shylock to dinner, taking on the hungry Lancelot Gobbo as an extra servant, and sending gifts to Portia. His attempt at unlimited generosity with his words complements Antonio's attempt at unlimited generosity with his money and his life. Bassanio's spontaneity is appealing, but there is something of a naive love of fine gestures in it, a romanticism of risk, magnanimity, and promise unqualified by a sense of responsibility.[24] In a comparison he himself uses in asking money from Antonio, he gives and takes like a child at play—who believes that he can give anything away and have it to give again.

Juxtaposed with these three male characters, however admirable, fascinating, or charming they may be at their best, Portia seems much better able to cope with the world in which she lives—indeed, to protect it from the dangers of extreme asceticism, individualism, or irresponsibility. From the beginning of the play, where she mocks all her suitors, she would fall short by traditional standards of perfect charity, but she succeeds by the standards of romantic comedy. We first meet her complaining about one of the limitations traditionally set on women—patriarchal control of marriage choice.[25] When she finds a way of dealing with this problem, it is not the blithe unconsciousness of limits that Bassanio shows, any more than it is passive self-sacrifice like Antonio's. In a situation that makes her an object to be chosen, her mockery of her suitors shows that she preserves her own wish to choose, and she defines her own requirements in a husband by observing what her suitors lack. For all the xenophobia in her wit, what she criticizes most are qualities that hinder mutuality of social interchange: "he doth nothing but talk of his horse. . . . He doth nothing but frown—as who should say, 'An you will not have me, choose!' He hears merry tales and smiles not; . . . he will fence with his own shadow. . . . You know I say nothing to him, for he understands not me, nor I him" (1.2.38–39, 43–45, 57, 63–64).

And because of her own skill in talking with people, she learns how to work with the limitations of the casket test. Although in its choice of imagery it *seems* to dramatize a definition of woman as an object, she can use it to disqualify those who so define her and would deny her an active role in a mutual relationship.[26] With Morocco and Arragon, she speaks much more of the rules of the game than of her own feelings, and by hurrying them to the caskets, she exposes their susceptibility to the possession-oriented mottos: "Who chooseth me shall gain what many men desire" and "Who chooseth me shall get as much as he deserves."

With Bassanio, by contrast, Portia can be much more than the passive object of quest. There is a new spontaneity in her language as she feels her way into trusting him with her thoughts:

There's something tells me, but it is not love,
I would not lose you; and you know yourself
Hate counsels not in such a quality.   (3.2.4–6)

By speaking of his company as something she does not want to lose, she first puts herself in the position of one who receives and asks for gifts; at the same time her language is generous. Perhaps by her own risk-taking, more than by any verbal hint, she reinforces his love of risk and encourages the frame of mind in which he chooses the casket demanding that he "give and hazard all he hath." Although she feels herself already his, she then speaks as active giver of herself. In light of all the economic imagery in this scene, it is interesting that her words to him here— "Myself and what is mine to you and yours / Is now converted" (3.2.166–67)—echo a medieval etymological pun often found in scholastic writings against usury: "A loan [mutuum] is so called from this, that mine [meum] becomes yours [tuum]."[27] As in a purely financial partnership, however, she can ask for a share in the outcome of his ventures: "I am half yourself, / And I must freely have the half of anything / That this same paper brings you" (3.2.248–50). When what it brings is news of Antonio's losses, her decision to help comes not from an impersonal generosity but from a personal sense of relationship, through Bassanio, with Antonio, "the semblance of my soul" (3.4.20). Antonio's friendship with Bassanio has been basically one-sided, since generosity with money and life costs more than generosity with words; Portia tries to make their relationship more mutual as she both insists that Bassanio meet his obligations and enables him to do so.

In the trial scene, Venice continues to emphasize its own generosity in trying to deal with Shylock. Each of the male characters tries to play out his role to the extreme, and limitations suggested earlier become apparent; only Portia can act effectively. Shylock talks only about a side of human existence the Venetians would prefer to forget—impulses to destroy. "Hates any man the thing he would not kill?" (4.1.67). While earlier he could explain his anger as a response to Antonio's contempt, here he refuses to make his case in public terms—"I'll not answer that, / But say it is my humor" (4.1.42–43)—except to point out the dependence of the Venetian slaveholding system on the inviolability of *private* bonds analogous to his with Antonio. Antonio also refuses to argue his case in the court. Initially he presents his surrender as a kind of moral victory:

> I do oppose
> My patience to his fury, and am armed
> To suffer with a quietness of spirit
> The very tyranny and rage of his. . . .   (4.1.10–13)

However, as the scene proceeds, some telling lines suggest that his sadness has its basis in his own anger turned inward, and they hint at the psychological basis for the peculiarly compelling quality in the confrontation between Shylock and Antonio:

> I am a tainted wether of the flock,
> Meetest for death. The weakest kind of fruit
> Drops earliest to the ground, and so let me.
> (4.1.114–16)

The startling self-disgust of these lines suggests the limits of Antonio's solution to the conflict between self-sacrifice and self-assertion.

Earlier Antonio's language made him seem asexual; now he makes the image more concrete by calling himself a "wether"—castrated. Both "tainted" and the likelihood of rottenness in "the weakest kind of fruit" that "drops earliest to the ground" suggest disease and corruption. Whether he is criticizing himself for his asexuality and sense of powerlessness—tainted because he is a wether—or for the sexuality that makes him feel tainted and that he therefore tries to deny—a wether because he is tainted—he is clearly accusing himself of both disease and weakness. Oddly echoing his earlier attack on Shylock as "a goodly apple rotten at the heart" (1.3.97), Antonio here seems to be calling himself a failure by two different sets of standards, goodness as valued by Christianity and power as valued by individualism. Again his words call for a psychological interpretation,

and psychoanalytic theory directly connects such self-criticism and depression with idealism and self-sacrifice. Freud
explains self-criticism in melancholia by saying that "the
more a man controls his aggressiveness, the more intense
becomes his ideal's inclination to aggressiveness against his
ego."[28] Applying this concept to the suicidal melancholic,
A. Alvarez describes his harsh internal ego-ideal as "an
unappeased Doppelgänger, not to be placated, crying out
to be heard."[29] Some of the power of the trial scene comes
from the confrontation between Antonio and a character
very much like this unappeased doppelgänger. The demands Shylock makes on Antonio coalesce with the demands Antonio makes on himself.

   Both Antonio and Shylock appear to want the same outcome for the trial. Antonio's death would, apparently, be a
victory for both of them according to their own opposite
standards. The values they speak for are, of course, very
much in conflict, and thus the conflict seems an impossible one to resolve. Where the play seems most clearly to
be dramatizing the conflict between the opposing values of
self-sacrifice and individualism, it dramatizes the conflict as
a deadlock.[30] Both the Duke and Bassanio attempt to medi-
ate, but they are too openly hostile to Shylock and too
similar to Antonio in their rhetoric and surface values.

   Only Portia, using her outsider's perspective, can act effectively. She closes her "quality of mercy" speech with an
admission such as none of the other characters has made
that Shylock has a case in justice, and this prepares for her
final ability to defeat him. Unlike the other characters, she
can establish a common language with him; an outsider
herself, she must be able to use language for more purposes than communion with friends or anger at other outsiders.

   After words of self-sacrificing devotion from Antonio
and Bassanio, it is Portia's disguised self-assertion that first
hints that something may prevent Antonio and Shylock
from acting out to the end their roles of giver and taker.

Bassanio responds to Antonio's emotional farewell by declaring:

> life itself, my wife, and all the world
> Are not with me esteemed above thy life.
> I would lose all, ay sacrifice them all
> Here to this devil, to deliver you.   (4.1.282–85)

Portia draws back from the immediate situation and reminds us of the greater awareness and detachment her disguise gives her, like the awareness and detachment that come from recognizing that one is playing a game in which the rules can be manipulated. She says, "Your wife would give you little thanks for that / If she were by to hear you make the offer" (4.1.286–87). The realistic literalism of her words punctures the emotional and idealistic mood. Her skepticism about self-sacrifice puts her in momentary alliance with Shylock, who says, "These be the Christian husbands!" (4.1.293). She is too vital to let her husband get away with talking about sacrificing her—even at a farewell to his best friend—and at the same time resourceful enough to voice her complaint in a joke entirely in character for the objective doctor of laws she is playing. While Shylock, observing her insistence on the law and her outsider's irony here, may think he has met his ally, we can see that he has actually met his match. Her use of language here—detached, witty, literal to the point of being unfair—directly prepares for her use of language to save Antonio herself rather than being sacrificed for him. "This bond doth give thee here no jot of blood; / The words expressly are 'a pound of flesh'" (4.1.304–5). Thus reading very literally the words that Shylock and Antonio agreed to as partners in the bond, she finds a way to force them out of their extreme positions—to compel Antonio to take and Shylock to give—for of course the court will seize on any means an apparently objective lawyer gives to defeat Shylock.

It is interesting to compare the trial scene with the somewhat similar deadlock that occurs in *Richard II* in the confrontation between Richard and Henry Bolingbroke, often seen as emblematic of the conflict between the Middle Ages and the Renaissance. Richard, like Antonio, presents himself as self-sacrificing, and even more explicitly compares himself to Christ. He says to Bolingbroke ironically, "They well deserve to have / That know the strong'st and surest way to get" (3.3.200–201). That play heads toward an outcome in which both win on their own terms, but the emphasis on conscience and sympathy is so great that whoever takes the throne appears to be in the wrong. In *The Merchant of Venice*, by contrast, Shakespeare avoids giving either Antonio or Shylock the victory on his own terms. Instead, the victory goes to Portia, and in spite of the cost to Shylock, it does not evoke the guilt of a purely egoistic victory of an isolated individual, since Portia wins it for Antonio's life as well as for the success of her marriage. Yet in the punishments she and Antonio can impose on Shylock for his intent because he is an outsider, we can see how pervasive the spirit of vengeance is in this play. No character is an ideal of perfect charity, although Antonio tries to be; the aggressive forces within and without are too strong.[31]

It has been suggested that Antonio is an ethical ideal because his attempt to sacrifice himself for his friend can be seen as an imitation of Christ. Yet by making him a melancholy and at times self-hating figure on the comic stage, Shakespeare deliberately exposes some of Antonio's limitations even to an audience uncritical of his anti-Semitism. Furthermore, it is not only her defeat of an adversary against which he is powerless that puts Antonio and Portia into direct contrast; Antonio makes the contrast both implicitly and explicitly. He presents his impending death as a defeat for Portia in a competition about who loves Bassanio most.[32]

> Commend me to your honorable wife.
> Tell her the process of Antonio's end,

Say how I loved you, speak me fair in death;
And when the tale is told, bid her be judge
Whether Bassanio had not once a love.   (4.1.271–75)

After he escapes death, furthermore, he continues to suggest that it is he, and not Portia, who loves Bassanio; he begs Bassanio to reward the lawyer with Portia's ring by saying, "Let his deservings, and my love withal, / Be valued 'gainst your wife's commandèment" (4.1.448–49). Bassanio's choice to give away the ring he has promised Portia to keep until death—a choice made only after the lawyer has left and Antonio has made this request—prepares for the fifth act's further development of the contrast between Portia and Antonio.

"I pray you know me when we meet again" (4.1.417) is Portia's farewell to Bassanio in the trial scene, and the pun on "know," which relates sexuality to recognition, anticipates her emphasis on sexual identity in the return to Belmont and her implicit victory over Antonio. In the trial, the threat of aggression has been removed by projection onto a scapegoat; at Belmont, it can be dissolved in play—mock hostility that unites the married couples more closely. In the trial the characters presented a general show of liberality from which only Shylock was excluded; at Belmont, Portia and Nerissa will incorporate some of Shylock's self-assertion and demand for his rights into their relationships with their husbands.[33] In the trial there has been a demonstration of *agape*, love that gives without asking for any return, in Antonio's willingness to die;[34] in the fifth act the focus is on love as *eros*, which desires also to receive.

When the returning wives make their husbands account for giving away their rings, the strongly sexual tone of the threats and counter-accusations makes it clear that the argument is in some way working out—or rather playing out—threats from sexuality at the same time that it is parodying threats from Shylock. Portia pretends possessiveness and promiscuity, parallels to the financial acquisitiveness and irresponsibility of earlier scenes. She assumes an inexorability like Shylock's, and Bassanio thinks she even makes a similar threat on his bodily integrity: he says, "Why, I were best to cut my left hand off / And swear I lost the ring defending it" (5.1.177–78).

But at the same time the threat is all controlled. Portia's quick conversational repartee with Bassanio has the formal parallelism of structure that one might find in a ritual or a rhetorical exercise. While acting angry at Bassanio, she is actually uniting the two of them more closely by emphasizing their sexual relationship. "Lie not a night from home" (5.1.230) is more an expression of desire than a warning.

Portia's play with Bassanio is echoed by Nerissa's with Gratiano: both of them include a number of jokes and equivocations about sexual identity.

> Nerissa   The clerk will ne'er wear hair on's face that
>   had it.
> Gratiano He will, an if he live to be a man.
> Nerissa   Ay, if a woman live to be a man.   (5.1.158–60)

Nerissa is exuberating in her own disguised participation in the trial scene; her jokes and Portia's break down the general identification of the Christians against Shylock in the trial, where no sexual distinctions or relationships appeared. The wordplay on change of sex calls attention to sexual differentiation, a physical parallel to the mock-hostility and playful self-assertion of this scene.

The joking byplay creates an atmosphere in which Antonio feels uncomfortable. "I am th'unhappy subject of these quarrels" (5.1.238), he says, in a line that seems somewhat presumptuous at first. In a sense, however, they are quarreling about him. It was Antonio whose trial caused Bassanio's departure from Portia on their wedding day; it was Antonio who finally persuaded Bassanio to give the lawyer the ring. Even when Bassanio tries to conceal Antonio's intervention in his explanation to Portia, the motives he gives are words he used earlier in describing Antonio's virtues:

I was beset with shame and courtesy.
My honor would not let ingratitude
So much besmear it.   (5.1.217–18)

These values of public generosity and individual reliability
here confront the value of mutuality identified with Portia
and marriage; we see Antonio's generous self-effacement
causing his lack of participation in the vitality of both jokes
and sexuality.[35]

In the final reconciliation between husband and wife,
the threats of possessiveness and promiscuity are both dis-
pelled, and the vision is one of a sexual relationship in
which both partners can maintain their own identity. At
the same time we are reassured that the idealism about
self-sacrificing friendship that Antonio and Bassanio express and the reciprocal sexual relationship that Portia demands need not finally conflict with each other. Portia
makes Antonio the intermediary when she returns her
ring; afterwards she announces that his argosies are safe,
and he pays tribute to her power, relinquishes his earlier
depreciation of her, and acknowledges that he himself can
receive as well as give. "Sweet lady, you have given me life
and living!" (5.1.286).

Like Shylock's, Portia's role involves both power and
powerlessness. Portia appears powerless at the beginning,
and Shylock at the end, as reflections of a society in which
women and Jews do not have equal rights; at other points
in the play we see them possessing a power that is partly
money, partly wit, and partly what Shakespeare's imagery
makes of the magic that their society projects onto them.
While the conclusion of the trial repeats the official power
relationships between Christians and Jews, the working
out of marriage relationships, by contrast, balances the official power in society. This reverses the situation in the
other early comedy that ends with an emphatic ritual acknowledgment of marital power, *The Taming of the Shrew*,
where Petruchio's roles as game-leader and patriarchal
husband coalesce. But Portia's purpose in her final game is

not, like Petruchio's, to get the spouse to play along; Bassanio, flexible and responsive, always follows the game-leader. It is, more accurately, to demonstrate to Antonio that she and Bassanio are in one game that excludes him—their marriage gives them a bond that takes precedence over other friendships—but that he can still play the role of friend to both of them. In trying to get Antonio with his ascetic idealism to accept the value of marriage, Portia and Shakespeare are acting analogously to those Renaissance humanists and puritans who were writing in praise of marriage, modifying traditional devaluations of women, and criticizing the application of the ideal of celibacy.

Earlier Gratiano and Salerio agreed that love was a constant and unstable pursuit of something new, and Gratiano added that like all other desires it leaves one "lean, rent, and beggared" (2.6.19), but the opposition between such passion and asceticism—between taking and giving—is transcended in the image of mutuality in love with which the play ends. Momentarily the three main characters fall into a tableau that could resemble the image of the Graces as deities of gifts, explained by Seneca in "De Beneficiis."[36] In this image, important in Renaissance iconology and especially in the Neoplatonic philosophy of love of Marsilio Ficino,[37] Seneca explains that the arrangement of the Graces "in a ring which returns upon itself" shows "that a benefit passing in its course from hand to hand returns nevertheless to the giver" ("De Beneficiis," 3:13, 15). Yet we are free to think of the psychology of the characters as in tension with the image of harmony, just as the psychology of the trial scene is clearly opposed to the ritual significance of Shylock's baptism.

Michael Goldman has suggested that the great characters of both comedy and tragedy act out an attitude to the extreme, live out a wish of the audience beyond the bounds of ordinary life, and then find their self-definition questioned.[38] The self-surrender of Antonio, the aggression of Shylock, and the responsiveness of Bassanio are all attitudes Shakespeare's audience had within themselves: alternative possible reactions to social change and personal loss. They are attitudes we all have within ourselves, and the play gives us a chance to dramatize our internal conflicts about them. It is the triumph of comic wish fulfillment that Portia can combine all three attitudes and finish the play bound in love and friendship with the representatives of the two attitudes the audience of Shakespeare's time honored most. Throughout, Portia is operating within limits—her father's will, her husband's departure, the laws of Venice, and the decision of the judge and Antonio. Yet she maneuvers superbly within those limits, and, unlike the other characters we have discussed, she is never humbled for going too far in any direction. In the final scene, she stops playing the role of the jealous and promiscuous wife at her own decision. Having already pronounced her submission to Bassanio with no prejudice to her autonomy in the trial scene or the ring game, she does not even make the gestures of self-subordination with which Rosalind and Beatrice end their plays.

Shakespeare's early poems and comedies, with their twins and their images of friendship, love, and marriage as double identity, show a fascination with the element of identification in love.[39] Their structure and themes also suggest a concern for ideals of community. But he, like his society, was also fascinated by the separateness and the desire for self-assertion of the individual. Shakespeare's characters must face the fact that they are different, other, separate from those they love; they must recognize that the possibility of giving and receiving requires this separate identity, that love involves a risk that identification, whether possessive or generous, would deny.[40] Like the threat of Shylock, whose trial postpones the consummation of marriages, otherness may seem an obstacle to love —and indeed, Shylock's conversion may be intended, among other things, as an exorcism of its threat. But the acceptance of Portia's self-assertion in The Merchant of Venice is also a celebration of the ways that people manage to love one another with all their differences. In the words of a nun who taught me in grade school, "Marriages are always mixed." In the tragedies, such acceptance is harder for the heroes to achieve.

Chapter Five
Tragic Women as Actors
and Audience

At the center of Shakespeare's comedies, as we have seen, there is frequently a female character who is acting a part—whether disguising herself as a boy or pretending in some more subtle fashion. These characters usually play roles that provide counter-roles for the men and draw them into participation. By the end of the play, characters of both sexes can be alternately actors and audience, cooperating in a relationship of mutuality.[1] Both meanings of "act" apply: the women's acting has been deed as well as pretense; their fictions have helped express, even create, some kind of truth. When the men finally discover that the women have pretended false identities, no shadow falls on the celebration.

In the tragedies, however, the image of the woman as actor is more problematic. The heroes' suspicion of female pretense darkens their view of the women, whether the women actually pretend or not. The men's own acting—whether deed or pretense—discourages female participation. When Shakespeare's tragic women do act, the men find it difficult to cooperate or be audience. Thus, the tragic women are often confined to being audience to the hero, mediating the offstage audience's sympathy with their own, as Ophelia does for Hamlet, Desdemona for Othello, and even Lady Macbeth for Macbeth. Furthermore, because of the men's suspicion of female pretense, the sympathy the female characters express often cannot reach them; the women are ultimately like the tragic audience in their sense of powerlessness and separateness, rather than like the comic audience, which, as we have seen, can be valued for its responsiveness and imagination.

To Hamlet, for example, even his mother's tears for his father seem "unrighteous" (1.2.154) because of her subsequent remarriage. He is enraged by the pretenses he sees in women—"God hath given you one face, and you make yourselves another" (3.1.143–44), he says to Ophelia. But Ophelia's shifting responses are less controlled pretense than the result of the audience-like passivity she brings to encounters with other characters. Even in the nunnery scene, on stage for her father and Claudius, she phrases her hurt at Hamlet's rejection as a kind of compliment on his acting:

> Hamlet I did love you once.
> Ophelia Indeed, my lord, you made me believe so. . . .
> Hamlet I loved you not.
> Ophelia I was the more deceived.   (3.1.115–16, 119–20)

At the end of his attack, though she is "of ladies most deject and wretched" (3.1.155), her tone is much more one of sympathy for Hamlet—"Th'observed of all observers, quite, quite down!" (3.1.154)—than of concern for herself. It has been argued that Ophelia and similar heroines speak such lines not in their own person but to guide audience reaction to the hero. The words do guide audiences to sympathy, I agree, but they also say something about the audience-actor nature of Ophelia's relationship with Hamlet; she is a mediator between him and the offstage audience. It is characteristic of them that when they watch a play together, Hamlet cannot bear to be just a spectator, while Ophelia is a spectator to both him and the play. She must go mad in order to escape social restrictions and take center stage.

At the beginning of Othello, Desdemona seems likely to be more successful as both actor and audience. The beginning of their love, as Othello lyrically describes it, seems the hyperbole of an ideal actor-audience relationship. "She loved me for the dangers I had passed, / And I loved her that she did pity them" (1.3.167–68). With her gestures, tears, and sympathy, her response to his storytelling is an actor's dream. Like the theater audience, furthermore, she identifies with him; she wishes, ambiguously, "That heaven had made her such a man" (1.3.163), and he recalls that she would "With a greedy ear / Devour up my discourse" (1.3.149–50); her listening is such an intense and incorporative activity that Othello can only compare it to eating, just as Norman Holland compares an attentive theater audience to a child wishing to merge with a mother who feeds it.[2]

Desdemona, however, goes beyond the audience's responsiveness. Because of the restrictions of her society, her acting-as-doing requires acting-as-pretending, and her abilities in both coalesce. In the emotional moment we have just heard Othello describe, she resourcefully finds a way to initiate courtship while seeming to him merely to be hinting:

> She thanked me;
> And bade me, if I had a friend that loved her,
> I should but teach him how to tell my story,
> And that would woo her.   (1.3.163–66)

Later examples of the two forms of acting, now separated, do not work so well. Her pretense that her handkerchief is lost and her commitment to Cassio—"If I do vow a friendship, I'll perform it / To the last article" (3.3.21–22)—both contribute to Othello's anger at her. In reaction, she again assumes the role of audience, trying to understand Othello, sympathizing with him, imagining him in pain.

> Something sure of state . . .
> Hath puddled his clear spirit. . . .
>   . . . let our finger ache, and it endues
> Our other, healthful members even to a sense
> Of pain.   (3.4.140, 143, 146–48)

But rather than seeing her pain, Othello describes her tears as "well-painted passion" (4.1.250) and casts her in the role of a prostitute who can act to suit her customer's fancy. "Sir, she can turn, and turn, and yet go on / And turn again; and she can weep, sir, weep" (4.2.246–47). She keeps trying to break into his nightmare world, to ask for a specific accusation so she can defend herself—but his insistence that she is false means that none of her words can persuade him; if he doubts her honesty in the Elizabethan sense of sexual fidelity, he can never believe in the honesty of her words. She lives in a society where women are always suspect, and Iago has used her own love and survival techniques against her: "She that, so young, could give out such a seeming / To seel her father's eyes up close as oak—" (3.3.209–10).

At the end she is still trying to act—both to conceal her feelings and to mend the situation—but she is also still the sympathetic audience who adds to her song the line "Let nobody blame him; his scorn I approve" (4.3.50):

> Emilia   I would you had never seen him!
> Desdemona   So would not I. My love doth so approve him
>   That even his stubbornness, his checks, his
>   frowns—
>   Prithee unpin me—have grace and favor in
>   them.   (4.3.17–20)

Her last combination of acting with audience-like sympathy occurs after her apparent death, when she speaks upon Emilia's return:

> Emilia   O, who hath done this deed?
> Desdemona   Nobody—I myself. Farewell.
>   Commend me to my kind lord.
>   (5.2.124–26)

Even in this absurd attempt to claim Othello's guilt as her own, he sees only sinful pretense: "She's like a liar gone to burning hell!" (5.2.130). After he discovers her truth, his words still suggest inability to appreciate her integration of sympathy and acting. He speaks of her as a kind of rejecting audience—"This look of thine will hurl my soul from heaven" (5.2.275)—identifies her chastity with coldness, and finally describes her as a pearl—an image where the beauty and value are no less striking than the absence of animate energy.

Different as Lady Macbeth is from Desdemona, she has a similar vicarious interest in her husband's achievements, and similar sympathy for his sufferings. Pursuing their goals involves both women in pretense and stirs their resourcefulness in crises. But Macbeth's progressive insistence on acting on his own turns Lady Macbeth to an isolated and powerless audience.

Initially she advises him on pretending innocence and can herself pretend quite effectively to be a loving hostess and a grieved one after the death of Duncan. But basically she is dependent on Macbeth's acting. Though he calls her his "dearest partner of greatness" (1.5.10–11), it is his greatness, his manhood, his ambition she speaks about even in her soliloquies. Her own ambition is expressed through playing the encouraging and taunting wife, concerned about her husband's career and self-esteem—a much more complex version of the unquenchable burning for a crown of her counterpart in Holinshed. Robert Egan has suggested that her influence on Macbeth here is very much the audience's influence on an actor.[3] I would agree, but would note that this influence is only one phase of her relation with Macbeth, and that influence is only one aspect of an audience's relation to an actor. Her influence is dependent on her inability to rule or kill directly, somewhat as the audience's influence is dependent on the agreement that its members will not act in the play they are watching. Lady Macbeth's words here express one attitude the offstage audience can take toward Macbeth—complicity and vicarious satisfaction in his self-assertion. After the murders, her role as audience and voice for some audience attitudes is clearer—since Macbeth will not let her help in his future plans or even tell her what they are, in

their scene alone together (3.2) all she can do is sympathize with him and encourage him in his plans to play the
jovial host. In the banquet scene she tries to keep the show
going on by improvising when he cannot hide his reactions to Banquo's ghost, but her performance is useless
without his cooperation. Afterward she is audience again—
the clearest feeling in her few words is sympathy: "You lack
the season of all natures, sleep" (3.4.141). But Macbeth has
grown so withdrawn that he can scarcely accept even her
sympathy, let alone her cooperative acting. She now, like
Ophelia, can take center stage only when her rational consciousness is suspended. Macbeth finally reacts to her suicide by speaking not about her but about the meaningless-
ness of life. His words expressing his discomfort in his
own role also suggest his growing inability to be a responsive audience to her or to anyone else:

> The time has been my senses would have cooled
> To hear a night-shriek, and my fell of hair
> Would at a dismal treatise rouse and stir
> As life were in't. . . .
> Life's but a walking shadow, a poor player
> That struts and frets his hour upon the stage. . . .
>   (5.5.10–13, 24–25)

While *Lear* includes two women who exemplify the pretense most tragic heroes fear, it gives the suspicion of that
pretense not to the hero but to Cordelia, who censors her
own words by it. She disclaims "that glib and oily art / To
speak and purpose not" (1.1.224–25); she exemplifies what
Jonas Barish calls the nontheatrical protagonist, characterized by rectitude rather than plenitude.[4] While other tragedies, like *Othello*, generally combine female pretense and
female attempts at autonomy, so that we may be confused
about which infuriates the hero more, here the two are
separated and it is clear that what Lear resents is the challenge to his desire for control. It should be noted, furthermore, that Cordelia refuses not only to pretend but also to

say anything that might be interpreted as pretense. The kind of acting that she refuses in the first scene is the emotional expression, on cue, of feelings that are really hers. She loves Lear, but she does not want him to control how she expresses that love.

But as Lear, cast out from society, becomes more critical of its pretenses, Cordelia, freed from her father's commands, expresses her feelings of love for him more openly. Shakespeare includes a choral scene to draw our attention to this: when Kent and the Gentleman discuss her reactions to the letters about her father, their descriptions and questions at times sound like those of a theater critic:

Kent	Did your letters pierce the Queen to any demonstration of grief?
Gentleman	Ay, sir. She took them, read them in my presence,
	And now and then an ample tear trilled down Her delicate cheek....
Kent	O, then it movèd her?
Gentleman	Not to a rage. Patience and sorrow strove Who should express her goodliest....
	Faith, once or twice she heaved the name of father
	Pantingly forth, as if it pressed her heart.

(4.3.9–13, 15–17, 25–26)

Kent and the Gentleman are extraordinarily interested in her expression of her feelings; this scene prepares us for what we will see in her later appearance and also makes a link between the role of actor and the role of audience. For Cordelia, in expressing her feelings for Lear, is also playing the role of audience here and in the next scene. In her sympathy for Lear, she is providing a voice, a mediation for the sympathy of the offstage audience. But at the same time her words and gestures accomplish something onstage— they give the recognition, love, and forgiveness that Lear needs and asks for:

Lear   As I am a man, I think this lady
              To be my child Cordelia.
Cordelia   And so I am! I am!
Lear   Be your tears wet? Yes, faith. I pray weep not.
          If you have poison for me, I will drink it.
          I know you do not love me; for your sisters
          Have (as I do remember) done me wrong.
          You have some cause, they have not.
Cordelia   No cause, no cause.
                                        (4.7.68–75)

She moves from audience-like sympathy to its expression
in tears, words, and gestures that finally reach Lear; she is
even willing to use the verbal pretense of "No cause, no
cause."

In an essay on *Lear* and the theatrical experience, Stanley
Cavell asks, "What is the difference between tragedy in a
theater and tragedy in actuality? In both, people in pain are
in our presence. But in actuality acknowledgment is incomplete, . . . unless we put ourselves in their presence, reveal
ourselves to them."[5] For the theater audience, however, no
self-revelation to those they see suffering is expected or
possible. Many of the examples of sympathy expressed by
the women discussed previously have been more like that
of a theater audience—incomplete by the standards of actuality—because they have been expressed in the hero's
absence; even in speaking to the hero, Lady Macbeth and
Ophelia often maintain something of the audience's refusal
to acknowledge themselves. Few as her words are, however, Cordelia's acknowledgment of her relationship to
Lear is extraordinarily powerful and seems complete. In
this reunion scene each can be moved by the other, like an
audience, and express feelings, like an actor, in a kind of
mutual dependence. But Cordelia reaches Lear here partly
because she has proved herself by her earlier refusal to say
anything that could be construed as pretense. Only in *Antony and Cleopatra* does the man enjoy the woman's ability to
pretend as much as he suspects it.

Antony and Cleopatra is the only Shakespearean tragedy that focuses on and indeed glorifies the woman as actor in both senses, doer and pretender, and, not coincidentally, as sexually active. Whether she is asking for a declaration of love from Antony or asking him to return to Rome, Cleopatra is likely to be role-playing. Antony does at times angrily accuse her of deception, but she, unlike the other heroines so accused, makes similar accusations to him:

> Good now, play one scene
> Of excellent dissembling, and let it look
> Like perfect honor.   (1.3.78–80)

Much more than the other tragic heroes, each of them can be mollified; their ability to forgive and start over is closely related to their ability to play many different roles. Furthermore, each of them can also be appreciative audience to the other:

> Fie, wrangling queen!
> Whom everything becomes—to chide, to laugh,
> To weep; whose every passion fully strives
> To make itself, in thee, fair and admired.   (1.1.48–51)

> His legs bestrid the ocean: his reared arm
> Crested the world: his voice was propertied
> As all the tunèd spheres, and that to friends. . . .
> (5.2.82–84)

In describing each other, each creates and shares the audience's admiration for the other; Cleopatra, especially, becomes artist as well as audience and actor. In the last of her visions, before her death modeled on Antony's ideals, the barriers between roles dissolve and each can be both actor and audience at once:

> Methinks I hear
> Antony call: I see him rouse himself
> To praise my noble act. I hear him mock
> The luck of Caesar. . . .   (5.2.282–85)

A skeptic may always refuse to believe in the love between Antony and Cleopatra. Love can never be proved
with mathematical certainty; attempts to show it can always be taken as pretense or self-deception. As Janet Adelman has suggested, the trust required of an audience to
believe in love onstage is analogous to the trust required of
lovers to believe in each other.[6] In *Hamlet, Othello, Macbeth,*
and *Lear*, the heroes tragically fail to achieve or maintain
their trust in the women who love them, and regain it, if
at all, when it is too late. In *Antony and Cleopatra*, by contrast, the lovers, for all their jealousy and wrangling, are
always willing to forgive each other and start over after
their fights; thus they accept the ambiguities in each other
and in their relationship and paradoxically achieve something more like trust than any of the other couples. The
role that each plays allows for and indeed demands the
partnership of a free and independent person.

Why this sharp contrast between Shakespeare's comic
and tragic men (with Antony in between) in their attitude
toward women as actors—in most of the tragic heroes a
suspicion that works to confine women to being audience,
in most of the comic heroes acceptance and participation?
The difference is clearly related not only to genre but also
to gender; women in the tragedies have no obsessive suspicion about men as actors. According to Michael Goldman, all major dramatic characters are actors in the extended sense that they "go beyond ordinary bounds in
ways that remind us of acting. They are capable of some
kind of seductive, hypnotic, or commanding expression."[7]
Thus audiences onstage and off see in them the *otherness* of
the professional actor. The character as actor is strange,
exotic, and therefore an object of both repulsion and attraction. I would suggest that within Shakespeare's tragedies, the women's reaction to the men as actors shows
much more the positive side of that ambivalence—the
sympathy and admiration. The tragic heroes' attitude to the
women as actors shows mostly the negative side. There the
suspicion of the actor as other coalesces with the general

cultural suspicion of the woman as other discussed by Simone de Beauvoir.[8] Much that Goldman says about one group could apply to both:

> The community focuses on them, makes them a cynosure, enjoys seeing them dressed up in their proper costumes at the proper times. But always the attraction springs from and exists in tension with an implied hostility. . . . They are elevated above the community by the role they take on, but their elevation exposes them [cf. woman on pedestal]; they serve at their audience's pleasure. (pp. 12–13)

Furthermore, for both women and actors, being seen as other also implies being identified with sexuality and physicality. Conditions of childbearing and traditions of childrearing associate women with the body; they have been seen as sexual temptresses since Eve became an archetype, and excessive female demands for sex were an Elizabethan commonplace.[9] Actors too, more directly than almost any other artists, use their own bodies in their work and have historically been attacked by moralists for their sexual behavior.[10] (pp. 5–6)

Shakespeare seems to have recognized and used further similarities between actors and women. Both are often seen not only as separate and alien but also as diversion. When Hamlet says, "Man delights not me" (2.2.305), the two possibilities for entertainment that occur to him and his companions are women and actors. Both are traditionally expected to survive by pleasing and are therefore dependent on others.[11] Thus in Shakespeare women often express a sense of kinship with the fool; Viola praises Feste: "He must observe their mood on whom he jests, / The quality of persons, and the time" (3.1.60–61). The necessity to please leads to much of the role-playing of which women are accused, which in turn makes them seem more strange and foreign to men who cannot determine what feelings are behind the roles. Paradoxically, however, this dependence on pleasing other people inclines both women and actors to study faces closely for clues to feelings, and thus it contributes to the ability of both groups to be audience as well, a point to which I shall return later.

Even in childhood, according to the psychologist Philip Weissman, "girls engage in play acting and play action more universally and with more spontaneous freedom than the average boy."[12] He further notes that acting begins when the infant "takes on the role of the mother, amusing her by borrowing her identity."[13] Identification with the mother is easier for girls because they are of the same sex; this ease of identification, perhaps combined with other restrictions, may be a cause of girls' early affinity for acting as well as of women's general greater ease in identifying with others, whether we see this as flexibility or weakness.[14] According to Weissman's theory, a man who becomes an actor is developing aspects of himself, shared by most women, which originate in his identification with his mother. The actor experiences "lack of differentiation of self from nonself"; his choice of profession is aimed at working out his uncertainty about how to define himself.[15] Goldman notes the universality of this need for self-definition, but if the actor, as he says (p. 122), lives closer to it, so do women. A consistent, and related, charge against actors has been "ontological subversiveness."[16] As Goldman paraphrases it, "A man is supposed to have only one being; what kind of creature can shift identities at will?" (p. 9). This same criticism can apply to women, whether they play only traditional feminine roles and mystify by their adaptability or flirtation, or traditional masculine roles and try to transcend conventional limits.

These similarities may help to explain why male actors have been effective in playing female roles in so many societies: their own experience of dependence and identification helps them in their interpretation, and since they are already "other" as actors, the audience sees them in many ways as it sees women.[17] My point here is not simply that actors are androgynous, but that traditional masculine and feminine qualities both exist in everyone to some degree.

The condition of actors mirrors the potentiality we all have to go beyond these categories—beyond all dichotomies—a potentiality threatening to believers in a neatly ordered world. As Jonas Barish points out, "The anti-theatrical prejudice belongs to a conservative ethical emphasis in which the key terms are those of order, stability, constancy, and integrity, as against a more existentialist view that prizes exploration, process, growth, flexibility, variety and versatility of response."[18] The worldview suggested by the anti-theatrical prejudice is the same one that would keep women silent and "in their place."

Paradoxically, this worldview is also part of the world-view of the typical Shakespearean tragic hero, actor though he is. He tries to be an actor-as-doer; he feels sullied by the necessity of pretending. He hates female pretense—what he sees in Ophelia, Gertrude, or Desdemona—partly because it exemplifies a way of life he is trying to transcend; he values constancy and integrity much as, like Macbeth, he may depart from them. The guiltier he feels about his own pretense, the harder it is for him to trust any woman. And the tragic genre itself is in accord with his emphasis on integrity.

The spirit of Shakespearean comedy, however, is much closer to Barish's "existentialist view." The basic explanation for the different treatment of women as actors in Shakespearean comedy and Shakespearean tragedy may be that most of the qualities which, as we have seen, are associated with both women and actors are more highly valued or more easily accepted in comedy than in tragedy. Sexuality, physicality, diversion, dependence, flexibility, compromise—all of these are much more at home in the comic world than in the tragic.

Yet actors and women are also associated with one quality that tragedy values—concern for feeling—and this concern relates closely to the characterization of women rather than men as sympathetic audiences. It is partly because emotions and their expression are so important in tragedy that the ability of the actor—or the suspected

ability of the woman—to express emotions felt only briefly
or not at all is such a threat. It is a commonplace of Elizabethan times as well as our own that women are allowed
by convention to cry when men are not; actors are also
expected to express emotions—in their performances—
more often than other people do in life. Members of a
theater audience too are there partly for the sake of the
feelings they experience and may allow themselves to cry
(or laugh) more freely than at other times. In concern for
feelings actors and audience meet; to the extent they can
respond to the feelings that an actor expresses, spectators
momentarily transcend their ambivalence toward the actor's otherness. As I have suggested, in Shakespearean
tragedy it is most often the female characters who provide
the audience with a model for this attitude. Their love of
the hero powerfully moves the offstage audience to sympathize with him, to experience the positive side of their
ambivalence. Shakespeare's women accept the otherness
of the actor in the men they love.

Perhaps we can see this most clearly when Shakespeare
uses different kinds of otherness to overlap with the otherness of the actor. Many of the characteristics shared by
women and actors are also shared by members of racial
minority groups. Certainly one of the reasons for the
power of Othello is the juxtaposition of the black man, who
knows he is seen as foreign, with the woman whom he
sees as foreign—in whom he punishes all the passions he
wishes to deny in himself, partly under pressure of his
society's expectations about his passionate nature. Similarly, both Elizabethan and modern writings show a set of
stereotypes attached to old people that also overlaps with
those for women and actors, and the confrontation between Lear and his daughters owes some of its power to
this coincidence.[19] The two plays that emphasize most the
hero's sufferings because of his membership in an alien
group are the two plays that emphasize most the women's
ability to sympathize as well as to act. It is as if Desdemona and Cordelia recognize the link between themselves

and the hero in sharing this experience of being considered other—and thus transform it into sympathy—while Goneril and Regan recognize it and reject their own possible reflection in Lear. "I pray you, father, being weak, seem so" (2.4.196), says Regan, using words frequently directed at women.

Although women in the comedies are more often actors than in the tragedies, and when they are audience it is frequently to wit rather than to feeling, there too we see women as onstage audiences responding with sympathy to an actor's emotions. For example, in *Two Gentlemen of Verona*, Julia, in her boy's disguise, tells a story about herself to Silvia, now pursued by Julia's fiancé Proteus:

> at that time I made her [Julia] weep agood,
> For I did play a lamentable part.
> Madam, 'twas Ariadne passioning
> For Theseus' perjury and unjust flight,
> Which I so lively acted with my tears
> That my poor mistress, movèd therewithal,
> Wept bitterly; and would I might be dead,
> If I in thought felt not her very sorrow!   (4.4.163–70)

Julia imagines the boy actor playing the role of a deserted woman, arousing the tears of a deserted woman (herself) in the audience, and responding to those tears with sympathy. The story arouses further sympathy in Silvia—"Alas, poor lady, desolate and left!" (4.4.172); and Silvia's response in turn arouses admiration and gratitude that restrain Julia's feelings of competition.

Of course, not all female audiences in Shakespeare are this sympathetic; Hippolyta, watching the mechanicals perform *Pyramus and Thisbe*, says, "This is the silliest stuff that ever I heard" (5.1.208). But her mockery is much less than what Demetrius, Lysander, and Theseus give that play, and in *Love's Labor's Lost* there is an even more obvious contrast between the mockery of the lords and the gracious response of the Princess to the Nine Worthies' Pageant. In neither situation do the ladies in the audience try to take over the focus of attention from the actors the way the men do.

Goneril and Regan aside, most of Shakespeare's women act using the same feelings that make them responsive audiences, and when they act they are concerned about the feelings of their audiences. In both comedy and tragedy, we can see the link between women's roles as actor and audience when their admiration or sympathy leads them to express themselves, directly or through a disguise, and actively reach out. In the comedies, the concluding rituals and marriages that result from the mutuality of this process symbolize the acceptance of compromise, dependence, physicality, ambiguity; in the tragedies, the central characters must die to prove that their emotions are felt with constancy and not simply pretended. In both comedy and tragedy, Shakespeare's women gain their dramatic power because they seem to live so close to the conflict between the desires to keep and to lose the self, between individuality and merging with others, between integrity and flexibility, which is part of the basis for the human interest in the theater.

Chapter Six
Violence, Love, and Gender in
Romeo and Juliet and *Troilus and Cressida*

As the previous chapter has shown, when we leave the comic world Shakespeare's plays show societies with a much more rigid sense of gender distinctions. However, it is not always the male character's desire to monopolize the role of actor and his suspicion of female pretense that enforce these distinctions. In three of Shakespeare's plays, female and male characters share the title. These plays all deviate from the male-actor–female-audience pattern that dominates in *Hamlet*, *Lear*, *Macbeth*, and *Othello* and resemble the comedies in other ways as well. In *Romeo and Juliet* and *Troilus and Cressida*, as in *Antony and Cleopatra*, the lovers begin as admiring audiences to each other. Juliet learns to pretend to protect her love of Romeo, and while her pretense fails, Romeo never distrusts her as the other heroes distrust women. Cressida pretends from the very beginning, and in the climactic scene Troilus is an audience to her infidelity with Diomedes. One hero lacks distrust of women, the other seems to learn it by painful experience (though we can find imagery suggestive of such distrust in his language earlier); unlike Lady Macbeth, Ophelia, or Desdemona, but more like the women of comedy, the women maintain or increase their ability to act throughout the play.

In these plays, then, suspicion of women's acting cannot be the cause of the disaster. But issues of gender politics are still important. Like the plays discussed in the previous chapter, and unlike the romantic comedies, these plays all include war or blood feud that calls on men to define their masculinity by violence.[1] In their private world, the lovers may achieve a mutuality in which both are active and genders are not polarized. But in the external world, masculinity is identified with violence and femininity with weakness; this is true in the tragedies discussed in the previous chapter as well. Romeo and Juliet establish a role-transcending private world of mutuality in love. But this world is destroyed, partly by Romeo's entanglement in the feud, partly by Juliet's continued life in her parents' house concealing her marriage. In *Troilus and Cressida*, the private world of the lovers contrasts with the military world less than usual in Shakespeare because both are so satirically treated. In both worlds we see self-centeredness, competition, mercantile values, appetite.[2] The war has stopped in the first part of the play, and the idleness of the soldiers and the "open" sexuality of the women, both satirized, make the genders less polarized than usual. But when the war revives and Cressida is exchanged, she submits with the weakness expected of her, while Troilus responds to her infidelity with a savage determination to define his masculinity by violence.[3]

The minor characters in *Romeo and Juliet* establish a background of common beliefs current in both plays: "women, being the weaker vessels, are ever thrust to the wall" (1.1.14–15) while men glory in their "naked weapon" (1.1.32). In the Nurse's view, there are compensations not found in *Troilus*—"women grow by men" (1.3.95)—but she assents to her husband's equation of female sexuality with falling backward.

Two different conventional images of this society link sex and violence. First, sexual intercourse is seen as the success of male attack.[4] For example, Benvolio consoles Romeo in his lovesickness for Rosaline by saying, "A right fair mark, fair coz, is soonest hit" (1.1.205). Romeo describes the futility of his courtship of her thus: "She will not stay the siege of loving terms / Nor bide th'encounter of assailing eyes" (1.1.210–11). Romeo has assayed this siege because he has already been hit with a different kind of violence—from "Cupid's arrow" (1.1.207). As Mercutio will later put it, he is "stabbed with a white wench's black eye; run through the ear with a love song; the very pin of his heart cleft with the blind bow-boy's butt-shaft" (2.4.14–16). Rosaline does not feel the same way, and thus "from Love's weak childish bow she lives unharmed" (1.1.209). Romeo's imagery conflates his sexual desire for Rosaline and his consequent desire that she fall in love with him—imagery of his attacking her and of love's attacking her.

When Romeo meets Juliet, he gives up using such violent imagery about sexual intercourse; when he uses it about falling in love, summing up to Friar Laurence in riddles, his emphasis is on the reciprocity of their feelings:

> I have been feasting with mine enemy,
> Where on a sudden one hath wounded me
> That's by me wounded.   (2.3.49–51)

Alternatively, he follows the image with a conceit that makes Juliet, if accepting, his protection:

> Alack, there lies more peril in thine eye
> Than twenty of their swords! Look thou but sweet,
> And I am proof against their enmity.   (2.2.71–73)

In general, with Juliet he gives up images of himself as violent aggressor. He speaks more of wanting to touch her than to conquer her, even if this means wishing away his own identity: "O that I were a glove upon that hand, / That I might touch that cheek. . . . I would I were thy bird" (2.2.24–25, 183).[5] Romeo is the only Shakespearean tragic hero who could offer to give up his name, who could say, "Had I it written, I would tear the word" (2.2.57). The strange nineteenth-century stage tradition of casting women as Romeo as well as Juliet may have been in part a response to his lack of violent imagery—except toward his own name—in their love scenes.

Nevertheless, lack of violence in the imagery does not

mean a lack of sexual energy and attraction, and Shakespeare's dialogue sensitively suggests the power of their
developing relationship. The openness and directness of
Romeo and Juliet stand out against the background of the
romantic comedies, which celebrate the gradual triumph
of love over the inhibitions and defenses of the lovers.
Only in The Merchant of Venice do two lovers (Portia and Bassanio) talk readily and without disguise at their first meeting. While the lovers in the comedies echo each other's
language and imagery as their affinity grows behind their
disguises, Romeo and Juliet at once match their shared
imagery with more emotional openness.[6]

Throughout this first meeting, Romeo takes the initiative; but at the same time, his language puts aggression at a
distance. He speaks humbly about his "unworthiest hand"
(1.5.93); if his touch is sin, it is "gentle" (1.5.94); if it is too
rough, he would prefer "a tender kiss" (1.5.96). Thus his
initiative is that of a pilgrim to a saint and claims to imply
the dominance of the woman, not the man. But his saint
does not simply stand motionless on her pedestal; she
talks back, picking up his imagery and quatrain form, and
accepts his hand as showing "mannerly devotion" (1.5.98).
Even when she claims that "Saints do not move" (1.5.105),
she is still showing her willingness for the kiss that cli-
maxes the sonnet their interchange has become:

Juliet   Saints do not move, though grant for prayers'
          sake.
Romeo   Then move not while my prayer's effect I take.
                                              (1.5.105–6)

After the kiss, Juliet gives up the imagery of sainthood:
"Then have my lips the sin that they have took" (1.5.108).
She insists on her sharing of his humanity.

The next time they meet, they share the initiative as well.
In the balcony scene, Shakespeare uses the soliloquy convention to show each of them in fantasy speaking to the
other first, but breaks that convention by showing Romeo
as the audience who responds to become actor along with

Juliet. Each speech sets the beloved outside the social framework: Romeo compares Juliet to the sun, her eyes to the stars; Juliet more consciously imagines removing him from society: "Deny thy father and refuse thy name" (2.2.34). It is when she makes a direct offer to her fantasy Romeo that the real one breaks in, and proposes a love that will create a private world between the two of them:[7]

> Juliet   Romeo, doff thy name;
>   And for thy name, which is no part of thee,
>   Take all myself.
> Romeo   I take thee at thy word.
>   Call me but love, and I'll be new baptized;
>   Henceforth I never will be Romeo.   (2.2.47–51)

Like a dreamer startled to find a dream materialize, Juliet is taken aback at Romeo's response. She breaks the fantasy of renaming—"What man art thou . . . ? . . . Art thou not Romeo?" (2.2.52, 60)—and momentarily appears to withdraw in fear. Thus the emphasis shifts from shared feeling to male persuasion, as Romeo speaks of the power and value of love, until Juliet responds and acknowledges to the real Romeo what she has said to the fantasy one—"Farewell compliment!" (2.2.89). When the interplay of caution and persuasion begins again, Juliet's anxiety oddly focuses on Romeo's oaths, as if his faith could be guaranteed by his not swearing. The unreality of her expressions of distrust adds to the charm of this exchange: there are no hints that she finds men untrustworthy, or that Romeo finds women untrustworthy, or even that the family feud leads either of them to doubts about the other (as distinguished from awareness of the practical difficulties). It is as if the only force working against their trust at this point is the feeling that their love is too good to be true. Romeo suggests this as he momentarily, in Juliet's absence, takes over the verbal caution:

>   I am afeard,
> Being in night, all this is but a dream,
> Too flattering-sweet to be substantial.   (2.2.139–41)

By this time Juliet has given up her hesitation; her avowal evokes the self-renewing power of their mutuality but at the same time grounds it in her own autonomy:

> My bounty is as boundless as the sea,
> My love as deep; the more I give to thee,
> The more I have, for both are infinite.   (2.2.133–35)

And as she has been more concerned with the external world in pointing out dangers, she takes the initiative in turning their love from shared fantasy and passion to social institution: "If that thy bent of love be honorable, / Thy purpose marriage, send me word tomorrow" (2.2.143–44).

As the movement of their scenes combines mutuality and male persuasion, the words they use about their love can imply both mutuality and patriarchy. "It is my lady" (2.2.10), says Romeo of Juliet at the beginning of the balcony scene, and near the end she promises that if they marry "all my fortunes at thy foot I'll lay / And follow thee my lord throughout the world" (2.2.147–48). This could reflect either reciprocity of service or a conventional shift from female power in courtship to male power in marriage.

Similarly, when Juliet anticipates her secret wedding night with Romeo, the imagery of female subordination is balanced by imagery of sharing. She speaks of losing her virginity as losing a game, but then it becomes a victory, and her virginity parallel to Romeo's, as she prays to Night, "Learn me how to lose a winning match, / Played for a pair of stainless maidenhoods" (3.2.12–13). Here and elsewhere, financial imagery turns Juliet into property more directly than it does Romeo: when she speaks of herself as possessing, the object is less Romeo than love:

> O, I have bought the mansion of a love,
> But not possessed it; and though I am sold,
> Not yet enjoyed.   (3.2.26–28)

Similarly, Romeo calls her "merchandise" for which he would adventure "as far / As that vast shore washed with the farthest sea" (2.2.82–83), while Juliet says "my true love is grown to such excess / I cannot sum up sum of half my wealth" (2.6.33–34).

Romeo and Juliet use the image of woman as property in a way that transcends its source in female social subordination; both of them are far from the financial interest that Lady Capulet suggests in her praise of Paris and the Nurse in her observation that Juliet's husband "shall have the chinks" (1.5.117). Nevertheless, the asymmetry in their use of financial imagery coheres with the asymmetrical demands that the male code of violence will make on Romeo and the female code of docility on Juliet.

Their use of other images is more symmetrical. Both lovers speak in words at once sensuously descriptive of beauty and celestially idealizing. Juliet, says Romeo,

> hangs upon the cheek of night
> As a rich jewel in an Ethiop's ear. . . .
> So shows a snowy dove trooping with crows.
> (1.5.45–46, 48)

Romeo, according to Juliet, "will lie upon the wings of night / Whiter than new snow upon a raven's back" (3.2.18–19). Romeo has imagined Juliet as the sun and her eyes as stars. Juliet overgoes Romeo's praise in saying that, transformed into stars,

> he will make the face of heaven so fine
> That all the world will be in love with night
> And pay no worship to the garish sun.   (3.2.23–25)

Unlike some of Shakespeare's more solipsistic early lovers, such as Berowne and Proteus, Romeo understands the value of reciprocity in love. He wants its ritual— "Th'exchange of thy love's faithful vow for mine" (2.2.127) —and explains to Friar Laurence, "She whom I love now / Doth grace for grace and love for love allow" (2.3.85–86); he speaks of "the imagined happiness that both / Receive in either by this dear encounter" (2.6.28–29). All this is far from the identification of sex and violence that the imagery of the servants and Mercutio suggests is more usual in Verona.

Why do Romeo and Juliet keep their love secret not only from their parents but also from their peers? Romeo never tells Benvolio or Mercutio of his love for Juliet, though neither one is so committed to the Montagues that they would necessarily be hostile. (Benvolio had no objection to Rosaline as a Capulet; Mercutio belongs to neither house.) This secrecy helps make Mercutio's fight with Tybalt inevitable. Romeo's exclusion of Mercutio from his confidence suggests that his love of Juliet is not only a challenge to the feud but also a challenge to associations of masculinity and sexuality with violence. How can Romeo talk of Juliet to someone whose advice is "If love be rough with you, be rough with love, / Prick love for pricking, and you beat love down" (1.4.27–28)?

It is in part because of the difference between their experience of love and Verona's expected distortion of it that Romeo and Juliet try to keep their relationship private. Yet this secrecy is avoidance of a problem that they cannot ultimately escape.[8] When Romeo tries to act according to his secret love of Juliet instead of according to the feud, Tybalt and Mercutio insist on fighting. And when Romeo's intervention—to stop the fight—results in Mercutio's death, it is clear that Verona's definition of masculinity by violence is partly Romeo's definition as well. "O sweet Juliet," he says, "Thy beauty hath made me effeminate" (3.1.111–12), as he prepares for the fight to the death that causes his banishment.

Just before their crucial fight, Tybalt and Mercutio, speaking of Romeo, quibble on the point that "man," a word so important as an ideal, has from the opening scene the less honorific meaning of "manservant."

> Tybalt   Well, peace be with you, sir. Here comes my man.
> Mercutio   But I'll be hanged, sir, if he wear your livery.
>
>   (3.1.55–56)

This pun is an analogue of the irony that it is precisely in his "manly" vengeance for Mercutio's death that Romeo most decisively loses control of his own fate and becomes, as he says, "fortune's fool" (3.1.134). In a sense, as Mercutio's elaboration of his pun suggests without his awareness, a commitment to proving manhood by violence makes one easily manipulated by whoever offers a challenge. "Marry, go before to field, he'll be your follower! / Your worship in that sense may call him man" (3.1.57–58). In the larger sense, the code of violence that promises to make Romeo a man actually makes him its man—its pawn.

If Romeo shares Mercutio's belief in the manhood of violence, he also shares the Friar's wish for reconciliation. But the Friar has his own version of gender polarization that also contributes to the disaster. He repeatedly uses "womanish" as a synonym for "weak" when speaking to both Juliet (4.1.119) and Romeo (3.3.110), and, more crucially for the plot, encourages Juliet to pretend obedience and death through his potion rather than helping her escape to Romeo (though she has expressed willingness to leap "From off the battlements of any tower, / Or walk in thievish ways"—4.1.78–79). His image of manhood (desirable as an ideal for both sexes) is emotional control: he chides Romeo for his fury and grief at banishment by calling him "Unseemly woman in a seeming man! / And ill-beseeming beast in seeming both!" (3.3.112–13). The Friar distrusts passionate love, and, like much of the conventional imagery of the play, identifies passionate love with violence: "These violent delights have violent ends" (2.6.9). It is consistent that he should not encourage Juliet to elopement but rather hopes to stage their reunion in a context of family reconciliation.

Juliet's confidante, the Nurse, has a more positive attitude toward sexuality, but she too underestimates the lovers' intense commitment to each other. Like the Friar, too, she keeps the love secret and encourages Juliet to appear docile to her parents, and finally to marry Paris, since Romeo, she says, "is dead—or 'twere as good he were / As living here and you no use of him" (3.5.226–27). Thus she is counseling Juliet to a conventional acceptance of the husband chosen by her parents. While Juliet refuses this advice, she follows the counsel of pretense that she receives from nurse and friar. The controlled stichomythia of her dialogue with Paris is a sad contrast to her spontaneous participation in Romeo's sonnet. Juliet's acceptance of their advice of pretense and mock death is the point analogous to Romeo's duel with Tybalt where failure to transcend the gender polarization of their society makes disaster inevitable.

Yet before their deaths, Romeo and Juliet can transcend the aggressions and stereotypes of the outside in their secret world. Fulfilling the promise of the balcony scene, they rename each other "love" in their aubade scene, and their imagery suggests the creation of a private world with a technique oddly similar to that of the crucial scene in *The Taming of the Shrew*. To keep Romeo with her longer, Juliet transforms the lark into the nightingale and then transforms the sun into "some meteor that the sun exhales / To be to thee this night a torchbearer" (3.5.13–14). Romeo, after initially contradicting her, showing the caution that was primarily hers in the balcony scene, goes along with the game and accepts her transformation, with awareness of the likely cost:

> Let me be ta'en, let me be put to death.
> I am content, so thou wilt have it so.
> I'll say yon grey is not the morning's eye,
> 'Tis but the pale reflex of Cynthia's brow.   (3.5.17–20)

The scene in which Kate joins in Petruchio's transformation of the sun into the moon and old Vincentio into a young girl is of course quite different in tone. Kate and Petruchio have been engaged in a farcical combat of wills; they are now returning to Kate's father's house, accompanied by Petruchio's friend Hortensio, rather than in a romantic solitude, and they are under no sentence of death or banishment. But both scenes use a verbal transformation of the world—a creation of a private world through words—as a metaphor for a relationship. Such a private world is crucial to Shrew's mediation between ideologies of patriarchy and companionship in marriage, as well as to the attempt that Romeo and Juliet make to love each other tenderly in a world of violence. The secrecy of their love heightens at once its purity and intensity and its vulnerability. When the private world is established it is already threatened. As soon as Romeo accepts the pretense "It is not day" (3.5.25), Juliet resumes her caution and returns them to the real world, where Romeo must flee. Nevertheless, they have an absolute trust in each other; on their departure there is no questioning of each other's truths such as we shall see in Troilus and Cressida.[9] Presciently, they imagine death as the only possible obstacle to their reunion.

Shakespeare changed his source to reduce the age of the lovers, and historical evidence suggests that he also made them much younger than the typical age of marriage for Elizabethan aristocrats (twenty for women, twenty-one for men), who married still younger than other classes (median age twenty-four for women, twenty-six for men).[10] However young the members of Shakespeare's original audiences were—probably a high proportion were in their late teens or early twenties—Romeo and Juliet were still younger than almost all of them. The extreme youth of the lovers emphasizes their innocence and inexperience. Anyone who has lived longer than Romeo and Juliet—anyone who has given up a first love—has made more compromises than they have. It is their extreme purity that gives their love its special tragedy. The play expresses both the appeal and the danger of a love in which two people become the whole world to each other. This little world precariously remedies the defects of the larger one—its coldness, its hierarchies, its violence—but the lovers cannot negotiate recognition by the outer world except by their deaths because of their residual commitment to the outer world and its gender ideals.

In *Troilus and Cressida*, by contrast, the lovers' world has all too much in common with the larger world of their society. Shakespeare juxtaposes the titular love affair to the analogous story of the Trojan War, in which Helen, though ostensibly glorified as "the face that launched a thousand ships," is actually reduced to a pawn in male competition. The combination is one of the most devastating pictures in the Shakespeare canon or anywhere else of the gender relations consequent on the treatment of women primarily as property.

Helen of Troy was kidnapped—ravished, as the prologue has it—by Paris, and whether she stays with him or returns to Menelaus will result not from her choice but from the outcome of the Trojan War. As the Trojans argue over her fate, they constantly evaluate her: Hector says, "She is not worth what she doth cost / The keeping" (2.2.51–52), while Troilus would keep her because "she is a pearl / Whose price hath launched above a thousand ships" (2.2.81–82). Her value is not in herself for Troilus:

> Were it not glory that we more affected
> Than the performance of our heaving spleens,
> I would not wish a drop of Troyan blood
> Spent more in her defense. But, worthy Hector,
> She is a theme of honor and renown,
> A spur to valiant and magnanimous deeds.
>
> (2.2.195–200)

The most emphatic argument to return her comes from Hector's application of the law of marriage: "What nearer debt in all humanity / Than wife is to the husband?" (2.2.175–76). Nowhere in the argument is Helen's own preference an issue; nowhere in the play is her own autonomous choice shown as a possibility. Yet in the two places where we see Helen, she seems adjusted to her condition: flirting with Troilus, as Pandarus reports it, and with Pandarus himself, as we see in 3.1, she neither grieves for her lost husband nor seems overwhelmingly in love with Paris.

By the end of the play, Cressida's condition has become almost a replica of Helen's.[11] The armies' decision to exchange her for Antenor has removed her from Troilus and given her to Diomedes, just as military decisions keep Helen with Paris; Cressida, like Helen, adapts by general flirtation (although some lines suggest more psychological struggle)—and the war begun over the exchange of one woman draws more energy from Troilus's anger at his loss of another.

Like *Romeo and Juliet*, *Troilus and Cressida* is set in a society where women are commonly associated with weakness, but while in the earlier play lines from the servants and the Friar establish most of this atmosphere, here more of it comes from the words of Troilus himself. Many of these lines, like Romeo's one, are self-criticism: Troilus implies, at the beginning, that because of his love for Cressida he is "weaker than a woman's tear" (1.1.9). When Aeneas asks why he is not afield, he says, "Because not there. This woman's answer sorts, / For womanish it is to be from thence" (1.1.102–3). Nevertheless, the lines reveal not only self-criticism but also condescension toward women; this is especially obvious because in the scene where these lines occur so much of the dialogue is about Cressida. When Troilus moves from his description of her as a pearl to his snappy comeback to Aeneas, we see his ambivalence toward women—his share in the cultural ambivalence that both glorifies and subordinates Helen.[12] By the end of the play, Troilus has not only given up any idealized vision of Cressida, he has also given up any "womanlike" reluctance to violence. "Brother, you have a vice of mercy in you," he says to Hector, "Which better fits a lion than a man. . . . Let's leave the hermit pity with our mother" (5.3.37–38, 45).

In the beginning, Troilus and Cressida seem rather similar. Each is introduced listening to Pandarus praise the other. Troilus is much more concerned with love than with fighting, and Cressida seems not to be bound by the usual sexual restrictions on women in Shakespeare's plays;

neither one acts according to polarized gender roles. Cressida says that in her love for Troilus she "wished myself a man / Or that we women had men's privilege / Of speaking first" (3.2.120–22), yet it is she, in the scene where they meet, who first invites him to the bedchamber and first declares her love. Their responses to Pandarus's praise do contrast—Troilus admits his love to Pandarus, Cressida only to the audience. Both associate their affair with violence, though in different ways. Troilus imagines love as inflicting on him wounds that Pandarus's words exacerbate: "Thou lay'st in every gash that love hath given me / The knife that made it" (1.1.59–60). Cressida, on the other hand, sees sex as violence: "If I cannot ward what I would not have hit, I can watch you for telling how I took the blow; unless it swell past hiding, and then it's past watching" (1.2.254–57).

The overall symmetries of their introduction will break down because of the gender politics implied in the Trojan council scene, where Trojan men decide Helen's fate with no attention to the intruding prophet Cassandra or to Helen's own wishes, and Troilus himself gives an argument that shows how close Helen and all women are to property in his mind:

> I take today a wife, and my election
> Is led on in the conduct of my will—
> 　　　... How may I avoid,
> Although my will distaste what it elected,
> The wife I chose? ...
> We turn not back the silks upon the merchant
> When we have soiled them, nor the remainder viands
> We do not throw in unrespective sieve
> Because we now are full.　　(2.2.61–62, 65–67, 69–72)

Mercantile images are pervasive in Troilus, but women are almost always objects of trade and appraisal, not buyers, possessors, or sellers as men are and as Juliet occasionally is.[13] This context helps to explain some of the cautiousness of Cressida's policy: "That she beloved knows nought that knows not this: / Men prize the thing ungained more than it is" (1.2.274–75). Cressida accepts the definition of woman as commodity and wants as high a price in power as possible.

Pandarus's ubiquity contributes to the sense of the characters' relations as detached, commodity-like. After praising each of them to the other, he leads Troilus to their first meeting and leaves them only briefly. While we see Shakespeare's other lovers developing relationships through conversations with each other, Troilus and Cressida instead talk with Pandarus and in soliloquies that show Troilus's erotic fantasies and Cressida's caution rather than contact with the other. Both of them are afraid of losing power in their sexual encounter—Troilus because of the intensity of the experience he anticipates, Cressida because it will deprive her of her status as "thing ungained." But these fears are not enough to deter them; at their first meeting, before speaking they kiss while Pandarus coaches "rub on, and kiss the mistress" (3.2.46–47) and talks on for six more long lines of prose.[14]

While the impression of physical attraction is strong, the domination of Pandarus—like a parody Cupid—and the lack of rapport in the conversation, by contrast to that of most of Shakespeare's lovers, suggest the weakness of any lasting bond from the very beginning. Cressida twice tries to initiate a trip to her bedchamber—"Will you walk in, my lord?" (3.2.57, 92)—but unlike, for example, Juliet's initiation of talk of marriage, these words get no response from Troilus; later she threatens, unexpectedly, to leave by herself, and finally it takes Pandarus to get them to bed. Troilus wants to talk about his past wishes, Cressida, apparently, about her fears—both guardedly. What they can most discuss, with no Pandarus to coach them, is the limitation on lovers' achievements—and the language modulates so that Troilus is speaking with the first person plural, identifying with other male lovers, and Cressida seems to be challenging his sexual prowess. In all Cupid's pageants, says Troilus, nothing is monstrous "but our undertakings when we vow to weep seas, live in fire, eat rocks, tame tigers, thinking it harder for our mistress to devise imposition enough than for us to undergo any difficulty imposed. This is the monstruosity in love, lady, that the will is infinite and the execution confined; that the desire is boundless and the act a slave to limit" (3.2.71–77). Cressida agrees: "They say all lovers swear more performance than they are able, and yet reserve an ability that they never perform, vowing more than the perfection of ten and discharging less than the tenth part of one" (3.2.78–81). As with the fighting ostensibly over Helen, the real issue is achievement, not love.

After Pandarus returns, Cressida makes a more direct avowal: "Prince Troilus, I have loved you night and day / For many weary months" (3.2.107–8). Troilus does not respond with a returning declaration of love, but with a question: "Why was my Cressid then so hard to win?" (3.2.109). She has already told us, and she gives him a hint: "If I confess much you will play the tyrant" (3.2.112). As she tells Troilus about her pretenses, she reveals so much awareness of the constant possibility of pretense as to make belief in her very difficult. Perhaps she herself cannot tell when she is pretending anymore:

> I love you now, but not, till now, so much
> But I might master it. In faith, I lie;
>
> .   .   .   .
>
> Perchance, my lord, I show more craft than love,
> And fell so roundly to a large confession
> To angle for your thoughts.   (3.2.113–14, 145–47)

Troilus has shown his own greater concern with his own power and its limits in their earlier speech; now Cressida shows hers. They cannot agree on a picture of the past: Troilus sees her as hard to win, while she, wishing for "men's privilege / Of speaking first," implies that he did not use that privilege with her. It is understandable that Troilus finds this complex message of caution and changing of mood hard to answer with words. The kiss that she asks for and then apologizes for is simpler. And then she confuses him further by threatening to leave.

The balcony scene in *Romeo and Juliet* includes an interplay of Juliet's caution and Romeo's initiative, but it builds to Juliet's declaration of love.[15] She briefly worries about Romeo's response:

> If thou thinkest I am too quickly won,
> I'll frown, and be perverse, and say thee nay,
> So thou wilt woo; but else, not for the world.
>
> (2.2.95–97)

and would withdraw her vow, "But to be frank and give it thee again" (2.2.131). For all her skepticism about oaths, Juliet has already said, "Dost thou love me? I know thou wilt say 'Ay'; / And I will take thy word" (2.2.90–91). It is not just a moralistic commonplace that the first play is about love and the second about lust; the contrast runs through every significant point of comparison. Romeo and Juliet see each other's beauty with sensuous appreciation, but they have little of the concern for performance and sensation evident in Troilus's lines and little of the flirtatious mixture of initiative and withdrawal of Cressida's. Romeo and Juliet reach rapport with their words; Troilus and Cressida do not. Their bond, something like those forged in a bed trick in the other problem plays, is a bond chiefly of unintegrated sexuality.

After Cressida challenges Troilus, "But you are wise, / Or else you love not" (3.2.147–48), he finally speaks at length in an oddly qualified and impersonal declaration that suggests both the idealized faith he would require and his doubts about any woman:

> O! that I thought it could be in a woman—
> As, if it can, I will presume in you—
> To feed for aye her lamp and flames of love;
> To keep her constancy in plight and youth,
> Outliving beauty's outward, with a mind
> That doth renew swifter than blood decays. . . .
>
> (3.2.150–55)

This speech and the next few are remarkably self-centered. Troilus emphasizes the value of the truth he possesses and doubts whether any woman can offer him equal value of truth in an exchange of commodities. He wishes

> that persuasion could but thus convince me
> That my integrity and truth to you
> Might be affronted with the match and weight
> Of such a winnowed purity in love.   (3.2.156–59)

His emphasis is not on his relation to her but on his own moral qualities. There is irony in the rhetorical complexity of his declaration: "I am as true as truth's simplicity, / And simpler than the infancy of truth" (3.2.161–62).[16]

In their most formal declaration to each other, we are reminded again of how much their love has in common with the war that surrounds it:

> Cressida In that I'll war with you.
> Troilus   O virtuous fight,
>   When right with right wars who shall be most
>   right!   (3.2.163–64)

Similar imagery occurs earlier in the scene: Troilus, when he anticipates his meeting with Cressida, says:

> I do fear besides
> That I shall lose distinction in my joys,
> As doth a battle, when they charge on heaps
> The enemy flying.   (3.2.24–27)

And Pandarus, observing their first kiss, says, "Nay, you shall fight your hearts out ere I part you. The falcon as the tercel, for all the ducks i' th' river" (3.2.48–50). In the context of the characterizations that we have seen, these are not simply stock Petrarchan images of love as war, like Troilus's reference to the "cruel battle here within" (1.1.3) at the beginning of the play. Rather, they reinforce a sense of the continued self-concern of the lovers—and also of the parallel between their use of rhetoric to mask appetite and pride and the similar pretenses by both armies: if we listened to each side's language alone, the Trojan War too might appear to be "virtuous fight / When right with right wars who shall be most right!"

In this context, the format of their vows as well is not simply the dramatic device of momentarily turning the characters into literary emblems. The Troilus who promises that "True swains in love shall in the world to come / Approve their truth by Troilus" (3.2.165–66) is recognizably the same as the one who in the council scene calls Helen

> a theme of honor and renown,
> A spur to valiant and magnanimous deeds,
> Whose present courage may beat down our foes
> And fame in time to come canonize us.   (2.2.199–202)

Shakespeare could have given Romeo lines predicting his future fame as a lover, already established in Elizabethan England from the narratives of Bandello, Boiastuau, William Painter, and Arthur Brooke, but such lines would have been as anomalous for the characterization of Romeo as they are consistent with the characterization of Troilus.

Similarly, when Cressida pledges her truth by cursing herself with the fate of becoming a byword if she is false, the twist is of course partly determined by Shakespeare's proleptic fitting the conclusion of the scene to the conclusion of the legend; but it also reinforces the doomed nature of the love by showing how prominent in everyone's imagination is the image of the woman as false. When Pandarus seals the bargain, saying, "Let all constant men be Troiluses, all false women Cressids, and all brokers-between Pandars" (3.2.194–96), his word choice suggests both masculine suspicion of women and Cressida's future in the established story—two mutually reinforcing conditions.

While Troilus and Cressida spend the night together, Calchas asks the Greeks to send their prisoner Antenor back to Troy to, as he says, "buy my daughter" (3.3.28), and they accept the proposal. Cressida is no longer "the thing ungained" for Troilus, and he seems anxious to be off in the world of men who think about other things than love. With condescending tenderness he puts Cressida in her place. She should not trouble herself to unbolt the gates or call her uncle:

> Sleep kill those pretty eyes,
> And give as soft attachment to thy senses
> As infants' empty of all thought!   (4.2.4–6)

He urges her back to bed so emphatically as to suggest he wants to leave quickly, and there is poignancy in her question, "Are you aweary of me?" (4.2.7), in spite of his attempt at a courteous reply.[17]

The morning is cold in more than the weather. Both are losing any sense of one another's uniqueness that they may ever have had.[18] "Prithee, tarry; / You men will never tarry" (4.2.15–16), she pleads pathetically. As she herself has predicted, once she has yielded Troilus will not give her enough attention to distract her from her loneliness. When Aeneas knocks on the door asking for Cressida, his response is simply, "How my achievements mock me!" (4.2.69).

But Cressida's attitude is similarly self-centered. When she maintains her love for Troilus it is by denying relationships to others:

> I have forgot my father;
> I know no touch of consanguinity—
> No kin, no love, no blood, no soul so near me
> As the sweet Troilus.   (4.2.95–98)

She enjoys playing the role of suffering lover—and makes a point of her beauty as she plans to "Tear my bright hair, and scratch my praised cheeks" (4.2.105).[19] Both of them maintain a kind of aestheticism of suffering. She declares, "The grief is fine, full, perfect, that I taste. . . . My love admits no qualifying dross" (4.4.3, 9); he boasts of his love's "strained . . . purity" (4.4.23). The self-centeredness of these images remains in the mercantile imagery of Troilus's parting speech:

> We two, that with so many thousand sighs
> Did buy each other, must poorly sell ourselves
> With the rude brevity and discharge of one.   (4.3.38–40)

Unlike Romeo and Juliet, they are insecure about each other's love, and as in their first enounter, Troilus muses on human powerlessness:

> sometimes we are devils to ourselves
> When we will tempt the frailty of our powers,
> Presuming on their changeful potency.   (4.4.94–96)

What we see most directly in the next scene is Cressida's powerlessness as the Greeks inflict kissing games on her—and she adapts. She proves pathetically unable to maintain her loyalty to Troilus, and in a climactic scene, as Troilus watches, she gives Diomedes the sleeve that Troilus has given her. Though Troilus feels powerless as spectator, nevertheless he can seek another kind of power in the war, and that he determines to do, without any scruples about humanity. "Let's leave the hermit pity with our mother" (5.3.45), he says.

Troilus's move toward rejecting qualities he considers feminine in himself and rejecting the woman he has valued parallels moves in Hector and Achilles. Hector begins the council scene by declaring his aversion to prolonging the war:

> There is no lady of more softer bowels,
> More ready to suck in the sense of fear,
> More ready to cry out, "Who knows what follows?"
> Than Hector is. . . .   (2.2.11–14)

Yet after this, he announces his decision to keep Helen and reveals the challenge he has sent to the Greeks. In 1.3 we see the delivery of this challenge by Aeneas, and in its wording a woman yet again appears as an object over which men fight. But in this situation it is even clearer how much the woman is an excuse—a "theme for honor and renown," as Troilus has said of Helen.[20] Hector's message is that

He hath a lady, wiser, fairer, truer,
Than ever Greek did compass in his arms;
And will tomorrow with his trumpet call,
Midway between your tents and walls of Troy,
To rouse a Grecian that is true in love.   (1.3.275–79)

The Greeks clearly recognize that this is a fight to establish valor, not one to establish truth in love: they assume it is directed to Achilles, although love of Polyxena is by no means salient in his characterization, and by the time Achiles repeats the challenge, and Hector tells the other Trojans, the women have dropped out of the message: Hector will, says Achilles,

Tomorrow morning call some knight to arms
That hath a stomach, and such a one that dare
Maintain—I know not what; 'tis trash.   (2.1.119–21)

Because of Ulysses' calculation, the Greek representative is Ajax, not Achilles, and nothing more is said about the woman. Indeed, when Andromache, whose wisdom Hector praises in his challenge, finally appears, it is to give Hector advice not to fight because of her dreams—advice that he ignores at the cost of his death.

Like Troilus and Hector, Achilles also compares himself to a woman before his return to fighting:

                          I have a woman's longing,
An appetite that I am sick withal,
To see great Hector in his weeds of peace. (3.3.237–39)

At first, this may suggest a longing for reconciliation, but the actual nature of the meeting bears out instead the association of "woman's longing" with irrational desires, such as women are thought to have in pregnancy. After many lines of gallant praise between Hector and the other Greeks, Achilles bursts out in verbal savagery and reduces Hector to the same level.

Achilles Tell me, you heavens, in which part of his body
          Shall I destroy him, whether there, or there, or
          there?

.   .   .   .

Hector I'll kill thee everywhere, yea, o'er and o'er.
                                        (4.5.241– 42, 255)

The move toward gender polarization in Troilus, Achilles, and Hector parallels the move from truce to war. As
Patroclus says to Achilles, "A woman impudent and man-
nish grown / Is not more loathed than an effeminate man /
In time of action" (3.3.217–19). The first part of *Troilus and
Cressida*, like the first part of *Romeo and Juliet*, has some
affinities with the world of the comedies with their less
rigid gender expectations; the second part has more affinities with the violent world of the tragedies.[21] (This reverses the pattern some critics have found in another
problem play, *Measure for Measure*, of beginning with a tragic
situation and ending with a comic solution.[22]) But both
parts of the play, and both plots, are dominated by imagery
of commodity relations and judged by imagery of disease
and decay.[23] When even Hector kills a Greek soldier for his
armor, the revelation of the soldier as a putrefied core epitomizes the moral condition of both Greeks and Trojans.
Cressida's attempt to keep her price high is like Achilles'
attempts to make the Greeks value him by withdrawing
and the Greeks' attempts to keep power over the Trojans
by sending Ajax instead of Achilles to fight with Hector:
"Let us, like merchants, / First show foul wares, and think
perchance they'll sell" (1.8.358–59). Characters are either
naively self-centered, disregarding others, or cynically self-
centered, manipulating others.

Paradoxically, Cressida is both self-centered and insuffi-
ciently autonomous. Gayle Greene argues that Cressida's
characterization demonstrates "the tendency of a woman
to define herself in 'relational' capacities, to derive self-
esteem from the esteem of others, and to 'objectify' her-

self."[24] But it is important to note that Cressida's "relational" identity differs significantly from the "relational" identity of Shakespeare's other female characters—for example, Juliet and Desdemona and Cleopatra, who die speaking of the men they love. Cressida's "relational" identity is unstable: apparently, she adapts herself to whatever man is nearest. The other women actively choose their relationships and commit themselves firmly; though they die, they affirm their identity and their relationship at the same time. Cressida is alive at the end of the play, but she can affirm neither.[25]

Antony and Cleopatra incorporates some of the satirical vision of Troilus and Cressida to make its vision of mutual love ending in death more comprehensive than in Romeo and Juliet. In Antony and Cleopatra we see flawed warriors and flawed lovers—Cleopatra may be even vainer than Cressida—but we also see the possibility of judging Antony as brave and generous, Cleopatra as loving and courageous.[26] More than any other play, it shows the love in the world of war (Enobarbus's bond with Antony even after his betrayal) and the war in the world of love; it dramatizes about as many battles between Antony and Cleopatra as between Antony and Caesar. But unlike Troilus and Cressida, they can re-create their relationship after its apparent destruction. Antony sees Cleopatra apparently betraying him, explodes in anger, and forgives her; Cleopatra hears of Antony's marriage, rages, and takes him back. As in the other two plays we have been discussing, observers comment on transgressions of customary gender behavior; conflicts occur sometimes because the lovers follow gender expectations (Cleopatra leaves the battle in fear), sometimes because they do not. But because both show the anger usually expected of men and the forgiveness usually expected of women, their relationship has more depth and stability than those in this chapter's plays of secret love as well as more equality than the others discussed in the previous chapter. Romeo and Juliet characteristically idealize each other, Troilus and Cressida their own feelings; Antony and Cleopatra also idealize their relationship itself:

> The nobleness of life
> Is to do thus; when such a mutual pair
> And such a twain can do't, in which I bind,
> On pain of punishment, the world to weet
> We stand up peerless.   (1.1.36–40)

They use imagery of giving, rather than of buying and selling, and for all their fights the giving occurs in actions and not just in words.[27]

In the plays of the previous chapter, the men are easily suspicious of women and usually at least middle-aged; the women are largely reduced to audience, and the central characters are bound by publicly recognized family ties. In the pattern discussed in this chapter, the men are young and not so suspicious, the women maintain or increase their ability to pretend, and the central love relationship is kept secret. The relationship creates a private world within which the women have relative equality—but unlike such worlds in the comedies, it is a precarious one, threatened by violence. Thus outside the comic world, where the usual conclusion with marriage keeps an ambiguity we have discussed earlier, Shakespeare's plays suggest a dilemma for his female characters: they can keep equality in a relationship if it is secret and not publicly recognized, but such a private relationship is inherently unstable, especially in a violent world. *Antony and Cleopatra* develops something from both traditions. The central relationship is adulterous—neither secret nor legally recognized. Cleopatra is like the (otherwise very different) women of this chapter in her continued ability to act, though at the end, in a tragic modulation of the comic pattern, she calls on Antony as her husband. Antony has the relative age more characteristic of heroes of the previous chapter, and occasional outbursts of mistrust of women such as they express more often, but he also shows a capacity for forgiveness without equal among Shakespearean heroes until the romances. But before we turn to the romances, let us look at two other tragedies—first one in which Shakespeare deals in even more depth with the problems of integrating the private world of love (and mutuality) with the public world of war (and patriarchy).

Chapter Seven
Marriage and Mutuality in *Othello*

In an article entitled "Marriage and the Construction of Reality," the sociologists Peter Berger and Hansfried Kellner say, "Unlike an earlier situation in which the establishment of the new marriage simply added to the differentiation and complexity of an already existing social world, the marriage partners are now embarked on the often difficult task of constructing for themselves the little world in which they will live."[1] By this definition, Othello and Desdemona seem to begin their marriage in a situation more modern than traditional. Othello is cut off from his ancestry; Desdemona is disowned by her father. They spend most of the play in Cyprus, a setting native to neither of them. Thus they have some of both the opportunities and the difficulties of constructing their own world that Berger and Kellner discuss. "The re-construction of the world in marriage," they continue, "occurs principally in the course of conversation. . . . The implicit problem of this conversation is how to match two individual definitions of reality."[2]

Marriage for Berger and Kellner, as, I have argued, for Shakespeare's comedies, involves a combination of ideals of mutuality and assumptions of patriarchy, though of course patriarchy takes a different form in twentieth-century America than in seventeenth-century England. Though the balance may tip in one direction or the other, the predominance of playfulness and of festive disguise helps to remove threatening elements. In Shakespeare's tragedies, however, the combination of patriarchy and mutuality breaks down. We never see Othello and Desdemona creating together a private game-like world of conversation onstage. All the early scenes where they both speak are public, and events in the outside world remain important to their relationship. Othello's public role as warrior is part of what Desdemona loves in him. Furthermore, Berger and Kellner assume a situation in which "the husband typically talks with his wife about his friend, but not with his friend about his wife"; in *Othello* the opposite is true.[3] One principal representative of the already existing social world stays with Othello and Desdemona—Iago. And accompanying his presence is the persistence of conventional attitudes from the outside world in Othello's mind. Othello cannot completely free himself from the conventional assumption that Desdemona's marriage to him is unnatural. He cannot keep distrust of women out of his marriage. Brabantio may not be physically present, but his message, "She has deceived her father, and may thee" (1.3.293), rings in Othello's memory. And after Othello has stopped believing anything Desdemona says, Iago's presence makes it impossible for Othello to keep out of his marriage a code of proving manhood by violent revenge. Between patriarchy and racism, the initial mutuality between Desdemona and Othello is destroyed. To restore it is the aim of Othello's suicide.

In Shakespeare's comedies we usually see mutuality being established; in *Othello* we hear the process described. Othello calls it, "How I did thrive in this fair lady's love / And she in mine" (1.3.125–26). While he told his life story to her father,

> This to hear
> Would Desdemona seriously incline;
> But still the house affairs would draw her thence;
> Which ever as she could with haste dispatch,
> She'd come again, and with a greedy ear
> Devour up my discourse. Which I observing,
> Took once a pliant hour, and found good means

To draw from her a prayer of earnest heart
That I would all my pilgrimage dilate,
Whereof by parcels she had something heard,
But not intentively. I did consent,
And often did beguile her of her tears
When I did speak of some distressful stroke
That my youth suffered.   (1.3.145–58)

Here Othello gives a description of a process of initiative
and response leading to further response—Othello talks,
Desdemona listens, Othello sees her listening and encourages it, hopes she will ask to hear more; she does, he
agrees, and she responds with tears of sympathy. Othello is
gratified by her initial interest in his performance and
draws her out for more active participation.

While this scene fits some conventions of patriarchy—
male activity and female response—the imagery by which
Othello's words become food that Desdemona devours
should signal that roles here are not altogether limited to
conventional ones. As Brabantio says, Othello's story por-
trays Desdemona as "half the wooer" (1.3.176). She goes
beyond the audience's responsiveness, as an earlier chapter noted, to initiate courtship by her hint. The content of
their conversation in this story is Othello's experience, not
Desdemona's, but we should notice how closely he has
observed her, how carefully he has elicited her request.
While Desdemona has been an audience to Othello's performance, he has also behaved like an audience in closely
observing her. In the narrative Othello tells, he has judged
Desdemona's feelings from her gestures, guessed at meaning beneath her words, and he has been right about her
interest in him—beyond his dreams. Othello describes a
powerful experience of emotional sharing—he has gone
back to his youth and relived his sufferings and she has felt
them along with him: "She loved me for the dangers I had
passed, / And I loved her that she did pity them" (1.3.167–
68).

Yet in spite of her active participation, Desdemona describes her loyalty to Othello as a matter of duty. Furthermore, Desdemona makes as many concessions as she can to her father in explaining her "divided duty" (1.3.181); she speaks first of her bonds as a daughter, and she compares her choice of Othello with her mother's choice of her father. One of few Shakespearean women who claim to imitate their mothers, she is trying to reassure Brabantio by putting her marriage into an orderly continuity of marriages, trying to remind him that his marriage too was won at the cost of separation from a father.

In these introductory statements by Othello and Desdemona, their marriage appears as a combination of patriarchy and mutuality. Othello makes the marriage proposal and keeps the title of lord, yet there is a genuine emotional sharing and companionship. Desdemona further emphasizes both these elements later on in this scene. "That I did love the Moor to live with him," she says,

> My downright violence, and storm of fortunes,
> May trumpet to the world.   (1.3.248–50)

She joins him in his imagery as in his career. "My heart's subdued / Even to the very quality of my lord" (1.3.250–51). She identifies with him in a way that subordinates her.[4] He does not, for example, ask that she accompany him to Cyprus until after she does, and he makes a point of saying that he asks it only as a magnanimous gesture, "to be free and bounteous to her mind" (1.3.265). Although his description of their courtship revealed the importance to him of her emotional response—the mutual dependence that they have created—he wants to deny his need of her and, most emphatically, to deny any sexual appetite that would clamor for satisfaction—"Not to comply with heat—the young affects / In me defunct" (1.3.263–64). Furthermore, while she values his world, his words here suggest that he scorns the domestic world she comes from; his curse to be imposed on himself if he neglects his duty because of her ends:

Let housewives make a skillet of my helm,
And all indign and base adversities
Make head against my estimation!   (1.3.272–74)

In their meeting in Cyprus, it is Othello who uses imagery that describes their love as a fusion of Desdemona's essence into his: he calls her "My fair warrior . . . my soul's joy" (2.1.180–82). In this reunion, as in his scene of self-revelation to her described earlier, social structures and temperamental differences may drop away and two people can create the illusion of unity; such scenes are the end of love as quest and of the typical plot of romantic comedy.[5] But what can follow them? Othello's words of joy are filled with apprehension. It is as if the hardships of his life have led him always to expect disaster:

        If it were now to die,
'Twere now to be most happy; for I fear
My soul hath her content so absolute
That not another comfort like to this
Succeeds in unknown fate.   (2.1.187–91)

It is easier for Othello to imagine a *Liebestod* than a love enduring the test of daily life; yet he sees their love not as the passion usually identified with *Liebestod* but as calm, content, comfort. This suggests, perhaps, the element in their love that involves regression to a relationship like that of mother and infant.

Desdemona's response, however, is more active and creative:

        The heavens forbid
But that our loves and comforts should increase
Even as our days do grow.   (2.1.191–93)

Othello quickly agrees, but the memory of his fear is there to mix with the ominous suggestions of Iago's asides.

Why is Iago so successful in his attempts to destroy the relationship between Othello and Desdemona? Many different approaches can work toward answers to this question; here I am interested in looking at what the play shows about the vulnerability of the combination of patriarchy and mutuality that we see in that relationship, and about how Iago manipulates Othello's persisting need for mutuality.

If mutuality and patriarchy are to be combined, as we have already suggested, the woman must make the gesture of subordinating herself to the man; in addition, in *Othello*, much more than in the comedies, the man believes he must subdue qualities in himself that he considers would make him woman-like or too dependent on a woman. Othello's need for control to assert his manliness often coalesces with the need for control to assert that he is civilized and not a barbarian slave to passion. It is important to note here the overlap between the stereotypes of the woman and of the Moor: conventional Renaissance European views would see both as excessively passionate.[6] Othello's first appearance, contrary to this stereotype, is an amazing show of self-possession under Brabantio's attacks. Even in his description of his life history, he recounts his adventures in a controlled tone. He is, however, moved when Desdemona cries over them; if he beguiles her of her tears, she can express his emotions for him. It further suggests his control, based on his sense of social distinctions, that *Desdemona* first speaks of love, and Othello can see himself as loving only in response, and therefore rationally. Indeed, he is, as we have seen, curiously emphatic about his lack of sexual passion.

Othello's stress on control of passion may add to the implications of his dismissal of Cassio. Just after the announcement that Othello has proclaimed a general festivity because of the coincidence of the victory over the Turks and the celebration of his nuptial, Othello says to Cassio:

Good Michael, look you to the guard to-night.
Let's teach ourselves that honorable stop,
Not to outsport discretion.   (2.3.1–3)

Here Othello seems to be identifying himself with Cassio, the potential drunkard, in a common need for control. A few lines later, Othello leaves with Desdemona, saying

> Come, my dear love.
> The purchase made, the fruits are to ensue;
> That profit's yet to come 'tween me and you.   (2.3.8–10)

After the first line, this is a rather business-like description for the sexual initiation of a wedding night. Again it suggests a concern for sharing, but it is odd that he should turn pleasure into financial imagery. Iago's words a few lines later suggest one kind of language Othello has avoided using: "He hath not yet made wanton the night with her, and she is sport for Jove" (2.3.15–17).

Thus, while Cassio drinks too much and gets into a fight with Rodrigo and then with Montano, the characters and the audience are frequently reminded that Othello and Desdemona are meeting in bed for the first time. Iago, in fact, brings this juxtaposition shockingly into focus when he describes the fight to Othello, who has been called back by its clamor:

> Friends all, but now, even now,
> In quarter, and in terms like bride and groom
> Devesting them for bed; and then but now—
> As if some planet had unwitted men—
> Swords out, and tilting one at other's breast
> In opposition bloody.   (2.3.169–74)

What Iago has described is perilously close to the reality of the wedding night, when at least briefly rational control must be abandoned and blood must be shed.

I suggest that, partly under Iago's influence, partly because of his own emphasis on self-control, Othello feels guilty about the passion involved in his intercourse with Desdemona; he identifies with the offender who has also let passion run away with him, and in effect he makes Cassio a scapegoat for himself. When he dismisses Cassio,

as later when he kills Desdemona, he insists that he is acting justly when he is really moved by his emotions. Here
he returns to Desdemona saying "All's well now, sweeting"
(2.3.242), because Cassio is dismissed, and so too, Othello
thinks, is the disturbing image of sexuality becoming violent with which Iago has associated him. Like Stanley
Cavell, I think that Othello's guilt about sexuality is an important subtext of the play;[7] but in addition to the guilt
about hurting Desdemona, which Cavell stresses, I see him
as feeling guilty for loss of control of his passions, such loss
of control as many medieval theologians whose views
were still reflected in some Elizabethan sermons thought
made sex inevitably suspect even within marriage.[8]

Of course, *Othello* is a play about passionate love; but part
of its impact comes from the tension between that passion
and the restraints that Othello is constantly trying to place
on it, as suggested by his words. Furthermore, Othello's
very idealization of Desdemona has a passionate compo-
nent. He is passionate in wishing her to be totally fused in
identification with him, in a symbiosis possible only for
the mother and infant before the infant's discovery of sex.
In one of his final confrontations with Desdemona, he describes her, in language that brings to mind the dependence of the infant at the mother's breast, as the place

> Where either I must love or bear no life,
> The fountain from the which my current runs
> Or else dries up.   (4.2.58–60)

C. L. Barber has suggested that many of Shakespeare's female characters have the resonance for the hero, and for
the audience, of the Virgin Mary; Shakespeare's audience
still had the fantasy of a total and pure relationship such as
one could have only with a mother who was perpetually a
virgin, and this fantasy could no longer be dealt with
through religious symbolism and ritual because of the Ref-
ormation. Thus Othello projects the kind of religious need

onto Desdemona that no merely human being could fulfill.[9]

In his description of the handkerchief and its provenance, there are more suggestions of Othello's fantasy of love as fusion with a woman both maternal and virginal. He describes a gypsy sorceress as telling his mother that the handkerchief,

> while she kept it,
> [would] make her amiable and subdue my father
> Entirely to her love; but if she lost it
> Or made a gift of it, my father's eye
> Should hold her loathèd.   (3.4.58–62)

In sharp contrast with Desdemona's description of her parents as bound by duty, here are the precarious bonds of magic. The mere chance loss of the handkerchief can turn one side of the polarized image—Othello's father entirely subdued to her love—to the other—loathing. Furthermore, by concluding the description with a reference to dye made from maiden's hearts, Othello calls up the image of dead women and associates it with the blood lost in the loss of virginity, which Lynda Boose has shown might well be visually suggested by the handkerchief.[10] Othello's words imply that if Desdemona could keep the handkerchief, could keep her fidelity safe from any accusation, could define herself as the virgin who shed her blood for him, then she would be like his mother and would keep his love.

Othello's desire for a love that is total fusion is, in part, his attempt to escape from his underlying sense of separateness. His blackness is a visual sign of how his history differs from that of the other characters; his narrative tells of an early life far from ordinary family and domestic connections. His ties in Venice, except with Desdemona, are those made by military service, and as Brabantio's behavior shows, they are precarious. Thus it is particularly easy for Iago to play on Othello's sense of separateness with regard to Desdemona, who is not only Venetian but also a woman. Othello is defenseless against commonplaces of antifeminism when couched as the insider's sociological observation:

I know our country disposition well:
In Venice they do let God see the pranks
They dare not show their husbands. (3.3.201–3)

It is at this key point that Iago's hints depend most on the structure of a patriarchal society; because of fathers' controls over their daughters, women can choose their husbands only through some deception—and that deception can forever after be held against them. "She did deceive her father, marrying you" (3.3.206). There is always a latent male alliance, which Iago brings to the surface here as a compensation for the sense of alienation he is arousing in Othello. By stressing Desdemona's youth, also, Iago makes her sound like a diabolically clever child:

She that, so young, could give out such a seeming
To seel her father's eyes up close as oak—
He thought 'twas witchcraft. (3.3.209–11)

The witchcraft charges originally applied to Othello have been projected to Desdemona. Othello's sense of being an outsider is evident as he resigns himself:

Haply, for I am black
And have not those soft parts of conversation
That chamberers have, or for I am declined
Into the vale of years—yet that's not much—
She's gone. I am abused, and my relief
Must be to loathe her. (3.3.263–68)

One of the reasons that Iago can play so easily on Othello's sense of separateness to break up his relationship with Desdemona is that he himself can supply a pretense of the mutuality Othello so longs for. It is ironic that Iago is one of the few characters in Shakespeare to use in his dialogue a form of the word "mutuality"; to him it is a suggestive word that can make Cassio's gestures of courtesy to Desdemona sound like foreplay: "When these mutualities so marshal the way, hard at hand comes the master and main exercise, th' incorporate conclusion" (2.1.255–57). To Iago, sincere mutuality of feeling is impossible, and most of the time he assumes that other people are as shallow in their relationships. He reduces love to a precariously matched set of appetites that he can easily manipulate.

It is unsettling to see, with Stephen Greenblatt, how well Iago's attitude toward Othello fits some definitions of empathy.[11] As W. H. Auden has noted, "Iago treats Othello as an analyst treats a patient except that, of course, his intention is to kill, not to cure. Everything he says is designed to bring to Othello's consciousness what he has already guessed is there."[12] Iago cleverly postpones making direct charges against Desdemona and Cassio. Rather he drops hints and raises questions, leaving Othello to imagine the charges himself. His technique here is particularly poignant because it plays on the attempt to read gestures and see unspoken thoughts which worked for Othello in his recounted conversation with Desdemona. While earlier we heard about Desdemona and Othello creating a mutual trust together, here we see Iago and Othello creating a union based on suspicion of Desdemona, pretended by Iago and believed by Othello. Furthermore, Iago speaks openly of his own love for Othello—knowing that Othello will respond—and uses this technique especially when Othello sounds as if he is likely to doubt him: "From hence / I'll love no friend, sith love breeds such offence" (3.3.379–80). Othello's growing fascination with Iago's words is heightened as Iago calls up the image of Cassio and Desdemona in bed, "as prime as goats, as hot as monkeys" (3.3.403), and then the image of Cassio in bed with Iago, mistaking him for Desdemona; the dream-like image of sexual union between two men parallels and charges the emotional union that Iago is creating with Othello. The excitement of the image adds to the tension of the conversation.

The parody marriage ceremony enacted when they kneel and vow murder, and Iago says, "I am your own forever" (3.3.480), offers a return to a relationship in one respect like the one Othello earlier had with Desdemona. In the worldview Iago offers, Othello again has someone's total dedication:

> Witness that here Iago doth give up
> The execution of his wit, hands, heart
> To wronged Othello's service!   (3.3.465–67)

Desdemona, by contrast, has given evidence that she extends her sympathy not only to Othello but also to Cassio.

In loving Desdemona, Othello has ventured outside of the man's world of war and made himself vulnerable to charges of being ruled by his emotions and therefore, in Renaissance terms, less than manly; remember his oath that if he neglects his duty because of Desdemona, "Let housewives make a skillet of my helm" (1.3.272). Iago plays on these fears as well by the way he acts the advocate of cold reason. His image of Cassio and Desdemona in bestial lust is introduced by "It is impossible you should see this" (3.3.402). The struggle between passion and control that initially was internal to Othello is now externalized; all of Iago's qualifications and admonitions to patience serve to enrage Othello further:

> Iago   And this may help to thicken other proofs
>   That do demonstrate thinly.
> Othello   I'll tear her all to pieces!
>   (3.3.430–31)

After Othello's emotions have surfaced so powerfully that he falls into a fit, Iago begins to harp on the issue of manhood.[13] "Would you would bear your fortune like a man. . . . Be a man . . . grief—a passion most unsuiting such a man" (4.1.61, 64, 76–77). By trying to emphasize the need for control, he is still promoting Othello's passion, but helping to channel it toward revenge:

Iago   Marry, patience!
          Or I shall say y'are all in all in spleen,
          And nothing of a man.
Othello   Dost thou hear, Iago?
          I will be found most cunning in my patience
          But—dost thou hear?—most bloody.   (4.1.87–91)

Under Iago's influence, Othello starts to name Desdemona in ways that fit more into the harshest potential of
the patriarchal structure of marriage than into a mutuality
of love. The images that he uses for Desdemona put her
into categories of objects to be controlled or possessed.
His sense of her as different from him becomes more and
more an image of her as strange, not quite human. He
compares her to a hawk, using one of Petruchio's more
patriarchal images:

                   If I do prove her haggard,
          Though that her jesses were my dear heartstrings,
          I'd whistle her off and let her down the wind
          To prey at fortune.   (3.3.260–63)

He cannot bear to think that total control of her is impossible—the impossibility seems to threaten reducing him to
an animal as well:

              O curse of marriage,
          That we can call these delicate creatures ours,
          And not their appetites! I had rather be a toad,
          And live upon the vapor of a dungeon
          Than keep a corner in the thing I love
          For others' uses.   (3.3.268–73)

"The thing I love"—that is now Othello's phrase for Desdemona. Emilia and Iago echo the word, with similar undertones of sexuality and a reductive approach to women, a
few lines later, when they gain possession of the handkerchief:

Emilia	I have a thing for you.
Iago	A thing for me? It is a common thing—
Emilia	Ha?
Iago	To have a foolish wife. (3.3.301–4)

The word suggests the reduction of woman to object and particularly to sexual object that has occurred in Othello's mind under Iago's influence.

When Othello starts to doubt Desdemona, he also uses more images of dirt, often associated with sexuality. Desdemona, instead of a clear fountain, becomes "a cistern for foul toads / To knot and gender in" (4.2.61–62). This dirt also becomes associated with blackness. Here too we see Othello showing more self-hatred in his imagery as his distrust of Desdemona grows. "Her name, that was as fresh / As Dian's visage, is now begrimed and black / As mine own face" (3.3.386–88).

This opposition between cleanness and dirt is another reason why the handkerchief becomes central to Othello's rejection of his love for Desdemona. "Such a handkerchief . . . ," says Iago, "did I today / See Cassio wipe his beard with" (3.3.437–39), and Othello explodes: "O, that the slave had forty thousand lives! / One is too poor, too weak for my revenge" (3.3.443–44). The handkerchief, something originally clean, is juxtaposed with dirt from Cassio's beard and for Othello it is as if that dirt soiled Desdemona herself.

When Othello becomes more distrusting of Desdemona, he also becomes more conscious of his passionate physical attraction to her, which earlier in the play he did not speak of, or denied.[14] While initially he called her "My soul's joy," now he speaks of "her sweet body" (3.3.346) and declares, "I'll not expostulate with her, lest her body and beauty unprovide my mind again" (4.1.200–202). The more he imagines her guilt, the more he feels his own attraction to her; he feels it more intensely, no doubt, because it appears split off from all her good qualities in which he no longer believes. He plans to kill her as a way to control his own unruly passion for her body as he punishes her passion.

In spite of this general tendency, Othello has moments even as he is planning the murder when he sees Desdemona not as an object to be controlled or punished but as an active, even civilizing woman. "So delicate with her needle! an admirable musician! O, she will sing the savageness out of a bear! of so high and plenteous wit and invention" (4.1.184–87). Struck by his admiration of her, Othello is moved to exclaim, "But yet the pity of it, Iago! O Iago, the pity of it, Iago" (4.1.192–93). But Iago can expel this mood in a moment by returning to the patriarchal imagery of possession: "If you are so fond over her iniquity, give her patent to offend; for if it touch not you, it comes near nobody" (4.1.194–95).

As Othello is torn by the conflict between his admiration and his disgust, Desdemona's synthesis of attitudes breaks up disastrously. After the marriage Desdemona's combination of initiative—which contributes to mutuality—and pretense—which accommodates to patriarchy—dissolves, and both forms of acting contribute to Othello's anger at her. Her commitment to Cassio is carried out with such vehemence that some critics have accused her of trying to take away Othello's military authority; on the other hand, her resort to the evasive technique of lying about the handkerchief causes his anger even more intensely.

Desdemona knows that in some ways she is transcending patriarchal categories in pleading for Cassio with Othello (although of course she would not have called it that); she uses images suggesting that she sees herself in roles held predominantly by men in Renaissance society: "His bed shall seem a school, his board a shrift. / . . . Thy solicitor shall rather die / Than give thy cause away" (3.2.24, 27–28). Furthermore, she asks that Othello pardon Cassio not as an obedient inferior asks for a favor from a condescending superior but with the suggestion that their marriage is one of mutual generosity: "I wonder in my soul / What you could ask me that I should deny / Or stand so mamm'ring on" (3.3.68–70). At the same time she goes on to suggest a different vision of their relationship: "Why, this is not a boon; / 'Tis as I should entreat you wear your gloves, / Or feed on nourishing dishes, or keep you warm" (3.3.76–78). This imagery suggests either that she is imagining total identification with him—she is asking for this because it is what he needs—or that she sees herself as taking care of him as a nurturing mother does a child. In the light of psychoanalytic theory it is easy to conflate these two suggestions and to see the lines as hints that she too participates in the fantasy of a union with Othello as close as that of mother and infant. It is at this point that she swears "By'r Lady [By Our Lady], I could do much" (3.3.74), and Othello dismisses her by saying, "Leave me but a little to myself" (3.3.85), words that suggest he feels his identity threatened by engulfment. He has wanted fusion, yes, but it is also threatening, especially for someone who values control as Othello does.

As Othello's jealousy becomes clearer, Desdemona's attitudes are a mixture of mature strength and evasion.[15] When openly accused she defends herself forcefully to Othello:

Othello   Are not you a strumpet?
Desdemona   No, as I am a Christian!   (4.2.82)

But after this scene she emphasizes her innocence in language that makes her seem more weak and passive:

> Those that do teach young babes
> Do it with gentle means and easy tasks:
> He might have chid me so; for, in good faith,
> I am a child to chiding.
>
> .   .   .   .
>
> Am I that name, Iago?   (4.2.111–14, 118)

She has been slow to see that Othello is jealous and even slower to see that he is jealous of Cassio: she has intuitions that she is in danger in her last scene with Emilia, but she dismisses them:

> Good faith, how foolish are our minds!
> If I do die before thee, prithee shroud me
> In one of those same sheets.   (4.3.22–24)

Early in the play she seems mature and aware of people's limitations ("I would not there reside, / To put my father in impatient thoughts / By being in his eye"—1.3.241–43) and worldly-wise enough to deal with Iago's antifeminist jokes with a cool "O heavy ignorance! Thou praisest the worst best" (2.1.143–44). She can be calm and tolerant about Othello's bad temper, although this tolerance sounds like evasion in the light of later events:

> Nay, we must think men are not gods,
> Nor of them look for such observancy
> As fits the bridal.   (3.4.148–50)

Near the end, with Emilia, she retreats into a willful ignorance, as her disillusionment with Othello leads her to cling harder, perhaps, to a belief in women:

Desdemona   O, these men, these men!
         Dost thou in conscience think—tell me,
            Emilia—
         That there be women do abuse their
            husbands
         In such gross kind?
Emilia   There be some such, no question.

         .   .   .   .

Desdemona I do not think there is any such woman.
                                             (4.3.58–61, 82)

At this point it is Emilia who takes over the articulate awareness that Desdemona showed earlier. She makes a speech attacking the institution behind Othello's assumption of his right to kill Desdemona—the double standard. Elsewhere than in this speech, the play alludes to adultery by men only in Iago's fantasies—and there, of course, he sees it as an offense against one man by another. Here, suddenly, the whole perspective changes, and we see adultery not as a world-shaking crime committed by women, but as one of a whole group of men's possible behaviors annoying to wives—in the same category as jealousy, violence, and stinginess. How different it is to see adultery as a violation of "there where I have garnered up my heart" and to see it as analogous to cutting an allowance. Emilia rejects the patriarchal valuation of female adultery as worse than male adultery:

> Let husbands know,
> Their wives have sense like them. They see and smell,
> And have their palates both for sweet and sour,
> As husbands have. . . .
> . . . And have not we affections,
> Desires for sport, and frailty, as men have?
> (4.3.92–95, 99–100)

Othello's murder of Desdemona is the epitome of his failure to accept the fact that both of them have what Emilia calls frailties and affections. When he sees her sleeping, his words show appreciation of her beauty as a passive object, which he can describe in static, lifeless terms—sensuous conversions of passion to coldness and art—"That whiter skin of hers than snow, / And smooth as monumental alabaster" (5.2.3–4). As he becomes more aware of the irrevocability of her death, the imagery changes:

> I know not where is that Promethean heat
> That can thy light relume. When I have plucked the
>   rose,
> I cannot give it vital growth again.   (5.2.12–14)

Yet this awareness falters: "I will kill thee, / And love thee after" (5.2.18–19). When seeing her sleeping, he talks tenderly of her, even kisses her, in spite of his intent to kill, and wants to give her time to confess her sins, but on confronting the awakened woman, who struggles for life and denies his accusations, he becomes enraged.

Again Desdemona defends her innocence stoutly in a mix of assertiveness, generosity, and naiveté:

>   I never did
> Offend you in my life; never loved Cassio
> But with such general warranty of heaven
> As I might love.   (5.2.58–61)

But her earlier resourcefulness and understanding of Othello have left her. She cannot believe that he will kill her. "Why I should fear I know not, / Since guiltiness I know not; but yet I feel I fear" (5.2.38–39), she says, after he has already begun to talk of killing. The best she can do for her survival, when she learns that Othello will not believe her and Cassio is dead, is to ask for a stay of execution.

In her last words, uttered after she is apparently dead and Emilia has returned, her first impulse is to proclaim her murder and thus to maintain her own innocence. But when Emilia asks her to name her murderer, Desdemona shows that she has forgiven Othello—"Commend me to my kind lord"—and for the last time uses a lie to try to cover up—this time Othello's guilt—"Nobody—I myself" (5.2.125–26).

Othello does not see her forgiveness but rather the lie that fits with his insistence on her dishonesty. But eventually he learns the truth, when Emilia tells the story of her own responsibility in the loss of the handkerchief—at the cost of her life. Yet Othello's words at the end show that he still fails to understand Desdemona. If she were true, he says, after Emilia has challenged his charges,

> If heaven would make me such another world
> Of one entire and perfect chrysolite,
> I'd not have sold her for it.   (5.2.145–47)

And at the end he compares her to a foolishly discarded "pearl . . . / Richer than all his tribe" (5.2.347–48). Value is evident in these images, but it is lifeless, inanimate—a possession: "Cold, cold, my girl? / Even like thy chastity" (5.2.276–77). His identification of her chastity with the coldness of death shows his inability to connect it with the warmth of her love; it is in keeping with this that he does not understand the forgiveness that she has already granted him:

> When we shall meet at compt,
> This look of thine will hurl my soul from heaven,
> And fiends will snatch at it.   (5.2.274–76)

At the end Othello seems again to regain control of himself and can finally admit his earlier lack of control, his passivity to "being wrought, / Perplexed in the extreme" (5.2.345–46). He maintains control of his own destiny by killing himself but also intends a return to mutuality. The final image of three people dead on a bed is on one level an image of the power of sexual passion to take life. Yet unlike the first two deaths, inflicted in passion, this one is calm. These deaths show not the simple destructiveness of passion but the more complicated destructiveness of passion combined with an attempt to control, closely related to social structures of sexual polarization.

Let us consider briefly three of the ways that Shakespeare's characters see sexual relations between man and woman. They can be seen as a sharing of passion and action in mutual responsiveness, as the man asserting his dominance over the woman, or as the man overcome by his passion for the woman. The second and third views come out of a mental structure of sexual polarization, in which either man = action and woman = passivity or man = control and woman = passion. In the comedies, the first view of sexuality (mutuality) balances the second (male dominance), as in The Taming of the Shrew, or the second and third (male submission to passion, represented by a woman), as in As You Like It. Comic game-playing helps keep this balance. Either male or female dominance can seem less threatening and less permanent if portrayed as a game, and the participation of the lovers in a game not understood by other characters adds to the sense of their existence in a shared world that dramatizes the strength of their relationship. This structure of play allows the lovers to try out the extremity of passion ("Then, in mine own

person, I die"—*As You Like It*, 4.1.84) and to draw back from
it ("No, faith, die by attorney"—*As You Like It*, 4.1.85). The
fears of betrayal and rejection surface and are dealt with.
Desdemona has something of the playful attitude, the
ability to try out situations through imagining alternatives.
But unlike the comedy heroes, Othello lacks any trace of
such flexibility. "Disport" seems a bad word to him. Unlike
them, also, he is matched with Iago, one of the most notable game-players in Shakespeare, who uses his abilities to
create false mutuality and destroy true mutuality. Under his
influence, Othello's wish to assert his dominance over
Desdemona and control their passions becomes desperate
and contaminated by the masculine code of revenge by
murder. When he discovers his guilt, however, Desdemona becomes identified with control ("Cold, cold as thy
chastity") and himself with passion. Then with his final act
he turns his activity against himself and tells us that this
gesture of control is intended as a union with her.

While in the first part of the speech, his guilt about his
excess of passion is apparent—"one that loved not wisely,
but too well" (5.2.344)—there is a section of it in which he
speaks of a kind of passion in himself that by implication
becomes healing:

> One whose subdued eyes,
> Albeit unusèd to the melting mood,
> Drop tears as fast as the Arabian trees
> Their med'cinable gum.   (5.2.348–51)

He is following Desdemona in weeping and in speaking of
himself as subdued. Furthermore, his image momentarily
suggests a reconciliation with nature and its fluids. Othello
has often used similar images of biological viscosity with
disgust—"The slime / That sticks on filthy deeds" (5.2.149–
50).[16] Now for perhaps the first time he sees something in
nature as healing. Furthermore, the gum is from Arabian
trees—from an exotic, non-European land, one closer to
Othello's heritage. It is a brief moment—only four lines—
of relative peace—with the trees and the tears that recall

Desdemona's willow song, where "Her salt tears fell from her, and soft'ned the stones" (4.2.45). Othello knows his heart is not the stone he once said it was. For these few moments he transcends the stereotype of masculine control to which he has elsewhere aspired. But he cannot accept as adequate the forgiveness that Desdemona has already granted him; he must return to the code of violence and control, and kill the passionate alien self that he earlier thought he was killing in Desdemona: "No way but this, / Killing myself, to die upon a kiss" (5.2.358–59).

The violent events of Othello dramatize, in hyperbolical form, many aspects of the predominant form of emotional symbiosis between men and women that remains in our society still. The references that I have occasionally made to echoes of the mother-child relationship in the imagery of the play are not intended as a prologue to comments about special pathologies in Othello's childhood, or Shakespeare's; rather, they are meant to underline the psychological influence that the restriction of child-rearing to women has had for centuries over the prevailing feelings of both sexes about women. Some of Othello's resonance comes from the imagery by which Othello's words about Desdemona evoke, at one moment, the way she gives him such joy as the mother gives the infant, and, at another moment, the way that his disillusionment with her re-creates the total desolation of the infant in a temporary state of frustration. I am following here the analysis of Dorothy Dinnerstein in The Mermaid and the Minotaur.[17] Dinnerstein believes that the boy raised by a woman feels "that the original, most primitive source of life will always lie outside himself, that to be sure of reliable access to it he must have exclusive access to a woman" (p. 43). Before the child has a defined self "a woman is the helpless child's main contact with the natural surround. . . . She is this global, inchoate, all-embracing presence before she is a person, a discrete, finite human individual with a subjectivity of her own" (p. 93). She is, perhaps, more a place than a person:

There where I have garnered up my heart,
Where either I must live or bear no life,
The fountain from the which my current runs
Or else dries up.   (4.2.57–60)

Initially, in her warmth and sympathy for him Desdemona seems to fulfill Othello's dreams of how a woman
ought to behave. Indeed, we in the audience know, though
Othello does not, that she never loses that warmth and
sympathy and that her only conflict with him arises because she also takes on the role of trying to help Cassio.

But that conflict does arise, and Othello's experience of
it, magnified by Iago's hints, has echoes of the discovery,
as Dinnerstein puts it, "that the infant does not own or
control the mother's body. Because this body has needs
and impulses of its own, its responsiveness to the infant's
needs is never totally reliable" (p. 60). "We can call these
delicate creatures ours / And not their appetites." We never
completely learn to deal with this truth, says Dinnerstein:
"That the other to whom we look for nurturance has, like
any sentient other, needs and a viewpoint separate from
and never wholly subject to our own" (p. 240). But conventional female behavior serves to hide this fact as much
as possible; "woman traditionally agrees to listen to man's
opinions and keep her own to herself, lets him hog the
limelight and offers herself as audience, allows herself activity only as it nourishes his projects" (pp. 239–40). Desdemona does more than this, but like many such women she
possesses what Dinnerstein calls "a monstrously overde-
veloped talent for unreciprocated empathy, an adult talent
that she must exercise in a situation in many ways as vulnerable as a child's" (p. 236).

Desdemona's "talent for empathy"—perhaps "sympathy"
is more accurate in view of her misunderstandings of
him—and her inability to fight back when her life is at
stake are symmetrical to Othello's military prowess and
inability to sympathize when he feels wronged. His role as

a soldier makes the point about the contrast between his and Desdemona's skills according to typical sex roles in the most emphatic way. Yet Desdemona admires Othello's military abilities and identifies with them so much that Othello calls her "fair warrior," and she later calls herself "unhandsome warrior" (3.4.151). They are re-creating the traditional woman's "privilege of enjoying man's achievements and triumphs vicariously" (p. 211).

When Desdemona hears of Othello's earlier experiences, her tears serve, as Dinnerstein suggests that women's tears often do, to help a man go on—"for she is doing his weeping for him, and he is doing what she weeps about for her" (p. 226). The flashback to his earlier life in this speech is the only time in the play when we have a glimpse of Othello acting without regard to Desdemona, and even that is put in the context of their relationship by its position in the story of their courtship. Thus we see his identity as a soldier as connected with his confidence in Desdemona's admiration and sympathy from almost the beginning of the play. It is in keeping with this connection that when he loses faith in Desdemona he says farewell not only to the tranquil mind but also to "the big wars / That make ambition virtue" (3.3.349–50). After he has regained belief in Desdemona's faith, at the end, he speaks again of his service to the state and he stages his suicide as a re-creation of an earlier battle against a Turk.

Dinnerstein's analysis illuminates the connections between three attitudes that we have seen linked in Othello: emphasis on control, rejection of physicality, and rejection of women. Her analysis suggests that the kind of mutuality at the beginning of Othello, moving though it may be, contains some of the seeds of the disaster that follows. Erikson defines mutuality, we recall, as a relationship in which partners depend on one another for the development of their respective strengths: after Dinnerstein's analysis, we may be more critical of that word "respective," if it implies a traditional differentiation of roles. As she puts it, "what each sex knows best has been distorted by . . . sealing off from what the other knows best" (p. 272). Finally, Othello's and Desdemona's definitions of reality diverge so much that no conversation can match them. Othello's limited development of sympathy combines with Desdemona's limited development of self-defense, and with all the powers that both of them *have* developed, to destroy both of them. And this destruction is more poignant because neither of them is simply stereotypical, because Desdemona has shown initiative and courage, because Othello has felt more love for her than he can kill. But finally they act out ideals of their own culture, ideals that are still part of our own culture. It is Shakespeare's genius that the play can suggest both the limitations and infantile roots of these ideals and their magnetic power.

Chapter Eight
Patriarchy, Mutuality, and
Forgiveness in King Lear

If *Othello* explores patriarchal behavior in the husband, *King Lear* explores it in the father. Critics of *King Lear* have frequently noted that Lear begins with the power of the archetypal king and father; many of them have also noted that his initial lack of self-knowledge springs in part from the prerogatives of kingship.[1] It has been less observed that the play includes implicit criticism of the prerogatives of the father and an exploration of some behavior that patriarchy fosters in men and women. The apparent mutual dependence of Lear and his older daughters, following conventional patterns of male and female behavior, is deceptive. What the characters need are bonds of forgiveness and sympathy based on a deeper and less categorized sense of human connection.

Maynard Mack emphasizes the importance of relatedness in *Lear*.[2] This concern, as I have been suggesting, pervades Shakespeare's plays. While the early comedies parallel many different kinds of mutuality, and accept them all, in tragedy mutuality is tested, and many of its varieties are found wanting. If a society is working, the principle of mutuality—or reciprocity, as the sociologist Alvin Gouldner calls it—offers its structure further justification.[3] Places in a hierarchy give reciprocal duties; the subject serves a benevolent master out of gratitude as well as obedience. However, if what the master needs of the subject includes forgiveness, this begins to call the social order into question. The emphasis on King Lear's need for forgiveness reinforces the challenge he makes to his society on the heath.

Although *Lear* is concerned with the mutuality between father and daughter, it deals with aspects of that mutuality which are also experienced by husband and wife in a patriarchal society, where the authority of fathers over their families, husbands over wives, and men in general over women are all related and analogous. Too great an imbalance in this power makes it likely that attempts at mutuality will be flawed by male coercion and female deception.

Lear's abdication scene provides a paradigm of this danger. He offers money and property in exchange for words of love:

> Which of you shall we say doth love us most,
> That we our largest bounty may extend
> Where nature doth with merit challenge. (1.1.51–53)

Of course, part of the problem with the contest is that it takes words of love as an adequate equivalent of love itself. But this is not just a problem with words; any means of expressing love may be used deceptively, and yet love requires the use of some kind of means. It is the power imbalance behind Lear's offer that makes deception both more likely and more impenetrable. Lear is really trying to coerce his daughters to a certain form of behavior; he sets up the terms and the contract. If a daughter wishes a different kind of contract, she is disowned. As king, Lear is the source of all money and property; in their dependence on him at this point the daughters resemble wives in a patriarchal marriage who can get money only by begging it from their husbands. Nora Helmer's performance in *A Doll's House* is a variant response to a similar situation. No matter how much the male depends on the female's response, if he has all the external power, the social approval, and the sole right to initiate, the mutuality is deeply flawed by coercion.

In such a situation, the obvious way for a woman to survive is to go along with the social order, as Goneril and Regan do at the beginning. In *The Taming of the Shrew*—closer to Lear than any tragedy or any other comedy in the large number of times the word "father" is used—this kind of survival is what Bianca practices from the beginning and part of what Kate learns by the end.[4] In a comedy we do not much mind Bianca's ability to gull Lucentio, and the ambiguity of Kate's final integration of her individuality and the social order still pleases most audiences or wins Kate more sympathy. But even that play shows in Bianca's final posture the cool self-interest that may underlie such compliance. The pretenses of Goneril and Regan have more devastating effects, but in flattering Lear they are doing a service that women are traditionally expected to do for men. Of them, as well as of his subjects, Lear could say, "They told me I was everything" (4.6.103–4).

Lear's childishness has been noted by many critics of the play, as well as the Fool and, self-interestedly, Goneril— "Old fools are babes again" (1.3.19); but it has been less observed that the similarity between king and child is in part in their assumptions of omnipotence encouraged— for different reasons—by the flattery of those who care for them.[5] Elizabeth Janeway has explained how traditional expectations of female behavior come from nostalgia for a mother's care in childhood.[6] Lear, in wishing to "unburdened crawl toward death," wants to become a child still omnipotent in his ability to control Cordelia's "kind nursery." The illusory omnipotence of the abdicating king can be compared to the illusory omnipotence of the head of the family within his household, which the sociologists Peter Berger and Hansfried Kellner call a "play area" where he can be "lord and master."[7] Lear really is lord and master at the beginning; but in the love contest he pretends to have more power over his daughters' feelings than he actually has, and this, of course, results in the loss of power that makes the split between his wishes and reality even more glaring later on. Although at first Goneril and Regan have seemed like good mothers in their compliance and words of total devotion, now they are punitive and emphasize Lear's powerlessness, as the Fool suggests: "thou mad'st thy daughters thy mothers; . . . when thou gav'st them the rod, and put'st down thine own breeches, / Then they for sudden joy did weep" (1.4.163–66). When Lear curses Goneril with his wish that she bear no children or a "child of spleen," it is partly because he feels that filial ingratitude such as he experiences is the worst possible suffering—but perhaps also because her behavior toward him makes him think of her as a bad mother.

The contrast between Goneril and Regan, on the one hand, and Cordelia, on the other, owes something to the traditional tendency in Western literature to split the image of woman into devil and angel, Eve and Mary.[8] Goneril and Regan are much less psychologically complex than most Shakespearean characters of comparable importance. Few of their lines carry hints of motivations other than cruelty, lust, or ambition, characteristics of the archetypal fantasy image of the woman as enemy. Shakespeare gives them no humanizing scruples like those provoked by Lady Macbeth's memory of her father. He does not allow them to point out wrongs done to them in the past as eloquently as Shylock does, or to question the fairness of their society's distribution of power as articulately as Edmund. If their attack on Lear can be seen as in part the consequence of his tyrannical patriarchy, they never try to explain it as an attack on an oppressor. Indeed, even if we follow Peter Brook's lead and imagine a Lear who knocks over tables, whose men really are a "disordered rabble," their cruelty to Lear and, even more, to Gloucester exceeds all provocation. Rather than attacking tyranny, they prefer to attack weakness, and sometimes compare those they attack to women in terms meant to be insulting. Regan says to Lear, "I pray you, father, being weak, seem so" (2.4.196). Goneril says, "I must change names at home, and give the distaff / Into my husband's hands" (4.2.17–18). One of the few suggestions of psychological complexity in their characteriza-

tion is this hint of a compensatory quality in their cruelty—
a hatred of others they consider weak because of a fear of
being weak themselves.[9] Here the play suggests that weakness, or the fear of it, can be as corrupting an influence
as power. This fear of weakness is, however, a standard
enough trait in the psychology of violence that it does little
to individualize them.

Cordelia, by contrast with her sisters, is much less stereo-
typed. Shakespeare's presentation of her shows sympathy
for the woman who tries to keep her integrity in a patriarchal world. Refusing pretense as a means of survival, such
women often try to withdraw from the coercive "mutuality" that patriarchy seems to demand. Cordelia initially attempts to say nothing; her asides tell us her wish to "love
and be silent." As she speaks further, in a mode completely
alien to the love contest, her difficulties with language add
to the audience sympathy with her; they make us imagine
that she feels much more than she says. She describes the
parent-child bond in language that emphasizes its mutuality, its elements of reciprocation and response; the possible coldness in her reference to "duties" is counterbal-
anced by her approximation of the marriage vow:

> Good my lord,
> You have begot me, bred me, loved me. I
> Return those duties back as are right fit,
> Obey you, love you, and most honor you.   (1.1.95–98)

Cordelia looks more toward the general parental gifts of
the past than toward munificent promises for the future;
all that she anticipates is a marriage and conflicting loyal-
ties. In Shakespearean comedy, Portia or Rosalind can joke
skeptically about professions of absolute and exclusive
love; in this tragedy, Cordelia's refusal of hyperbole continues the challenge to Lear's wish to be loved alone and his
delight in his special power, and it precipitates her rejection. Lear wants more than the ordinary mutuality of parent and child, but his ability to disown Cordelia when such
ordinary mutuality is all she will promise springs from the

superior power of fathers in a patriarchal society. Lear's
rejection is total: "Better thou / Hadst not been born than
not t'have pleased me better" (1.1.233–34).

It is retributive, however shocking and disproportionate,
when Lear's older daughters use the power they receive
with a coercion like Lear's own. As the Fool says, "I marvel
what kin thou and thy daughters are. They'll have me
whipped for speaking true; thou'lt have me whipped for
lying" (1.4.173–75). What Lear criticizes in them, however,
is not their general tyranny and cruelty but their lack of
mutuality—their ingratitude to him. Along with this preoccupation goes a preoccupation with his own generosity: "Your old kind father, whose frank heart gave all—"
(3.4.20). Perhaps this suggests something of the intent of
his gifts.

But as he experiences the sufferings of the poor and the
outcast, Lear begins to imagine less self-interested kinds of
giving. He shows concern for the Fool and acknowledges
his own responsibility for the condition of the "poor naked wretches" he now wishes to help. And after the fantasy
trial he starts to speak of his daughters in different terms as
he moves to more general social and existential concerns:
"Is there any cause in nature that makes these hard hearts?"
(3.6.75–76). In the next scene he denounces the false mutuality that would say "ay" and "no" to everything he said.
Here is his longest attack on women: it begins by pointing
to someone who could be Goneril or Regan as we see
them, but he does not name her, and he attacks her not for
ingratitude but for lust and hypocrisy:

> Behold yond simp'ring dame,
> Whose face between her forks presages snow,
> That minces virtue, and does shake the head
> To hear of pleasure's name.
> The fitchew nor the soilèd horse goes to't
> With a more riotous appetite. . . .   (4.6.117–22)

His words are antifeminist commonplaces of Elizabethan
England, but the context suggests a basis in revulsion

against pretense and sexuality in general more than against women. A bit later he shows deeper insight about the origin of such antifeminist commonplaces:

Thou rascal beadle, hold thy bloody hand!
Why dost thou lash that whore? Strip thy own back.
Thou hotly lusts to use her in that kind
For which thou whip'st her.   (4.6.157–60)

We punish others for our own faults; this is a general phenomenon that Lear denounces here and that Shakespeare often illustrates and describes elsewhere. More specifically, this passage implies the relationship of such scapegoating to patriarchal society's split of human qualities, both vices and virtues, into masculine and feminine. Patriarchal society exerts social and psychological pressure on men to deny qualities in themselves that would be seen as feminine and instead to project them on to women. This analysis suggests that Lear's disgust with women's lust is so strong because it is really disgust with himself; at the same time, his initial expectations of Cordelia's "kind nursery" are so high because he identifies her with nurturing qualities and vulnerabilities not easily admitted by a king whose royal symbol is the dragon.

Both textual and structural details in *Lear* support this emphasis on projection of feminine qualities; furthermore, it is closely related to the play's concern with connections between people. Lear's own words to Goneril suggest something of his identification with her:

We'll no more meet, no more see one another.
But yet thou art my flesh, my blood, my daughter;
Or rather a disease that's in my flesh,
Which I must needs call mine.   (2.4.215–18)

Sometimes he seems unable to recognize his daughters as persons separate from himself: "Is it not as this mouth should tear this hand / For lifting food to 't?" (3.4.15–16). At other times he blames himself for begetting them, in language that again suggests revulsion from the sexuality with which, as women, they are linked in the imagination of Western culture: "Judicious punishment—'twas this flesh begot / Those pelican daughters" (3.4.72–73). Just after Lear gags at imagining the stench beneath women's girdles, he acknowledges the smell of mortality on his own hand.

From this vision of universal guilt, Lear moves to a vision of universal suffering, the basis for a different kind of mutuality. He responds to Gloucester's sympathy, recognizes him, and speaks with him using the "we" of identification and common humanity.

> We came crying hither;
> Thou know'st, the first time that we smell the air
> We wawl and cry. . . .
> When we are born, we cry that we are come
> To this great stage of fools.   (4.6.175–77, 179–80)

His use of "we" contrasts with his earlier assumption of the royal prerogative of the first person plural and with the "I" of his felt isolation; the imagery of crying makes an equally insistent contrast to his earlier stance:

> let not women's weapons, water drops,
> Stain my man's cheeks. . . .
>   . . . You think I'll weep.
> No, I'll not weep.   (2.4.272–73, 277–78)

And while earlier he described the alienation between himself and his daughters as like an attack by one part of his body on another, now he imagines himself giving part of his body to supply another's disability: "If thou wilt weep my fortunes, take my eyes" (4.6.173). At the same time as he acknowledges his own identity and Gloucester's, and their fellowship, he acknowledges his share in a vulnerability to suffering and a need to express it—the powerlessness of the child, and not its illusory omnipotence—which he had previously relegated to women. And the tears in his vision of all crying for their own suffering quickly become tears of compassion.

The association of tears and women is a commonplace in Shakespeare and in our culture, even though in Shakespeare at least the association is most frequently made by men who do cry themselves (Laertes, Sebastian in *Twelfth Night*). Nevertheless, it is remarkable both how often Cordelia's tears are mentioned in *King Lear* and how the imagery strives to make them powerful rather than pathetic. Cordelia credits them with arousing France's sympathy and persuading him to help Lear (4.4.25–26); she prays that they will help restore Lear's health:

> All blessed secrets,
> All you unpublished virtues of the earth,
> Spring with my tears!   (4.4.15–17)

And at the climactic moment of their reunion, Lear, whose own tears "scald like molten lead" (4.7.48), touches her cheek and says, "Be your tears wet? Yes, faith" (4.7.71).[10] With Cordelia's tears, as with other aspects of her characterization, Shakespeare is suggesting a kind of power different from the coercion dependent on political rank or violence; it is the power of nurturing, of sympathy, of human connection as an active force.

The physical connection of parenthood, on which Lear relied earlier in his reproaches to Goneril and Regan, has proved too often only a torment to him; in his reunions with Gloucester and, even more, with Cordelia, Lear experiences a connection—based on shared suffering—which can also be called physical insofar as it involves touching and being touched by others, weeping and being wept for.[11] This kind of sympathy underlies Cordelia's ability to restore the parent-child bond rather than simply responding with the revenge Lear expects when he says, even after he has felt her tears,

> If you have poison for me, I will drink it.
> I know you do not love me; for your sisters
> Have (as I do remember) done me wrong.
> You have some cause, they have not.   (4.7.72–75)

The creative power of Cordelia's compassion transcends the mechanism of revenge; nor, her words suggest, is her sympathy confined to relatives.

> Had you not been their father, these white flakes
> Did challenge pity of them. Was this a face
> To be opposed against the jarring winds?
> . . . Mine enemy's dog,
> Though he had bit me, should have stood that night
> Against my fire.   (4.7.30–32, 36–38)

But for all the universality of her sympathy, she expresses it in the context of their particular relationship: to Lear's "as I am a man, I think this lady / to be my child Cordelia," she responds, "And so I am! I am!" (4.7.69–70). She is too tactful to speak of forgiveness; guilt and innocence seem irrelevant to her sympathy. But it is forgiveness that Lear needs, and finally he can ask for forgiveness instead of praise and gratitude: "Pray you now, forget and forgive. I am old and foolish" (4.7.84).

In his final vision of what their relationship would be, alone and happy together in prison, he says, "When thou dost ask me blessing, I'll kneel down / And ask of thee forgiveness" (5.3.10–11). In Shakespeare's England, Lawrence Stone tells us, kneeling to ask blessing was a common gesture of respect from child to parent, a symbol of generational hierarchy.[12] In Lear's vision, parent kneels to child. The need for forgiveness reverses hierarchies of both age and sex, and suggests their limitations.

Northrop Frye, noting the emphasis on forgiveness in Shakespeare's comedies, claims that it results from "impersonal concentration on the laws of comic form."[13] This does not, however, account for the importance of forgiveness, explicit and implicit, in a tragedy like *Lear*, and I think there are more basic reasons for the emphasis on the need for forgiveness in Shakespeare's tragedies, problem comedies, and romances. Shakespeare's plays are concerned with both power and relationship. Lear, for example, depends on power—even though he thinks he wants to give it up—and he wants love. Frequently, Shakespeare shows a man's attempt to get, preserve, or control a relationship with a woman resulting in disaster because he abuses his power. Lear and Angelo are the most obvious examples. From the problem comedies on, Shakespeare suggests that in a patriarchal society mutuality between man and woman must include the mutuality of forgiveness and repentance, because the powerful are so likely to abuse their power.

However, before the female characters forgive, the balance often shifts: Lear and Angelo lose power, Cordelia and Isabella gain some. Alternatively, like Desdemona, they forgive when their forgiveness cannot possibly promise to help them. In either case, the forgiveness is freely chosen, not coerced by dependence on their men like the apparent forgiveness of a battered wife who has nowhere else to go. When Shakespeare's tragic and tragicomic heroes receive forgiveness, they have generally given up all expectations of it. Perhaps the women's forgiveness of them comes as even more of a surprise because it avoids the distancing of such self-righteous forgiveness as Prospero's words to his unrepentant brother:

> For you, most wicked sir, whom to call brother
> Would even infect my mouth, I do forgive
> Thy rankest fault—all of them.   (5.1.130–32)

Rather, their forgiveness is acceptance. Reversing the mechanism of projection and scapegoating, it implies a recognition of their own limitations as well, somewhat like the forgiveness Prospero begs from his audience: "As you from crimes would pardoned be, / Let your indulgence set me free" (Epilogue, 19–20).

However structurally important forgiveness is in Shakespeare's comedies and romances, where R. G. Hunter finds frequent affinities to the ritual stages of the sacrament of penance, it is worth noting how much more psychologically realistic and dramatically compelling are Lear's repentance and Cordelia's forgiveness.[14] Nor does *Lear* leave us with the sense of the inadequacy of forgiveness that Howard Felperin suggests in the problem comedies.[15] Cordelia's forgiveness cannot stop the political consequences of Lear's acts, to be sure, but there is no denying the emotional power of their reunion scene.

We can never completely account for *Lear*'s power to move us, of course, but it is worth considering the possibility that some of the intensity of this scene comes from an element in the play that would seem to move in an entirely opposite direction from sympathy and forgiveness—its portrayal of anger. The experience of *Lear* depends on the paradox that people are at the same time connected and separate, a paradox to which both sympathy and anger are responses. The intensity of anger may measure the intensity of feelings of loss; it also demonstrates how much sympathy is willing to forgive. Anger and sympathy are both signs of human vulnerability and relationship. In Lear's last scene his sorrow and anger at losing Cordelia merge:

> Howl, howl, howl! O, you are men of stones.
> Had I your tongues and eyes, I'ld use them so
> That heaven's vault should crack.   (5.3.258–60)

As he imagines the power his emotions could have with his listeners' help in expressing them, the effect in the theater is that he is also addressing the offstage audience. Before the intensity of his expressions of grief for Cordelia, our responses to our own losses, as well as to him, seem inadequate. We cannot heave our hearts into our mouths.

Earlier I suggested that the mutuality between characters in Shakespeare's comedies is analogous to the mutuality between actors and audience. Stanley Cavell has proposed that in *Lear* the inevitable separation between actors and audience mirrors the ultimate isolation of the characters, and all of us, from each other: we cannot stop the characters from acting wrongly, from suffering pain, just as they cannot stop each other, just as we cannot stop those closest to us.[16] Yet, although Lear cannot save Cordelia, nor she him, before this ultimate loss he does experience her acceptance. This acceptance includes tragic perception—it is combined with knowledge of his faults. It does not condescend, but it supports Lear in his own new willingness to acknowledge his limitations.

Perhaps this acceptance is a model for our relationship to Lear, and through him, to the play. Cordelia's attitude toward Lear mediates the attitude of the audience toward him. We can neither change Lear nor admire him uncritically, any more than Cordelia can, but we can join her in feeling with him. It is interesting that Shakespeare not only emphasizes his characters' capacity for sympathy, but also, in his descriptions of audiences, frequently presents sympathy as an important aspect of audience response. It may be the experience of feeling sympathy for someone we cannot change, whose faults we accept as we accept our own faults, that Shakespearean tragedy brings to its highest artistic expression, both within the play and between the play and the audience.

There is so much sympathy with Lear at the end that it seems cold to turn from feeling with him to any further analysis of the play in terms of sex-role behavior, but it is worth noting that part of the effect of the play is to impress on us the suffering created by these behavior patterns and then to show how inadequate they are. The forms of suffering in literature reflect the social structure, either directly or indirectly, and it is significant that much of Lear's and Cordelia's sufferings are related to the particular vulnerabilities of men and women in a patriarchal society, as I have shown. But when Lear enters with Cordelia dead in his arms, the visual image in itself suggests a change in him. The allusion to the pietà that many critics have seen here includes the fact that Lear is at this point taking on a posture much more characteristic of women than of men in our society—holding a child, caring for the dead. His patient watch over Cordelia, looking for a sign of life, may recall his expectation of her answer in the opening scene, but it is very different in tone. A performance might emphasize this change in Lear by making the gestures of his attempts to find life in Cordelia similar to the gestures of her attempts to wake him before their reunion. Though he still clings to some of his traditional images of male and female virtues, when he says, "Her voice was ever soft, / Gentle and low" (5.3.273–74), it is his own gentleness we see.[17] Now he would give to her in a way that would be nurturing and not coercive, but it is too late.

His suffering includes a sense of guilt for misusing his past power, but before the ultimate fact of death he feels the powerlessness that we all feel, king and subject, man and woman. At the end of the play, the surviving characters can for the most part only watch Lear's sufferings like the offstage audience, and the only acts they can perform are gestures of sympathy. All Edgar says in the concluding speech establishing his dominance is about feeling and sympathy for Lear. Thus in the sympathy that is the audience's only power we are united with the surviving characters. Cordelia's values spread beyond her and outlive her, but this is no matter for complacent intellectualization. Shakespeare probes in *King Lear* to the very heart of loss. Although here, unlike the parallel explorations of *Antony and Cleopatra* and *Othello*, the issue of sexuality as such remains mostly submerged, he shows with great depth the vulnerabilities to each other that the contrasting social roles of men and women intensify. The only consolation that he offers—and in a theater it is a significant one—is that we feel each other's loss because of our basic connection.

Chapter Nine

Transformed Images of Manhood
in the Romances

The previous chapters have suggested that most Shakespearean tragic heroes, like the traditional masculine stereotype of our own society, are afraid of qualities within themselves that they consider female and try to deny them by asserting their own male identity through violence. They cannot bear to be passive or uncertain; their ability to nurture others is undeveloped.[1] While the events of the tragedies show the inadequacy of this version of manhood, still their language often surrounds it with heroic grandeur.

In Shakespeare's romances, by contrast, the inadequacy of the traditional masculine stereotype is much more obvious. Men's attacks on women are presented as both more obviously wrong-headed and more ineffectual. Masculine violence in general is less glamorized, and the ideal of controlling emotional attachment has, usually, less appeal. The romance heroes are more readily resigned to being passive, more apt to express their sense of insecurity and vulnerability, more able to weep and to do penance, and more concerned about their own and others' children. They can take on occupations usually held by women and compare themselves to women without the anguish such imagery usually gives the tragic heroes.

Let us begin with the contrast between the tragedies' portrayal of the mistrust of women and that of the romances, focusing on the three self-styled cuckolds, Othello, Leontes, and Posthumus.[2] While Shakespeare gives many indications that Othello's suspicions of Desdemona are not justified, he helps the audience sympathize with Othello by juxtaposing him with the diabolically clever Iago and by showing Othello's complexity of feeling, his awareness of the uncertain case for his jealousy, and his memory of the qualities for which he loves Desdemona even after he is convinced of her guilt. There is no Iago in the romances; Leontes clearly creates his own suspicions, and Posthumus's are evoked by the much less threatening Iachimo. But Posthumus and Leontes experience less vacillation in their sense of their wives' guilt before attempting murder. Once Posthumus sees Imogen's bracelet and hears Iachimo's story, he is convinced. He speaks briefly of the falsity of her appearance of chastity: "A pudency so rosy, the sweet view on't / Might well have warmed old Saturn" (2.5.11–12)—but he has no other admiring words about her before he gives orders to kill her. Leontes, at the beginning of his suspicions, experiences some uncertainty about his accusations but soon abandons it:

> This entertainment
> May a free face put on, derive a liberty
> From heartiness, from bounty, fertile bosom,
> And well become the agent. 'Tmay, I grant,
> But to be paddling palms and pinching fingers. . . .
>   (1.2.111–15)

These quick misjudgments of the romance heroes make them seem even more blind than Othello, and their consequent behavior makes them seem more ineffectual.

In his suspicions Posthumus utters a sweeping manifesto of antifeminism that explicitly links distrust of women to distrust of aspects of men:

> Is there no way for men to be, but women
> Must be half-workers? We are all bastards,

And that most venerable man which I
Did call my father was I know not where
When I was stamped. . . .
                         . . . Could I find out
The woman's part in me! For there's no motion
That tends to vice in man but I affirm
It is the woman's part. Be it lying, note it,
The woman's; flattering, hers; deceiving, hers;
Lust, and rank thoughts, hers, hers; revenges, hers;
Ambitions, covetings, change of prides, disdain,
Nice longing, slanders, mutability . . .   (2.5.1–5, 19–26)

Yet it is notable that Posthumus never says what he would
do could he find out the woman's part in himself. And in
fact there is hardly anything left that he could do with his
hypothetical remaining "manly" self, since what he calls the
woman's part includes so much of human behavior. His
speech undercuts itself by its own hyperbole and then collapses into anticlimax:

    I'll write against them,
Detest them, curse them. Yet 'tis greater skill
In a true hate to pray they have their will.   (2.5.32–34)

And this anticlimax echoes the anticlimax of Posthumus's
more specific rage at Imogen:

O, that I had her here, to tear her limb-meal!
I will go there and do't i'th' court, before
Her father. I'll do something.   (2.4.147–49)

While Othello kills Desdemona himself, with his own
hands, horrifying us by his firmness of purpose against his
feelings of love and assuring himself that Desdemona cannot escape, the romance heroes delegate the killings they
plan. Posthumus sends his loyal servant Pisanio to murder
Imogen, but Pisanio's loyalty has its limits. Leontes holds a
public trial for Hermione, and when she faints, Paulina

takes charge and miraculously preserves her life. Because both the heroes attempt killing by intermediaries, rather than by their own hands, there is more room for events to deviate from their purposes and for the women to survive. Thus the heroes' ineffectuality here has benign consequences.

Both plays also demonstrate the instability of the hero's purpose—to similarly benign effect—by showing his repentance following immediately on his reception of the news that his wife is dead. Unlike Othello, who repents his murder only after Emilia's story about the handkerchief convinces him that Desdemona is innocent, Posthumus repents, more notably—and uniquely in Shakespeare—when he still believes Imogen is guilty:

> You married ones,
> If each of you should take this course, how many
> Must murder wives much better than themselves
> For wrying but a little!   (5.1.2–5)

Leontes begins to repent when he hears of his son's death, and when told of Hermione's, says, "I have too much believed mine own suspicion" (3.2.149).

In *Cymbeline*, unlike *The Winter's Tale*, military violence does play a significant part in the plot, but it is more like the episodic test of the comedies than the glamorous career of the tragedies. Posthumus does penance for his crime against Imogen by changing sides in the war and fighting for her Britain. He claims to be seeking death in war but cannot find it, and his repeated complaints about this make for an odd impression of heroism mixed with incompetence, which he continues by changing back to Roman costume. He has taken part in a legendary victory against odds, but his role in the legend is "a fourth man, in a silly habit" (5.3.86). His clothes remove the superficial military mythology somewhat as does Pericles' rusty armor. Furthermore, far from the usual glamorous image of the heroic warrior, the other participants in the battle are the aging Belarius and the young boys Guiderius and Arviragus.

In Cloten, Posthumus's rival for Imogen, the image of masculine violence is not merely demythologized but parodied. When we first meet him, he has been engaged in what a lord calls "the violence of action" (1.2.1–2)—a fencing match—but the main effect of it has been, as the lord says, that he "reek[s] as a sacrifice" (1.2.2) and needs to change out of his sweaty shirt. He breaks the head of a bystander who criticizes him for swearing, and is constantly spoiling for a fight. "Every jack-slave hath his bellyful of fighting, and I must go up and down like a cock that nobody can match" (2.1.19–20). He is determined to fight with Rome and not to pay tribute to Caesar, and he makes this point mainly with pugnacious jokes about Roman noses. He finds Imogen's whereabouts by threatening to rip Pisanio's heart to find the secret, and plans to confront her and Posthumus: "With that suit upon my back I will ravish her; first kill him, and in her eyes" (3.5.135–36). Plans that might be terrifying in Othello are ludicrous in Cloten; the justice of strangling Desdemona in "the sheets she has contaminated" has turned into the justice of killing Posthumus while wearing Posthumus's "meanest garment," which Imogen has praised while rejecting Cloten. When Cloten is killed, his literal loss of his head is emblematic of the folly that has been his throughout the play. In spite of his violence, he is even more ineffectual than Posthumus, with whom he shares a "Martial thigh, / The brawns of Hercules" (4.2.310–11) by the implications of Imogen's mistake. In Cymbeline and the other romances, the values of Mars and Hercules are superseded by the values of fertility and peace, and the recognition of Posthumus and his companions for their valor comes as a trifle by contrast to the restoration of Posthumus's marriage, Cymbeline's lost family, and, finally, to Posthumus's forgiveness of Iachimo and Cymbeline's "Pardon's the word to all" (5.5.422).

It is a similar sign of the repudiation of military values that Prospero renounces revenge and that Leontes, to atone for his crime against his wife, chooses not suicide but the penance of daily visits to a chapel honoring his wife and son, public notice there of his guilt, and finally "tears shed there / [for his] recreation" (3.2.237–38). As we have noted, most of Shakespeare's tragic heroes find themselves compelled to weep only after a long and bitter resistance, or with a profound sense of shame about the tears themselves, more than about what causes them. Thus it is particularly notable that Leontes *chooses* tears as his repentance and one of the same counselors who brought the oracle from Apollo eventually affirms that his repentance has indeed been effective. In *Cymbeline*, the line "The boy has taught us manly duties" (4.2.397) is spoken not about the young warriors but about Imogen/Fidele's plan to bury, pray, and *weep over* what she thinks is Posthumus's dead body. Furthermore, in the recognition scenes of all the romances, heroes weep unashamedly as a sign of joy. Pericles weeps at being reunited with Marina, Leontes at being reunited with Polixenes. Cymbeline, on his recognition of Imogen, says, "My tears that fall / Prove holy water on thee" (5.5.268–69). Prospero greets Gonzalo by saying, "Mine eyes, ev'n sociable to the show of thine, / Fall fellowly drops" (5.1.63–64). Tears are no longer "woman-like."

In the romances, some kind of relation to the young is important to many more of the characters, male and female, than in the tragedies. Parents may be nurturing, possessive, or rejecting, but their parental role is part of their characterization and they are more apt to express emotions about their children directly.[3] Other adults, like the Old Shepherd and Belarius, and even older children, like Arviragus, can readily take on quasi-parental attitudes. Posthumus's father, "Fond of issue . . . Took such sorrow / That he quit being" (1.1.37–38) when his older sons died in battle; in his place, Cymbeline "Breeds him and makes him of his bedchamber" (1.1.42). Posthumus's later dream-vision is an epiphany of continuing parental care, though his father's words express a sense of powerlessness as well: Sicilius asks, "Hath my poor boy done aught but well, / Whose face I never saw?" (5.4.35–36), and he attacks Jupiter for not taking over his fatherhood for Posthumus. When Jupiter appears, he claims that he has been looking after Posthumus all the time, but in a way that almost collapses the distinction between nurturance and its opposite: "Whom best I love I cross; to make my gift / The more delayed, delighted" (5.4.101–2). Whether he is crossing Posthumus or delighting him, the play suggests, Jupiter is concerned about Posthumus, as in the romances in general the gods are concerned about human life and the old are concerned, even if wrong-headedly, about the young.

It is characteristic that for vengeance Belarius turns not to murder or theft of property but to kidnapping, and that he cares about the boys so much that we can understand his calling it "nursing" (5.5.322). He raises them in a pastoral world where activities are not rigidly divided according to sex: though hunting is more valued, all three males cook as well. Belarius sees his boys as sharing in both the gentleness and roughness of the goddess Nature. They extend their care to Imogen; when she seems dead, Arviragus bears her in his arms in a tableau that, as Meredith Skura has discussed, recalls Lear's entry with the dead Cordelia as well as the pietà and more conventional images of mother and living child.[4] This masculine community does not in principle exclude women: the memory of Belarius's wife is honored, and Imogen does not really need her disguise to be accepted. Guiderius says to her, "Were you a woman, youth, / I should woo hard but be your groom in honesty" (3.6.68–69).

However, women do seem to be consciously excluded from the similar relationships between males associated with nature and with childhood in *The Winter's Tale*—the friendships between Polixenes and Leontes at the beginning, projected into an idyllic past and re-created in the father-son relationships of the present. As Patricia Southard Gourlay has noted, Polixenes contrasts the innocence of youth with the temptations of later life by saying to Hermione, "Your precious self had not then crossed the eyes / Of my young playfellow" (1.2.78–79).[5] And Leontes, fascinated by the absoluteness of Mamillius's resemblance to him, refuses to see such resemblance in Perdita.[6]

But in The Winter's Tale as in Cymbeline, some of the male characters show a nurturing concern for children who are not biologically theirs, and exclusion because of sex seems to dissolve along with exclusion because of blood. In Bohemia the Old Shepherd takes Perdita up for pity, and in the sheep-shearing scene he presides over another natural idyll, more accepting of both women and sexuality.[7] By the fifth act Leontes too has learned more generosity: he can extend his concern to Florizel and his bride while jokingly acknowledging and relinquishing his wish to beg her for himself. The interventions of Paulina, Autolycus, and Camillo—the latter two are explicit about their wish to help themselves at the same time as helping the young—combine to bring about the reunions of the happy ending.

Men in the romances are not only more interested in young children than are the tragic heroes, but they are also more apt to apply to themselves imagery of women's close biological relationship with children. When Camillo describes his wish to see his king and country, a wish he acts to fulfill, he calls it "a woman's longing" (4.4.656)—a phrase usually suggesting that the woman is pregnant. While men in the tragedies compare themselves to women most when they feel afraid or tearful, men in the romances more often compare themselves to women with reference to pregnancy or childbirth. When Cymbeline recognizes his children, he expresses his joy by saying,

> O, what am I?
> A mother to the birth of three? Ne'er mother
> Rejoiced deliverance more.   (5.5.368–70)

Why should a father compare himself to a mother upon finding his lost children? The point is in the emphasis on birth—an event that involves the mother immediately in action and suffering, the father only vicariously. The unraveling of the plot, he is suggesting, has been as laborious and as joyful as childbirth.

Before he knows her identity, Pericles responds to the reunion with his daughter with similar imagery, although the meaning initially sounds opposed to Cymbeline's: "I am great with woe, and shall deliver weeping" (5.1.107). His sorrow comes from the same source that he will soon discover should be a source of joy—the resemblance of Marina to his wife. As curiosity about her continues to revive him from his lethargy, he says,

> Tell thy story.
> If thine considered prove the thousand part
> Of my endurance, thou art a man, and I
> Have suffered like a girl.   (5.1.35–38)

Pericles' use of cross-gender imagery, while closer than that of other romance figures to that of the tragic heroes, is nevertheless different. Pericles begins by insisting that he has suffered more; but is "I have suffered like a girl" self-deprecating, or a simple acknowledgment of the fact that he has suffered like this girl? Either way, his language suggests that it is in terms of endurance that he defines manhood—and endurance is an accomplishment that has always been open to women as well.

The emphasis on endurance, characteristic of the romances, is one of the generic features that produce these transformed images of manhood. The romance heroes are generally more resigned to being passive for much of the play, and often achieve their purposes not through their own unilateral action (which tends to be wrong-headed when it occurs) but by the coalescence of the acts and interventions of many people.[8] Posthumus, although banished, makes no attempt to change the king's attitude or elope with Imogen—he expects to

          abide the change of time,
    Quake in the present winter's state, and wish
    That warmer days would come.   (2.4.4–6)

Leontes' willingness to accept sixteen years of penance, and more if need be, shows a similar willingness to let an organic process work itself out; Pericles shows a less hopeful passivity when he calls himself

    A man, whom both the waters and the wind
    In that vast tennis court have made the ball
    For them to play upon.   (2.1.58–60)

Prospero's control of the elements makes him something of an exception here, but even his power depends on cooperation and patience. He tells Miranda

    By accident most strange, bountiful Fortune
    (Now, my dear lady) hath mine enemies
    Brought to this shore; and by my prescience
    I find my zenith doth depend upon
    A most auspicious star, whose influence
    If now I court not, but omit, my fortunes
    Will ever after droop.   (1.2.178–84)

He too works through delegating power—to Ariel and his other spirits. He knows or learns his limits; he cannot reform his brother, or keep his daughter to himself, and he ends the play with the epilogue that speaks of weakness and dependence:

    Now my charms are all o'erthrown
    And what strength I have's mine own
    Which is most faint.   (Epilogue, 1–3)

While in the tragedies the possibility of human action and the distinction between activity and passivity are important issues, in the romances the perspective is different. In these plays, the characters' relationship to their parents and children (or to the other young they nurture) seems more important than their degree of activity. Indeed, the context of such relationships makes clearer the limitations on active control in every human life. Thus, the epiphany of the family in *Cymbeline* leads to the image of the newborn Posthumus as "crying 'mongst his foes, / A thing of pity" (5.4.46–47). We can, to some extent, choose the identities of our spouses and friends, but not those of our parents and children; the beginning of every relationship between parents and children involves utmost vulnerability and dependence on the part of the children, uncertainty on all sides, and usually, especially in Shakespeare's time, the physical risks of childbirth. A conscious choice to have children, even specific choices of children in adoption, gives no control over what they will turn out to be like, and whatever control parents may establish over their children's behavior, they must be prepared to give up.

As C. L. Barber has suggested, it is largely because their sense of the importance of children is so strong that the men in the romances are more interested in the female experiences of pregnancy and childbirth than are the men in Shakespeare's earlier plays.[9] These experiences give concrete physical immediacy to the generative concern of men in the romances. Furthermore, pregnancy epitomizes the possible productiveness of the waiting in ignorance that these men often experience; childbirth is a metaphor for the crucial moment at which they must respond in a way that transcends the opposition between activity and passivity.

The concern for the young in the romances is not simply altruistic: the older generation, for all its uncertainty, benefits from the relation as well as the younger. Polixenes says of Florizel,

> He makes a July's day short as December,
> And with his varying childness cures in me
> Thoughts that would thick my blood.   (1.2.168–70)

Similarly, Prospero says to Miranda, recalling his escape with her,

> Thou didst smile,
> Infusèd with a fortitude from heaven,
> When I have decked the sea with drops full salt,
> Under my burden groaned; which raised in me
> An undergoing stomach, to bear up
> Against what should ensue.   (1.2.153–58)

And Pericles acknowledges Marina with the riddling words, "Thou that beget'st him that did thee beget" (5.1.197). Because she is still alive, she has granted him "another life" (5.1.209). Regeneration in this scene occurs not only because Marina reminds Pericles of Thaisa, her mother, but also because she reminds him of the possibility of resilience after suffering; she restores his fatherhood to him and his connection with ongoing life.

For the full implication of this line, we should note that "beget" is customarily applied to the father's role in generation, or to that of both parents together, not to the mother's. In the background is the assumption of then-current physiology that the father's seed originally provided life and the mother then nourished it in her womb. Thus Pericles is granting Marina the procreative powers that she has restored to him by her return. Here, as when Pericles applies imagery of pregnancy and childbirth to himself earlier in the scene, the interchange of sexes suggests that the distinction between male and female experience has become less important than a sense of general human vulnerability and of the interdependence between generations. This imagery culminates the pattern in which the play shows the parallel sufferings experienced by Pericles and Marina.[10] As Marina says,

> She speaks,
> My lord, that, may be, hath endured a grief
> Might equal yours, if both were justly weighed.
>   (5.1.87–89)

While Shakespeare focuses more on male development in both the tragedies and the romances, there are contrasts in the characterization of women as well. If more of the men use imagery of pregnancy and childbirth, more women bear children in the romances than in the trage-dies.[11] Furthermore, while there are many intense mother-son relationships earlier in Shakespeare, the mother-daugh-ter bond, at least in *Romeo and Juliet* and *Merry Wives of Windsor*, seems rather cool. By contrast, though both Thaisa and Hermione are separated from their daughters for most of the play, their scenes together have an emotional intensity far surpassing those between mothers and daughters in the earlier plays. Thus, in some ways, women as well as men are characterized in more parental terms in the romances. Women who are not literal mothers also use imagery of maternity. Imogen, waiting to see her husband, compares her experience to pregnancy: "Never longed my mother so / To see me first as I have now" (3.4.2–3). Furthermore, in earlier plays, mothers of young children are likely to ap-pear powerless victims: Lady Macduff and her son, for ex-ample, are helpless against Macbeth's soldiers. In *The Win-ter's Tale*, by contrast, Hermione says that it is her love for her daughter that has kept her alive:

> I,
> Knowing by Paulina that the oracle
> Gave hope thou wast in being, have preserved
> Myself to see the issue. (5.3.125–28)

The consistent strength of Paulina herself is likewise un-precedented in the earlier plays. In Paulina's confrontation with Leontes, the issue of female subordination is raised and resolved in a way that, while unorthodox, leaves no doubt of Paulina's autonomy:

> Leontes   What, canst not rule her?
> Paulina From all dishonesty he can. In this,
>   Unless he take the course that you have done,
>   Commit me for committing honor, trust it,
>   He shall not rule me. (2.3.46–50)

Throughout the play she takes on Leontes as an equal, undaunted by his tyranny. When she speaks of herself as "a

foolish woman" (3.2.225), it is plainly only a rhetorical gesture. Unlike Beatrice, who feels powerless to defend her
falsely accused friend, or Emilia, who dies in vindicating
hers, Paulina can survive while restoring Hermione to
Leontes' esteem and finally to his presence. While Leontes'
concluding arrangement of her marriage to Camillo may
seem an odd attempt to place her back in a patriarchal
framework, we should notice that, unlike most of the powerful women of the comedies, she has already demon-
strated unambiguously how little marriage subordinates
her.

Even the younger women of the romances, whose relationships with their lovers spring up with fewer defenses
than in the comedies, know how to maintain their own
identity and are quite willing to disagree with their lovers
or pompous elderly visitors in public. When wronged by
their husbands, Imogen and Hermione reproach them at
much greater length than do Hero and Desdemona in
similar situations. These women are never inarticulate at
injustice. Many of them go beyond the polarity between
reproach and forgiveness visible in the contrast between
Emilia's and Desdemona's attitudes toward Othello at the
end. Imogen embraces her husband saying, "Why did you
throw your wedded lady from you?" (5.5.261), and Miranda
declares to Ferdinand, "Sweet lord, you play me false. . . .
Yes, for a score of kingdoms you should wrangle, / And I
would call it fair play" (5.1.172, 174–75). In Paulina and
Hermione, especially, Shakespeare presents much more
integrated images of women than infantile visions of Good
Mother and Bad Mother, toward which the tragic women,
however individualized, still tend. It is in keeping with this
integration that we can see Hermione asking her ladies to
baby-sit for a few minutes, because "He so troubles me. /
'Tis past enduring" (2.1.1–2), with the security that soon
she will say, "Come, sir, now / I am for you again" (2.1.21–
22).

Nevertheless, except with Imogen, the romances give
little attention to wives' development after marital disruption, compared to the focus on husbands', or even on

daughters'. Thaisa's temple and Hermione's cell are the plays' concern chiefly as symbols of withdrawal and dramatic expedients that permit the husband to believe his wife dead and find her as if returned to life. In the comedies we could see women's activity developing mutuality; here, since the couples appear together so infrequently after disturbance in their marriage—even Imogen and Posthumus do not meet again until the end—what makes convincing the restored mutuality of the reunion is often partly the man's evidence of feeling in other situations, even in other relationships.

But in the background of the romances is the belief that, with the aid of forgiveness, marriage as well as family can ultimately be indissoluble. The romances are less about mutuality between young lovers, or relationships being developed, than about mutuality between repentance and forgiveness, however reproachful—they concern relationships as given, lost, and then refound. These plays emphasize relationships with the long and intimate history that makes them part of what constitutes the individual's identity. This stress on acceptance, forgiveness, and family ties is further reinforced by the images of physicality in the recognition scenes.

In all the romances, recognition scenes involve imagery of natural, biological ties, of the physicality, the flesh and blood, of the characters. This imagery, partly a result of the characters' need to assure themselves that others are really alive, calls attention to the characters' bodies and their intimate link with powers of generativity. By contrast, in the comedies, Shakespeare gives no implicit stage directions for embraces of the reunited characters: Viola tells Sebastian, "Do not embrace me," and their token of recognition is a mole on their father's brow. Claudio says only "Another Hero," and the language of the reunited Antipholus family in The Comedy of Errors is similarly rather abstract. Pericles asks Marina, "But are you flesh and blood?" (5.1.154). His reunion with Thaisa, though much briefer, is longer than most reunions between husband and wife, or between lovers or betrothed couples, in the earlier comedies. Even the reunion between Egeon and Emilia (also a nun), who have been separated for a similarly long time, involves joy that is more cautious and restrained. Pericles' language puts much more emphasis on physical contact with his wife; he uses two images that both picture an embrace as a loss of the identity of one in the other:

> You shall do well
> That on the touching of her lips I may
> Melt and no more be seen. O, come, be buried
> A second time within these arms!   (5.3.41–44)

In the first sentence he disappears; in the second Thaisa disappears in him. These images of merging assimilate the physical connection of husband and wife to the physical connection of parenthood celebrated here and elsewhere in the play. The words of the nurse Lychorida, "this piece / Of your dead queen" (3.1.17–18), present childbirth as an event in which one being becomes two; here two people appear to become one. When Marina greets her mother, she uses similar language, "My heart / Leaps to be gone into my mother's bosom" (5.3.44–45), and Pericles introduces her as "Flesh of thy flesh, Thaisa" (5.3.46).

Similarly, in the long recognition scene of *Cymbeline*, Belarius introduces Guiderius and Arviragus to their father thus, "They are the issue of your loins, my liege, / And blood of your begetting" (5.5.330–31). Furthermore, to intertwine the recognition even more with literal flesh, Cymbeline recalls that "Guiderius had / upon his neck a mole, a sanguine star" (5.5.363–64), and Belarius shows him "that natural stamp" (5.5.366). Even Prospero's very different recognition of his brother uses the same imagery that elsewhere suggests amazement and delight to express a paradoxical disgusted acceptance. From one standpoint, this reproachful forgiveness seems self-righteous; from another, it shows that he accepts his own anger as well as his brother:

> Flesh and blood,
> You, brother mine, that entertained ambition,

Expelled remorse and nature . . .
          . . . I do forgive thee,
Unnatural though thou art.   (5.1.74–76, 78–79)

Alonso uses the same phrase more conventionally to Prospero: "Thy pulse / Beats, as of flesh and blood" (5.1.113–14).

In the final scene of The Winter's Tale, Leontes' long contemplation of Hermione's statue resembles the prolonged confrontation of Pericles and Marina. The moment of stasis leading up to the final achieved reunion stretches out as inhibitions are dramatized. And, like Pericles, both Hermione and Leontes must break out of passive postures. The pretense that Hermione is a statue generates verbal imagery of warm flesh and cold stone that identifies the contrast between emotion and control with that between life and death. Here the warmth of life blends with the warmth of responsiveness and generosity to deepen the vitalizing biological ties of fertility and sexuality.

The focus on the "statue" of Hermione allows for much emphasis on physicality, which reverses the disgust that colored Leontes' allusions to parts of the body in earlier scenes. Not only does he note the wrinkles on the statue, but the veins, the eye, and the breath. While earlier he noted his disgust at Hermione by calling Polixenes "he that wears her like her medal" (1.2.306), now Polixenes and Camillo observe, "She embraces him. . . . She hangs about his neck" (5.3.111–12).

It is only in the romances that Shakespeare gives these direct textual indications of embraces of the reunited characters, though of course directors often add them in other plays. The physicality of reunions in the romances coheres with the greater emphasis on generativity in these plays: perhaps the body is valued more because its generative powers are more important; perhaps greater acceptance of the body leads to a greater appreciation of its ability to generate new life.[12] In Othello, the hero suspects Desdemona when he finds her hand "Hot, hot and moist"

(3.4.39), and he trusts her again when she is "Cold, cold, . . . / Even like thy chastity" (5.2.276–77). For Leontes, by contrast, the miracle of Hermione at the end is that, as he exclaims, "Oh, she's warm!" (5.3.109).

As some recent critics have noted, the emphasis on physicality and procreation in the romances can be taken as reinforcing patriarchy. They see exclusion of women when male characters incorporate imagery of pregnancy and childbearing, and confinement of women when it is in procreative roles that women are honored.[13] Once again, these plays symbolically reconcile patriarchy and mutuality. Pointing toward mutuality is the vindication that *Cymbeline* and *The Winter's Tale* give to their female characters.

Male characters' images of childbearing often suggest the transformation and reversal of the suspicion of women that the romance heroes express earlier. In both *Cymbeline* and *The Winter's Tale*, this suspicion is explicitly linked with women's childbearing powers. Posthumus begins his antifeminist tirade with what Janet Adelman has called a fantasy of male parthenogenesis: "Is there no way for men to be, but women / must be half-workers?" (2.5.1–2). In this speech he clearly links Imogen with his mother:

> Some coiner with his tools
> Made me a counterfeit; yet my mother seemed
> The Dian of that time. So doth my wife
> The nonpareil of this.   (2.5.5–8)

Such an identification coheres with much else that the play shows of their relationship. Posthumus seems insecure about his tie to Imogen: in giving her a bracelet as she gives him a diamond, he says,

> As I my poor self did exchange for you
> To your so infinite loss, so in our trifles
> I still win of you.   (1.1.120–22)

This sounds like more than the conventional modesty of a comic hero; similarly, his idealization of Imogen seems extreme. He calls her "My queen, my mistress" (1.1.92) and makes the note of distance rather than intimacy explicit when he later calls himself her "adorer, not her friend" (1.4.62). If he is rejecting the sexual connotation of "friend," as the Arden editor says, his sense of taboo becomes even clearer: Juliet has no qualms about calling Romeo "husband-friend" (3.5.43).[14]

The idealization and sense of taboo and discomfort fit psychologically to the biography the play gives Posthumus: in marrying a woman who grew up in the same household, he chooses someone who stands to him as something like a sister and, because of his mother's death in childbirth, even more like a mother.[15] The absence of direct childhood recollections avoids calling our attention to this explicitly, but some sense of strangeness remains, heightened by the fact that we see them together only in this early scene of parting. Posthumus is at the same time uncomfortably close to and uncomfortably distant from his wife. Unlike Othello, he has a long history with her and her family; but he is genetically an outsider in that family, and, as an orphan who never knew his parents, a kind of outsider to the biological family as an institution. But after he repents of killing her, he takes on a new sense of identity with his family; his doubts about his legitimacy disappear after he sees Imogen's hypothetical adultery as "wrying but a little" (5.1.5). His dream of his family includes not only a vision of his father's and mother's concern but also a more abstract emphasis on the nurturing power of nature and heredity:

Great Nature like his ancestry
  moulded the stuff so fair
That he deserved the praise o'th'world,
  as great Sicilius' heir.   (5.4.48–51)

This epiphany helps prepare for the imagery of natural growth and fertility that Posthumus uses when he finally speaks to Imogen in recognition: "Hang there like fruit, my soul, / Till the tree die" (5.5.263–64). If he is the tree and she is the fruit, then he is metaphorically making her his offspring, repairing the imbalance of identifying her too much with his mother, as well as undoing his earlier hostile attitude toward "the woman's part" in himself (2.5.1–2, 19–24).[16]

In *The Winter's Tale*, the connection between male jealousy and female childbearing is clearer. Leontes' sudden suspicions of Hermione strike him during a scene that emphasizes her pregnancy. His speeches of jealousy alternate with lines about his physical similarity to his son: "What, hast smutched thy nose? / They say it is a copy out of mine" (1.2.121–22):

> methoughts I did recoil
> Twenty-three years, and saw myself unbreeched.
>
> .   .   .   .
>
> How like, methought, I then was to this kernel,
> This squash, this gentleman.   (1.2.154–55, 159–60)

He loves his son, but there is the ghost of a doubt about ancestry even with him—he refers to Mamillius as one "Who I do think is mine and love as mine." These lines suggest a ready-made motive for him to envy Hermione, who must be sure her children are hers.

If childbearing ability is seen as something to be envied in these plays, then the emphasis on this characteristic of women is not necessarily a sign of a patriarchal worldview. Peter Erickson points out that Leontes keeps governmental power when Hermione returns, but what can Leontes do with this power that would matter to him as much as his family? We hear nothing about any military or governmental campaigns he has waged during his sixteen years of penance. The only other concern as important to him as family is his friendship with Polixenes, and his suspicion of Hermione implies the suspicion that this too can be as much in his wife's sphere as in his own. That he can punish her for this groundless suspicion is a significant limitation on *her* power, to be sure, but for Leontes it is a compensatory gesture, undertaken because he thinks he has lost what he really wants. Similarly, in Cymbeline all the military achievement is undercut by the final submission to Rome, and the fate of the government pales by comparison with the reconciliations in marriage and family. And it is only reunion with Marina that can pull Pericles out of his lethargy.

The romances were written and observed against the background of a public life much more involved than that presented within them. Even more than most plays, they are presented as consciously fictitious creations, "like an old tale" (The Winter's Tale, 5.2.28). Yet this should not deprive their choice of subject matter of importance—it is this, we are being told when we watch or read them, that it is really important to present in a play.

In The Tempest, perhaps most self-conscious of all, it is more difficult to argue that the most important events of the play occur in the sphere of the family, including women, rather than in the sphere of governmental or military power, excluding women. Miranda is clearly important to Prospero, to be sure—but so are the dukedom and his ability to confront his brother by means of his power over the spirits of the island. Yet this is not ordinary governmental or military power—it is magic; as such it is more related to Rosalind's ability to produce Hymen in her masque, or Helena's ability to save the king in All's Well That Ends Well, than to Henry V's power over England, or to Hamlet's power to take revenge. But if Prospero's power is in part magic, it is in part also something else more familiar. For all their other meanings, Ariel and Caliban are also children that Prospero is raising. This enchanted island that often seems the projection of Prospero's own mind has in it elements of both family and state. And it is, of course, back to the family that we trace the conflict between Prospero and Antonio, as well as through the family that we see the resolution of the conflict between Prospero and Alonso. Yet in spite of all the importance of the family and family analogues in The Tempest, there is no mother, and the

incorporation of child-nurturing by Prospero is an exclusion of mature women as much as an image of male
wholeness. Unlike, say, Belarius's dead wife, Prospero's
is never mourned and barely mentioned ("Thy mother was a
piece of virtue, and / She said thou wast my daughter"—
1.2.56–57). But few spectators notice this, so much is our
attention drawn to Prospero's struggle with his feelings
about Miranda, Antonio—he whom Prospero tells Miranda, "next thyself / Of all the world I loved" (1.2.68–
69)—and even Ariel. Finally, this is a play of relinquishment, in which we focus more on the separation that marriage will bring than on the union. This is not so in the
other romances, which involve the restoration of husband-
wife as well as parent-child relationships

Yet while *The Tempest* differs from the other romances in
this respect, it is like them in the way the emphasis on
generativity moves away from the private/public conflict;
all move toward dissolving this conflict by making the
whole society a family. In these plays the contrast between
different kinds of courtships—usual to Shakespeare's
comic pattern—is not as important as the juxtaposition of
marriage and courtship with other family relationships.
The images of a private world of love are more threatening—Antiochus's incestuous bond with his daughter and,
perhaps, the maternal attachment that, in Dionyza and
Cymbeline's Queen, becomes murderous to their own
child's rival.[17] Prospero transcends his temptation to such a
bond with Miranda. Perhaps it is the final irony of the fam-
ily-centered transformation of Shakespeare's vision that the
marriage of Miranda and Ferdinand, however loving, has as
one of its main functions the uniting of two families and
that, unlike the similar marriage between Perdita and Florizel, it is so planned by Prospero; it is as if Capulet had
secretly arranged Juliet's encounter with Romeo with a
view to civic reconciliation.

At the heart of the romances is a man's need for his
family. The man recognizes his interdependence with his
family; at the same time, he is the father (except for

Posthumus) and therefore in a position of household power. Fatherly love of a young daughter, inevitably patriarchal (except perhaps after an agonizing wrench like Lear's), is juxtaposed with a relationship suggestive of mutuality in the younger generation. While there may be comparatively more characterization of women as mothers in the romances than in the other genres, their presence still pales (except perhaps in The Winter's Tale) by contrast to the focus on fathers. It is the comparative absence of the mother, combined with her evil incarnation in the Queen and Dionyza, that ensures the plays' assimilability within patriarchy. Ironically, the use of pregnancy and childbirth imagery makes this absence more noticeable.

Yet the emphasis on mutuality continues in these plays and receives reinforcement from their transformation of the conflict between emotion and control. In these plays, rejection of attachment, such as Leontes and Posthumus attempt, is shown to be madness and a deliberate hardening of heart; Pericles' lack of interest in life after his unwitting abandonment of Thaisa and Marina is pathology, not virtuous detachment. Even though Leontes admits that believing Hermione is alive seems like madness, he seems saner in that belief than in his earlier doubt of her. Analogously, Prospero claims both feelings and his "nobler reason" (5.1.26) as motives to show mercy to Alonso's party. Thus Prospero's version of self-control is antithetical to the ideal identified by Stone, since it includes forgiveness based on a sense of common humanity and leads to restraining anger (though not eradicating it).

Once the image of manhood shifts so that family ties become more important than military identity, conflicts take on a different form. Cymbeline is torn between his love for his wife and his love for his daughter; Prospero struggles between two different forms of love for his daughter—possessiveness and generous desire for her welfare. Lear, who gave up Cordelia in anger, had to learn the importance of their continuing bond; Prospero, who knows the importance of his bond with Miranda, has to give her up anyway. The tragic heroes at their best learn the value of their attachments; Prospero acknowledges this value and detaches himself, reaching an emotional control quite different from the denial that apparently constituted an Elizabethan cultural ideal. Yet so dialectical is the vision of The Tempest that even Prospero's acting out of his possessiveness has the function of deepening Miranda's relationship with Ferdinand—"lest too light winning make the prize light" (1.2.452–53). Prospero's turning to the audience for reciprocal forgiveness is the continuation of the turn outward from a private relationship to ongoing life that we see in all the romances.

Chapter Ten

Shakespeare's Imagery of Gender
and Gender Crossing

In an earlier chapter I connected the fact that Shakespeare's female characters were played by males on the Elizabethan stage with affinities between actors and women; now it is time to make explicit the more general analogy that his plays suggest between gender and theatrical role. The kings in Shakespeare were played by commoners; that fact, like the use of boy actors, gave rise both to moralists' complaints about the disorder of the stage and to Shakespeare's dramatization of the theatrical nature of social roles—in this case, of kingship. Just as Shakespeare found his imagination struck by the stage's transformation of subject to king and back again, he seems to have been fascinated by the image of gender as role. In five plays (*Two Gentlemen of Verona*, *The Merchant of Venice*, *As You Like It*, *Twelfth Night*, and *Cymbeline*), major female characters pretend to be male; in five other plays, mostly minor male characters briefly pretend to be female (the page in *The Taming of the Shrew*, Francis Flute in *Midsummer Night's Dream*, Falstaff and the boys who pretend to be Anne Page in *The Merry Wives of Windsor*, the boy actor of the Player Queen in *Hamlet*, and Ariel in *The Tempest*). There is, in *Antony and Cleopatra*, one other lengthy reference to boy actors of female roles. The two most explicit discussions of this practice, conveniently, occur in one early play and one late one, both plays in which the female character's acting is also an explicit theme.

In the Induction to *The Taming of the Shrew*, the lord directs his page how to take the role of Christopher Sly's wife. The main problem he expects can be solved easily:

> if the boy have not a woman's gift
> To rain a shower of commanded tears,
> An onion will do well for such a shift.
> (Induction, 1.123–25)

The words of the second passage maintain that it is much more difficult for a boy to act a woman well; but they are spoken by a female character, and in that context suggest Shakespeare's confidence in the best boy actors in his troop and their capacity to gain the audience's belief. When Cleopatra anticipates her capture by Caesar she imagines this humiliation:

> I shall see
> Some squeaking Cleopatra boy my greatness
> I'th' posture of a whore.   (5.2.219–21)

Here is the suggestion of a specifically female greatness that—contrasted not only to "boy" but also to "whore"—not all women can achieve—and not all boy actors either. The power of these lines onstage—especially on the Elizabethan stage—includes their celebration of the transforming power of the imagination.[1] But they also include a celebration of the particular kind of being the actor and the audience's imagination have created—the female Cleopatra. If the play succeeded, at the same time as the Elizabethan audience imagined a boy who could not play Cleopatra, they saw one who could—partly because his creator made him admit onstage that it was more than a matter of smelling onions.

While I am not claiming that Shakespeare at the beginning of his career agreed with the lord in *The Taming of the Shrew*, I think that the juxtaposition of these passages suggests something—though not all—of the transition in Shakespeare's imagery of gender and gender crossing. But to see the full dimensions of this change we must look also at female characters who disguise themselves as men, at descriptions of characters' behavior as appropriate either to their own gender or to the other, and at the relative symmetry or asymmetry of characters' behavior according to gender within the various genres.[2] What I will suggest is that Shakespeare's use of gender and cross-gender imagery changes significantly from the comedies through the tragedies to the romances; my evidence will recapitulate and develop the associations of different gender relations with different genres that this book has explored. In both the comedies and the romances, the activities of the sexes are generally not as polarized as they are in the tragedies. The tragedies focus much more on ideals of manhood; the romances use cross-gender imagery more often to show men transcending a narrow masculinity, while the comedies use such imagery more often to show women transcending conventional limitations.

For the most part, what most of the lovers do in the comedies is talk about love, whichever gender they are. Unlike the tragedies, these plays are not set in military backgrounds that give the men a different goal. The women hold their own in conversation and are far from being chiefly spectators or assistants to the men. They don their masculine disguises with high spirits, making fun of men's appearances of courage at the same time. Rosalind declares

> in my heart
> Lie there what hidden woman's fear there will,
> We'll have a swashing and a martial outside,
> As many other mannish cowards have
> That do outface it with their semblances.   (1.3.114–18)

Portia similarly promises to

> speak of frays
> Like a fine bragging youth, and tell quaint lies,
> How honorable ladies sought my love. . . .

> . . . I have within my mind
> A thousand raw tricks of these bragging Jacks.
> (3.4.68–70, 76–77)

She implies that the men she imitates also lie and that if a masculine show of courage is a disguise for women, it may also be a disguise for men. Sir Toby makes a related point in advising poor Sir Andrew Aguecheek: "a terrible oath, with a swaggering accent sharply twanged off, gives manhood more approbation than ever proof itself would have earned him" (3.4.166–68).

Men do act violently in some of these comedies, to be sure. Orlando wrestles with Charles and saves his brother by fighting with a lioness. Sebastian fights as Viola—and Andrew—cannot. But these incidents of violence are not the men's main projects during the play, rather responses to tests that they meet. One of Orlando's gestures of violence—drawing his sword to get food—is censured by the gentle and generous exiles who welcome him to their table in the forest. In general, these characters wear their masculinity lightly. Most of them, for example, do not think it should prevent them from weeping. The Duke and Orlando include in their definition of the civilized life "drops that sacred pity hath engend'red" (2.7.123). Even Sebastian, who feels discomfort at being "so near the manners of my mother," weeps at thinking his sister dead, claiming to "drown her remembrance again with more" salt water (2.1.36, 28). For the most part, they are not apt to struggle hard for power. Sebastian submits readily to Olivia, and Orlando is ready to take instructions from Rosalind in her disguise as Ganymede. In the principal exceptions, *The Taming of the Shrew* and *Much Ado About Nothing*, the hot temper and ready wit of both man and woman means that in these plays, too, gender difference does not necessitate polarized behavior in the central couple throughout.

Nevertheless, an important scene in *Much Ado About Nothing* makes more of the relationship of violence to masculinity. "O that I were a man . . . ," says Beatrice, "or that I had any friend would be a man for my sake!" (4.1.312–13)—and she wants to be a man specifically to fight a duel with Claudio—or to "eat his heart in the marketplace" (4.1.302). In the same scene she complains about the degeneration of manhood, mocking cowardice and braggardism somewhat as Rosalind and Portia do, but in a very different tone. "But manhood is melted into cursies, valor into compliment, and men are only turned into tongue, and trim ones too. He is now as valiant as Hercules that only tells a lie and swears it" (4.1.313–16). When she refuses to accept Benedick as her lover until he promises to challenge Claudio to a duel, we approach the tragedies' concern with manhood. But Claudio repents and Benedick never has to fight. And the play offers some other definitions of manhood. Margaret observes that Benedick used to resist love and "now is he become a man" (3.4.78); Benedick describes his wit as "A most manly wit, Margaret: it will not hurt a woman" (5.2.14–15).

In *As You Like It*, an analogous scene in its dependence on conventions of gender difference in regard to violence is the one in which Oliver tells Rosalind of Orlando's fight with the lioness and then shows her his bloody napkin. Rosalind faints, and tries to cover up: "I pray you tell your brother how well I counterfeited" (4.3.167–68)—pretending to be Ganymede pretending to be Rosalind. Their dialogue sums up the parallel between female disguise as male and male disguise as brave:

> Oliver   Well then, take a good heart and counterfeit to be a man.
> Rosalind So I do; but, i'faith, I should have been a woman by right.   (4.3.172–75)

Has the crisis of Orlando's wound taken the characters to the bedrock of sexual differentiation—to gender as ultimate reality, as Sandra Gilbert identifies the view of the male modernist?[3] Or does the imagery that recalls the boy-actor convention remind us that the femininity presented on the Elizabethan stage is always counterfeit? As so often,

Shakespeare allows us to have it both ways. Rosalind and the other disguised heroines joke both about how well they pretend—"I must comfort the weaker vessel, as doublet and hose ought to show itself courageous to petticoat" (2.4.5–7)—and about their underlying femaleness—"Dost thou think, though I am caparisoned like a man, I have a doublet and hose in my disposition?" (3.2.185–87). What difference does it make that these lines were spoken by Elizabethan boy actors? The first becomes merely a joke about the importance of underlying maleness only to an audience that resists the theatrical illusion and sees actors rather than characters.[4] If we see the actor-as-character-as-actor—as Rosalind succeeding or failing to play Ganymede—remembering the boy-actor convention adds another dimension of awareness of gender as construction to both jokes. If boys can play women and characters that we think of as women can play boys, this reminds us doubly that gender can be seen as role rather than as biological given.

In the comedies, references to gender transcendence are not only frequent but also generally favorable. Orsino believes Viola/Cesario will be an effective wooer because

> Diana's lip
> Is not more smooth and rubious; thy small pipe
> Is as the maiden's organ, shrill and sound,
> And all is semblative a woman's part.   (1.4.30–33)

Phebe says of Rosalind/Ganymede:

> There was a pretty redness in his lip,
> A little riper and more lusty red
> Than that mixed in his cheek; 'twas just the difference
> Betwixt the constant red and mingled damask.
>
> (3.5.119–22)

Orlando and Olivia have less detailed speeches of admiration. The only character who finds androgynous figures distasteful is Malvolio, who describes Viola/Cesario thus: "He is very well-favored and he speaks very shrewishly.

One would think his mother's milk were scarce out of him" (1.5.153–55). Malvolio seems as disgusted as he is with all disorder.

When we move from the comedies to the tragedies, the role of gender changes. Even in Romeo and Juliet, contemporary to the comedies, the young couple who in their scenes together seem partners in love are dealing with a society more rigid about gender.[5] The expected relation of masculinity to violence, femininity to weakness, is crucial to the outcome of the play. Romeo calls his reluctance to fight with Tybalt "effeminate" (3.1.112) and to avenge Mercutio engages in a fight to the death that brings about his banishment. The friar repeatedly uses "womanish" as a synonym for "weak" when speaking to both Juliet (4.1.119) and Romeo (3.3.110), and he encourages Juliet to pretend obedience and death through his potion rather than helping her escape. He chides Romeo for his fury and grief at banishment with an image of androgyne as monster: "Unseemly woman in a seeming man! / And ill-beseeming beast in seeming both!" (3.3.112–13)

Most other male tragic heroes are even more concerned about masculinity. In Hamlet, manhood suggests standards of control and action: Claudius tells Hamlet his grief is unmanly, and Hamlet in his powerlessness to do more than speak compares himself to a whore or a drab. He goes to the duel that will kill him disregarding what he calls "such a kind of gain-giving as would perhaps trouble a woman" (5.2.204–5). The women in the play do not have enough strength to counter his conviction that "Frailty, thy name is woman" (1.2.146). In the military world of Troilus and Cressida, also, women are constantly associated with weakness. Troilus at the beginning calls himself unfit for war because he is "weaker than a woman's tear" (1.1.9). Cressida claims that she would like to transcend conventional female behavior, and in talking about her long attraction to Troilus she says, "I wished myself a man, / Or that we women had men's privilege / Of speaking first" (3.2.120–22). After they are separated, she would like to remain faithful to Troilus, but ultimately she behaves with the weakness expected of her.[6] And this reinforces Troilus's determination to seek manhood in violence: "Let's leave the hermit pity with our mother" (5.3.45). Here, as in *Romeo and Juliet* and *Hamlet*, imagery of androgyny is used as an insult rather than with the appreciation of the comedies. As Patroclus says to Achilles:

> A woman impudent and mannish grown
> Is not more loathed than an effeminate man
> In time of action.   (3.3.216–18)

Even in *Lear*, where the hero is not a soldier or bound to revenge, self-definition as masculine is important. "Let not women's weapons, water drops, / Stain my man's cheeks" (2.4.272–73), Lear says, "No, I'll not weep" (278). Yet his experience eventually leads him beyond Troilus's image of manhood, and he learns that he must weep, for "We came crying hither" (4.6.175).

This discovery that one's conception of masculinity is too narrow is a recurrent feature of Shakespearean tragedy, but the heroes usually make it only after their desire to be men has led them to murder. Othello kills Desdemona partly to avoid the pain of doubting her, which leads him to lose control in a way that Iago keeps reminding him is not manly. Macbeth is persuaded to kill Duncan because he believes Lady Macbeth's words: "When you durst do it, then you were a man" (1.7.49). Macbeth feels fear is not manly, yet, having killed Duncan and Banquo, he cannot help fearing Banquo's ghost, and becomes, according to Lady Macbeth, "Quite unmann'd in folly" (3.4.74). To live out his ideal of manhood, he eventually realizes, he has deprived himself of "honor, love, obedience" and friends (5.3.25).

In both of these plays, the hero's violence in defense of his masculinity also contributes to the destruction of his marriage. Different as they are, both Desdemona and Lady Macbeth attempt some kind of partnership with their husbands, some degree of joining in their enterprises, but the enterprises are violent, and in both plays only men can directly commit acts of violence. Othello uses cross-sex imagery of Desdemona—"My fair warrior" (2.1.180)—and she imagines herself as Cassio's "solicitor" (3.3.27) making Othello's bed "a school, his board a shrift" (3.3.24). These images of Desdemona as lawyer, teacher, priest have some of the charm of the cross-sex imagery of the comedies. But Othello cannot see her as partner here—the army is a man's world, not a woman's—and her insistence contributes to provoking him to jealousy.

Macbeth's "dearest partner of greatness" (1.5.10–11) uses more ominous cross-sex imagery of herself. What she wants to gain by transcending her gender is "cruelty" (1.5.41); otherwise the process is subtraction—"Unsex me here" (1.5.39). But her relation to violence is still vicarious; Macbeth praises her courage in terms of her procreative powers:

> Bring forth men-children only;
> For thy undaunted mettle should compose
> Nothing but males.   (1.7.72–74)

Both of them are trying not to be woman-like, but it is Macbeth who strikes the blow. And his guilt separates them and destroys the relationship that began in partnership.

Antony and Cleopatra contains both of these motifs—a soldier who attempts to maintain his manhood and a woman who attempts partnership with him. But Antony, while he criticizes himself for acting under the influence of "this enchanting queen" (1.2.124), is much less insistent than the other heroes on a narrow conception of masculinity, and Cleopatra has more scope as well. In the eyes of Rome this leads to a confusion of gender as unattractive as in *Troilus:* Antony

> is not more manlike
> Than Cleopatra, nor the queen of Ptolemy
> More womanly than he.   (1.4.5–7)

Cleopatra, however, finds delight in her memory of playful transvestism:

> I drunk him to his bed;
> Then put my tires and mantles on him, whilst
> I wore his sword Philippan.   (2.5.21–23)

When he goes off to fight without her, she arms him and welcomes him in victory, and he calls her "squire" (4.4.14). But as a head of state, she can go further than the other women in accompanying her man in battle:

> A charge we bear i'th'war,
> And as the president of my kingdom will
> Appear there for a man.   (3.7.16–18)

Twice Antony loses the battles in which she shares: she flees in the middle of the first, fulfilling the expectation of women's weakness. After the second, her use of pretense—the false message that she is dead—to bring about reconciliation follows the related stereotype of female deviousness.

But at the end, it is Antony who, having decided on suicide, is less skillful at it than his servant Eros. It is Cleopatra who, unlike the other heroines, stages her death scene with care and control, saying, "My resolution's placed, and I have nothing / Of woman in me" (5.2.238–39). But as death approaches, her words acknowledge her femaleness. By her death she will claim true partnership with Antony: "Husband, I come: / Now to that name my courage prove my title!" (5.2.286–87). She dies combining a call to Antony with words imagining a baby at her breast, and thus she affirms her gender while finally transcending the image of feminine weakness.

If several of the romantic comedies show women pretending playfully to be men for a time and many of the tragedies show men more seriously attempting to play the masculine role as they see it, in the romances playing the man is less important or means something different. As we have seen in the previous chapter, romance heroes can take on occupations usually held by women and compare themselves to women without the anguish such imagery usually gives the tragic heroes.

In general, the cross-gender imagery in the romances emphasizes the primacy of generativity over aggression. Imogen's assumption of masculine disguise, for example, does not lead her to mockery of male assertiveness as it does the earlier disguised women; rather, she observes after a while, "I see a man's life is a tedious one" (3.6.1). Thus it is not so different from the female experience of pregnancy to which she has earlier compared her waiting: "Ne'er longed my mother so / To see me first as I have now" (3.4.2–3). When Leontes uses cross-gender imagery against Paulina, calling her "A mankind witch" (2.3.67), she has occasioned it not by her participation in war or violence but by her assertions in defense of a baby's parentage.

Among the young lovers in the romances, as in the comedies, the genders are not polarized in their activities. But as in the tragedies, partnership in one sphere—love—is balanced against another sphere where one sex has primacy over the other. In the tragedies that other sphere is violence, where men have primacy; in the romances it is the sphere of procreation, where in imagery women have primacy, and, as we have seen, a father can express his joy at finding his children by comparing himself to a mother (Cymbeline, 5.5.368–70). But while in the tragedies the attempts of both sexes to live by ideals of violence is disastrous, in the romances the assimilation by men of the values of generativity leads to the final harmony.

In the tragedies, and to some extent even in the comedies, "woman" seems to be associated with qualities—emotions, fears—one has against one's will, and "man" with a preferable mode of existence. Men are exhorted to be men, and women, playfully or seriously, often attempt to imitate male behavior. The reverse is much less often true. One of the few occasions where a character is told to be a woman still shows the relative rank given to the sexes.

Angelo, attempting to seduce Isabella, says, "Be that you are, / That is, a woman; if you be more, you're none" (2.4.134–35). Both women and men often say they have too much of woman-like qualities in them; only Kent admits that he "Having more man than wit about me, drew" (2.4.41), and it is more a boast than a confession. The imagery of the romances is the most significant exception to the rule that Shakespeare's male characters identify themselves with women only in embarrassment, farce, or plays within the play.[7]

Some of the associations I have been developing may make the Elizabethan convention of boy actors understandable on another level. If manhood is a condition that males can achieve, then the sexes begin in a similar state. Boys and women are linked together and opposed to men: actors can be, as Rosalind playing Ganymede tells Orlando that she can be, playing Rosalind, "for every passion something and for no passion truly anything, as boys and women are for the most part cattle of this color" (3.2.387–89). This viewpoint runs interestingly parallel to that of contemporary psychologists who suggest that all children begin with an identification with their mother—or primary caretaker, almost always female—which typical socialization pressures boys to reject.[8] But as we noted in an earlier chapter, boys who become actors are more likely to have kept some of this identification, and this prepares for their ease in later identifying with the characters they play.[9] If this is true of contemporary males who act male roles, it is even more plausible for males who acted female roles.

These connections make an interesting background for the transitions in Shakespeare's use of cross-sex imagery. In the comedies and the tragedies, the use of boy actors to play women parallels the conventional classification of both groups as emotional and immature by comparison to men; when they show control and maturity we have the sense of their resourcefulness in rising above their limitations. But in the romances the male characters who compare themselves to women suggest the possibility of a different meaning for the boy actor of female characters: playing women can itself be maturing, whether in him or in the incorporation of nurturing and generative qualities, considered feminine, by characters like Cymbeline, Belarius, Pericles, Leontes, and Prospero.

Many different cultures have barred women from the theatrical profession and accepted males in female roles onstage: classical Greek and Japanese Noh drama are similar to Elizabethan in this respect, though their styles are more formal and their male actors are adult.[10] In Greek drama, at least, the cross-gender imagery tends to be like that of Shakespearean tragedy, which criticizes men for acting like women and—occasionally and ambivalently—praises women for acting like men. But these other theaters do not portray female characters in male disguise anywhere nearly as often as Shakespeare does, nor, so far as I know, do they use imagery of femaleness positively as Shakespeare does in the romances, though this would be interesting to explore further. These contrasts help reinforce the point that Shakespeare's use of cross-gender images, visual and verbal, cannot come simply from the requirements of stage conditions. Rather, I believe it results from Shakespeare's ability to see through the limitations of conventional gender expectations. In the comedies the disguised heroines reflect his understanding of women's wish to transcend the roles they are customarily expected to play. But in the tragedies he explores in even more depth the destructiveness of conventional gender expectations for men if carried to the extreme. Perhaps this led him to the new appreciation that the romances show of specifically female experiences of childbearing, pregnancy, and nursing, and of masculine participation in the realm of generativity and nurturing.

Keats wrote, "Shakespear led a life of allegory: his works are the comments on it."[11] Shakespeare's first grandchild was born in 1608, just before he wrote *Cymbeline, The Winter's Tale,* and *The Tempest;* that biographical fact by itself might not have led him to the emphasis on adults' relationships with children in these plays, but the birth seems to have coincided with a point in his playwriting career when his exploration of human experiences had led him to start looking at these relationships with new interest.[12] In play after play, he had treated adults' relations with other adults, including their parents (most notably, it seems, Hamlet in 1601, the year his father died, and Coriolanus in 1607, when his mother died). Anachronistic though it may sound, the tragedies, especially Coriolanus and Macbeth, include a sense of the inadequacy of the pursuit of power. Such an attitude would make a plausible motivation for a wish to turn to relationships with children and an increased interest in forgiveness between adults. With our hindsight, we can wonder how much this thematic shift found its inevitable completion in his return to his home in Stratford.

When I began this book, I was interested in how Shakespeare's comedies had, however unprogrammatically and ambivalently, anticipated feminist concerns with freeing women from conventions. Now I see how the tragedies and romances are relevant to recent reanalyses of masculinity and to the public rediscovery of parenthood in 1980s America. A few years ago a critic who had recently had a serious eye operation called attention to the eyes of the actors in the Kozintzev film of Lear. His own experience had made him especially interested in eyes, but such a concern is clearly relevant to a play in which one character is blinded and all characters use sight imagery. Similarly, I believe that concerns about relations between the sexes are demonstrably present in Shakespeare's plays and that feminist theory's refusal to take those relations for granted helps analyze the plays. My point is not to suggest that Shakespeare transcended his time enough to foresee everything, but rather to emphasize the variety and complexity of human relationships and attitudes his plays explore. He could imagine attachments between the sexes and between members of the same sex, across generations and between peers. He was writing—as he lived through his twenties, thirties, and forties—for a divided audience, and he understood its divisions intimately; he could probably see in himself both the appeal of mutuality and the appeal of patriarchy, both the desire to express emotions openly and the desire to control expressions of emotions. He used the potential of the theater to personify opposite attitudes and play them off against each other. This dramatic use of ambivalence gives as good an illusion of presenting all sides of human relationships as our theatrical heritage so far possesses.

Notes

Chapter One

1. Quoted in Gordon S. Haight, *George Eliot: A Biography* (Oxford: Oxford University Press, 1968), p. 146.

2. Juliet Dusinberre, *Shakespeare and the Nature of Women* (New York: Barnes and Noble, 1975), p. 308. See also, for example, Irene Dash, *Wooing, Wedding, and Power: Women in Shakespeare's Plays* (New York: Columbia University Press, 1981).

3. Implications of patriarchy for Shakespeare's male characters are explored in Coppélia Kahn's *Man's Estate: Masculine Identity in Shakespeare* (Berkeley: University of California Press, 1980).

4. Erik Erikson, *Insight and Responsibility* (New York: Norton, 1964), p. 231. Comparatively early uses of this term in Shakespeare criticism include Edward Hubler, *The Sense of Shakespeare's Sonnets* (Princeton: Princeton University Press, 1952), p. 42: "With Shakespeare, however, the essence of love is mutuality"; and L. C. Knights, *Further Explorations* (Stanford: Stanford University Press, 1965), p. 21: "Aware as he is of the need for mutual relationship within society, he does not merely preach this; rather he explores—with a maximum of concreteness and immediacy—the nature of mutuality and its opposite."

5. Related points have been made, for example, by Hubler, *Shakespeare's Sonnets*, pp. 106–7; Maynard Mack, "Engagement and Detachment in Shakespeare's Plays," in *Essays on Shakespeare and Elizabethan Drama in Honor of Hardin Craig*, ed. Richard Hosley (Columbia: University of Missouri Press, 1962), pp. 275–96; Richard Wheeler, *Shakespeare's Development and the Problem Comedies* (Berkeley: University of California Press, 1981); and, from a feminist perspective, Marilyn French, *Shakespeare's Division of Experience* (New York: Summit, 1981).

6. Henry Smith, *A Preparative to Marriage* (1591), pp. 56, 28, 96, 10, and 32.

7. William and Malleville Haller, "The Puritan Art of Love," *Huntington Library Quarterly* 5 (1941–42): 247. For evidence about the complex relation between puritanism and theater, see Margot Heinemann, *Puritanism and Theatre: Thomas Middleton and Opposition Drama under the Early Stuarts* (Cambridge: Cambridge University Press, 1980), pp. 18–36.

8. Lawrence Stone, *The Family, Sex, and Marriage in England, 1500–1800* (New York: Harper and Row, 1977), p. 141; Kathleen M. Davies, "Continuity and Change in Literary Advice about Marriage," in *Marriage and Society: Studies in the Social History of Marriage*, ed. R. B. Outhwaite (New York: St. Martin's Press, 1981), pp. 61–66. For further earlier examples of the ideal of mutuality in the theory of marriage, see John T. Noonan, Jr., *Contraception: A History of Its Treatment by Catholic Theologians and Canonists* (Cambridge, Mass.: Harvard University Press, Belknap Press, 1965), pp. 305–30.

9. Lawrence Stone, *The Crisis of the Aristocracy, 1558–1641* (Oxford: Clarendon Press, 1965), p. 661.

10. Ibid., pp. 611–12.

11. Stone, *Family, Sex, and Marriage*, pp. 195–202 (hereafter cited in the text as FSM).

12. Keith Wrightson, *English Society, 1580–1680* (London: Hutchinson, 1982), pp. 92–104; Louis B. Wright, *Middle-Class Culture in Elizabethan England* (1935; reprint, Ithaca: Cornell University Press, 1958), pp. 485–507. For a summary of conflicting views on the position of women in Elizabethan England, see Carolyn Ruth Swift Lenz, Gayle Greene, and Carol Thomas Neely, Introduction to *The Woman's Part: Feminist Criticism of Shakespeare*, ed. Carolyn Ruth Swift Lenz, Gayle Greene, and Carol Thomas Neely (Urbana: University of Illinois Press, 1980), pp. 7–8. Few historians now credit Queen Elizabeth's status with improvement of the position of women in general; see Allison Heisch, "Queen Elizabeth I and the Persistence of Patriarchy," *Feminist Review* 4 (1980): 45–56.

13. See, for example, Joan Kelly-Gadol, "The Social Relation of the Sexes: Methodological Implications of Women's History," *Signs* 1, no. 4 (1976): 809–24.

14. Clara Claiborne Park, "As We Like It: How a Girl Can Be Smart and Still Popular," *American Scholar* 42 (Spring 1973): 262–78; reprinted in Lenz, Greene, and Neely, eds., *The Woman's Part*, pp. 100–116.

15. In discussion after Heilbrun's talk on "Marriage and Fiction" at the Center for the Humanities, Wesleyan University, Middletown, Connecticut, February 1980.

16. Macfarlane's review appears in *History and Theory* 18 (1979): 103–26, Trumbach's in *Journal of Social History* 13 (1979): 136–42. In *The Origins of English Individualism* (New York: Cambridge University Press, 1978), Macfarlane says that "the majority of ordinary people in England from at least the thirteenth century were rampant individualists, highly mobile both geographically and socially, economically 'rational,' market-oriented and acquisitive, ego-centred in kinship and social life" (p. 163), and notes the "loneliness, insecurity and family tensions which are associated with the English structure" (p. 202). In his review, Trumbach agrees with Stone that the quality of parental attachment improved in the eighteenth century, although he emphasizes that it was not absent earlier (p. 139); in *The Rise of the Egalitarian Family* (New York: Academic Press, 1978), pp. 230–35, he postulates that the male aggressiveness and female hysteria that he finds more pronounced before 1750 result from lack of sufficient attachment to a primary maternal figure. Other critical reviews are E. P. Thompson, "Happy Families," *New Society*, Sept. 8, 1977, pp. 499–501; Keith Thomas, "The Changing Family," *Times Literary Supplement*, October 21, 1977, pp. 1226–27; and Richard Vann, *Journal of Family History* 4 (1979): 308–14.

17. Stephen Greenblatt, *Renaissance Self-Fashioning* (Chicago: University of Chicago Press, 1980).

18. Trumbach discusses related issues in his review and in *Egalitarian Family*, pp. 237–85. See also Joseph E. Illick, "Child-Rearing in Seventeenth-Century England and America," in *The History of Childhood*, ed. Lloyd DeMause (New York: Harper and Row, 1975), p. 312; and David Leverenz, *The Language of Puritan Feeling* (New Brunswick, N.J.: Rutgers University Press, 1980), p. 105.

19. See Dorothy Dinnerstein, *The Mermaid and the Minotaur* (New York: Harper and Row, 1976), and also the discussions of psychoanalytic theories of male development and of the historical circumstances of Elizabethan patriarchy in the introductory chapter of Coppélia Kahn's *Man's Estate*.

20. Macfarlane, review in *History and Theory*, p. 125.

21. Louis Adrian Montrose, "'The Place of a Brother' in *As You Like It*: Social Process and Comic Form," *Shakespeare Quarterly* 32 (1981): 38. See Alfred Harbage, *Shakespeare's Audience* (New York: Columbia University Press, 1941), pp. 79–80.

Ann Jennalie Cook agrees that among the privileged in London, who she believes made up most of Shakespeare's audience, the late marriage age and high birthrate produced "a disproportionate number of unmarried men"; see *The Privileged Playgoers of Shakespeare's London, 1576–1642* (Princeton: Princeton University Press, 1981), p. 95.

22. See Montrose, "'The Place of a Brother,'" p. 39. See also Keith Thomas, "Age and Authority in Early Modern England," *Proceedings of the British Academy* 62 (1976): 205–48; Peter Laslett, *The World We Have Lost*, 2d ed. (New York: Charles Scribner's Sons, 1973), pp. 85–86; and Stone, *Family, Sex, and Marriage*, pp. 46–54.

23. Greenblatt contrasts Coriolanus's attempt at self-fashioning with those of Marlowe's heroes on p. 212. My view of Coriolanus has been much influenced by Janet Adelman's essay "'Anger's My Meat': Feeding, Dependency, and Aggression in *Coriolanus*," in *Representing Shakespeare: New Psychoanalytic Essays*, ed. Murray Schwartz and Coppélia Kahn (Baltimore: Johns Hopkins University Press, 1980), p. 188.

24. Cf. Greenblatt, *Renaissance Self-Fashioning*, pp. 248–51.

25. In 5.9 of Plautus, *The Twin Menaechmi*, trans. Richard W. Hyde and Edward Weist, in *Anthology of Roman Drama*, ed. Philip Whaley Harsh (New York: Holt, Rinehart and Winston, 1960), p. 46, the following exchange occurs:

Menaechmus I.   Oh, welcome, beyond all hope, after all these years!
Menaechmus II. Welcome, dear brother! Sought with such misery and toil, and found with joy at last!

26. Sherman Hawkins, "The Two Worlds of Shakespearean Comedy," *Shakespeare Studies* 3 (1967): 65–69.

27. See Norman Rabkin, *Shakespeare and the Common Understanding* (New York: Free Press, 1967), and *Shakespeare and the Problem of Meaning* (Chicago: University of Chicago Press, 1980).

28. Cf. Stanley Cavell, "The Avoidance of Love," in *Must We Mean What We Say?* (New York: Charles Scribner's Sons, 1969), p. 339.

Chapter Two

1. Lawrence Stone, *The Crisis of the Aristocracy, 1558–1641* (Oxford: Clarendon Press, 1965), p. 649. The spelling has been modernized. The quotation in the chapter title is from *Twelfth Night*, 5.1.365.

2. John Macmurray, *Persons in Relation* (London: Faber, 1961), p.

69; see also Erik Erikson, *Insight and Responsibility* (New York: Norton, 1964), p. 231, and for a sociological discussion of a synonymous concept, see Alvin W. Gouldner, "The Norm of Reciprocity: A Preliminary Statement," *American Sociological Review* 25 (April 1960): 161–78.

3. Cf. Madeleine Doran, *Endeavors of Art* (Madison: University of Wisconsin Press, 1954), p. 173; Richard Hosley, "The Formal Influence of Plautus and Terence," *Elizabethan Theatre*, Stratford-upon-Avon Studies 9, ed. John Russell Brown and Bernard Harris (New York: St. Martin's Press, 1967), p. 137.

4. Robert V. Merrill, "Eros and Anteros," *Speculum* 19 (1944): 265–84.

5. See, for example, James L. Calderwood, *Shakespearean Metadrama* (Minneapolis: University of Minnesota Press, 1971), pp. 59–76; and Malcolm Evans, "Mercury versus Apollo: A Reading of *Love's Labor's Lost*," *Shakespeare Quarterly* 26 (1975): 120–24.

6. See Richard Wheeler, *Shakespeare's Development and the Problem Comedies* (Berkeley: University of California Press, 1981); and Meredith Skura, *The Literary Use of the Psychoanalytic Process* (New Haven: Yale University Press, 1981), pp. 243–70. The ideas of both of these critics have influenced my thought on other plays as well.

7. In the other plot, Claudio's second marriage attempt with Hero is also set up to appear as a recompense.

8. Richard B. Young, "English Petrake: A Study of Sidney's *Astrophel and Stella*," in *Three Studies in the Renaissance: Sidney, Jonson, Milton* (New Haven: Yale University Press, 1958), p. 10.

9. See D. J. Palmer, "Art and Nature in *As You Like It*," *Philological Quarterly* 49 (1970): 30–40. For a wide-ranging and stimulating study of the relation of brotherhood to other social structures, see Louis Adrian Montrose, " 'The Place of a Brother' in *As You Like It*: Social Process and Comic Form," *Shakespeare Quarterly* 32 (1981): 28–54.

10. Cf. Norman Holland, *Dynamics of Literary Response* (New York: Oxford University Press, 1968), p. 253. The use of food imagery also reflects the variations in the characters' relationships in *Much Ado*.

11. Cf. C. L. Barber, *Shakespeare's Festive Comedy* (1959; reprint, New York: Meridian, 1963), p. 252. My view of the comedies is much indebted to this book.

12. Porter Williams, Jr., "Mistakes in *Twelfth Night* and their Resolution," *Publications of the Modern Language Association* 76 (1961): 198.

13. Cf. Alan Downer, "Feste's Night," *College English* 13 (1952): 259.

14. Plato, *Dialogues*, trans. Benjamin Jowett, 3d ed. rev., 2 vols. (1892; reprint, New York: Random, 1937), 1:317.

15. Marsilio Ficino, *Commentary on Plato's "Symposium,"* trans. Sears Jayne, University of Missouri Studies 19 (Columbia: University of Missouri Press, 1944), pp. 144–46.

16. Rainer Maria Rilke, *Letters to a Young Poet*, trans. M. D. Herter (New York: Norton, 1934), p. 35; quoted by Nancy Reeves in *Womankind: Beyond the Stereotypes* (Chicago: Aldine Publishing Co., 1971), p. 29. See also Walter N. King, "Introduction," in *Twentieth-Century Interpretations of "Twelfth Night,"* ed. Walter N. King (Englewood Cliffs, N.J.: Prentice-Hall, 1968), pp. 11–12; and Carolyn Heilbrun, *Toward a Recognition of Androgyny* (New York: Knopf, 1973), p. 40. My reading of *Twelfth Night*, at this point and many others, owes much to conversations with the late Diane Janeau.

17. Cf. Downer, "Feste's Night," p. 259.

18. Malvolio's word "revenged" (5.1.380) echoes Feste's "revenges" (5.1.379); Ficino finds "a most just vengeance in reciprocal love" (*Plato's "Symposium,"* p. 145).

19. Muriel Bradbrook, *The Growth and Structure of Elizabethan Comedy* (Berkeley: University of California Press, 1956), p. 41.

20. Ibid., p. 25. Cf. Northrop Frye's discussion of communion with the audience at the end of a comedy in *Anatomy of Criticism* (1957; reprint, New York: Atheneum, 1969), p. 164.

21. Cf. Holland, *Literary Response*, pp. 76–79.

22. Anne Barton, "*As You Like It* and *Twelfth Night*: Shakespeare's Sense of an Ending," *Shakespearian Comedy*, Stratford-upon-Avon Studies 14, ed. D. J. Palmer and Malcolm Bradbury (New York: Crane, Russak and Co., 1972), p. 176.

23. Holland, *Literary Response*, pp. 279–80.

24. Cf. Palmer, "Art and Nature," p. 30.

25. Victor Turner, *The Ritual Process* (Chicago: Aldine Publishing Co., 1969), pp. 166–203.

26. See, for example, Clara Claiborne Park, "As We Like It: How a Girl Can Be Smart and Still Popular," *American Scholar* 42 (Spring 1973): 262–78; reprinted in *The Woman's Part: Feminist Criticism of Shakespeare*, ed. Carolyn Ruth Swift Lenz, Gayle Greene, and Carol Thomas Neely (Urbana: University of Illinois Press, 1980); Peter Erickson, "Sexual Politics and the Social Structure in *As You Like It*," in *Patriarchal Structures in Shakespeare's Drama*, forthcoming from University of California Press.

27. Natalie Zemon Davis, "Women on Top," in *Society and Culture in Early Modern France* (Stanford: Stanford University Press, 1975), p. 143.

28. See Lynda Boose, "The Father and the Bride in Shakespeare," *Publications of the Modern Language Association* 97 (1982): 325–47, for Shakespeare's pervasive use of this ritual.

29. See Norman Rabkin, *Shakespeare and the Problem of Meaning* (Chicago: University of Chicago Press, 1980), esp. pp. 34–35; E. H. Gombrich, *Art and Illusion: A Study in the Psychology of Pictorial Representation*, 2d ed. rev., Bollingen Series 35, no. 5 (1961; reprint, Princeton: Princeton University Press, 1969), p. 5.

Chapter Three

1. See, for example, Muriel Bradbrook, "Dramatic Role as Social Image: A Study of *The Taming of the Shrew*," *Shakespeare-Jahrbuch* 94 (1958): 142–43; Charles Brooks, "Shakespeare's Romantic Shrews," *Shakespeare Quarterly* 11 (1960): 354; John Russell Brown, *Shakespeare and His Comedies*, 2d ed. (1962; reprint, London: Methuen, 1968), p. 98; Cecil C. Seronsy, "Supposes as the Unifying Theme in *The Taming of the Shrew*," *Shakespeare Quarterly* 14 (1963): 19–23; Ronald Berman, "Shakespearean Comedy and the Uses of Reason," *South Atlantic Quarterly* 63 (1964): 4–8; E. M. W. Tillyard, *Shakespeare's Early Comedies* (New York: Barnes and Noble, 1965), p. 83; Theodore Weiss, *The Breath of Clowns and Kings* (New York: Atheneum, 1971), p. 68; Ralph Berry, *Shakespeare's Comedies* (Princeton: Princeton University Press, 1972), pp. 54–71; and Robert Heilman, Introduction to *The Taming of the Shrew* (New York: New American Library, 1966), p. xxix.

2. Michael Goldman, *The Actor's Freedom* (New York: Viking, 1975), integrates discussion of the psychology of children's play into a theory of drama that I have found very useful here; see, especially, pp. 36–37, 82–89.

3. Cf. Juliet Dusinberre, *Shakespeare and the Nature of Women* (New York: Barnes and Noble, 1975), pp. 105–10. Coppélia Kahn, in *Man's Estate* (Berkeley: University of California Press, 1981), pp. 104–18, emphasizes the farce, but her interpretation coheres with mine at many points. So does that of John C. Bean, "Comic Structure and the Humanizing of Kate in *The Taming of the Shrew*," in *The Woman's Part: Feminist Criticism of Shakespeare*, ed. Carolyn Ruth Swift Lenz, Gayle Greene, and Carol Thomas Neely (Urbana: University

of Illinois Press, 1980), pp. 65–78, who emphasizes the romance. For a discussion that explains male dominance as a metaphor for sexual initiation, see Michael West, "The Folk Background of Petruchio's Wooing Dance: Male Supremacy in *The Taming of the Shrew*," *Shakespeare Studies* 7 (1974): 65–73. On the ambivalence aroused by all major dramatic roles, see Goldman, *The Actor's Freedom*, pp. 12–18.

4. For contrast between external and internal change, see Maynard Mack, "Engagement and Detachment in Shakespeare's Plays," in *Essays on Shakespeare and Elizabethan Drama in Honor of Hardin Craig*, ed. Richard Hosley (Columbia: University of Missouri Press, 1962), pp. 279–80; see also Seronsy, "Supposes as the Unifying Theme," p. 19.

5. Johan Huizinga, *Homo Ludens* (Boston: Beacon, 1955), pp. 9–10.

6. Elliott M. Avedon and Brian Sutton-Smith, *The Study of Games* (New York: John Wiley, 1971), p. 6.

7. Jean Piaget, *Play, Dreams, and Imitation in Childhood*, trans. C. Gattegno and F. M. Hodgson (New York: Norton, 1962), p. 148.

8. Peter Berger and Hansfried Kellner, "Marriage and the Construction of Reality," *Diogenes* 46 (Summer 1964): 17.

9. Ibid., p. 7.

10. Roger Caillois, *Man, Play, and Games*, trans. Meyer Barash (Glencoe, Ill.: Free Press, 1961), p. 12.

11. Ibid., p. 8.

12. Ibid., p. 39.

13. Ibid., p. 13.

14. William Willeford, *The Fool and His Scepter* (Evanston, Ill.: Northwestern University Press, 1969), p. 13; cf. West, "Petruchio's Wooing Dance," pp. 66–67.

15. Cf. Brooks, "Shakespeare's Romantic Shrews," p. 352, and George Hibbard, "*The Taming of the Shrew*: A Social Comedy," in *Shakespearean Essays*, ed. Alwin Thaler and Norman Sanders (Knoxville: University of Tennessee Press, 1964), p. 24.

16. Antoine de Saint-Exupéry, *Le Petit Prince* (Paris: Gallimard, 1946), pp. 66–67.

17. See Lawrence Stone, *The Crisis of the Aristocracy, 1558–1641* (Oxford: Clarendon Press, 1965), pp. 28–29.

18. Willeford, *The Fool and His Scepter*, pp. 15–16.

19. Berger and Kellner, "Marriage," p. 13.

20. Marvin Spevack, *A Complete and Systematic Concordance to the*

Works of Shakespeare, 8 vols. (Hildesheim: George Olms, 1968–75), 1:925 and 4:984–88.

21. Cf. William J. Martz, *Shakespeare's Universe of Comedy* (New York: David Lewis, 1971), p. 54.

22. Cf. Sears Jayne, "The Dreaming of *The Shrew*," *Shakespeare Quarterly* 17 (1966): 53n.

23. Ann Whitfield is called a hypocrite because she frequently claims to be following her parents' wishes when she is really following her own. She explains, "Women who are not hypocrites go about in rational dress and are insulted and get into all sorts of hot water." In the "Epistle Dedicatory" to this play, Shaw wrote, "Woman, projecting herself dramatically by my hands . . . behaves just as Woman did in the plays of Shakespear," *Man and Superman* (1903; reprint, Baltimore: Penguin Books, 1952), pp. 204 and 18. But perhaps this similarity has to do with English social traditions as well as comic ones. Zevedei Barbu has suggested that talking about interests and drives in terms of conscience and accepted social values was the typical English solution to the emotional conflicts of the Renaissance; see his *Problems in Historical Psychology* (London: Routledge and Kegan Paul, 1960), p. 207.

24. Cf. Susanne Langer, "The Comic Rhythm," in *Feeling and Form* (New York: Charles Scribner's Sons, 1953); reprinted in *Comedy: Meaning and Form*, ed. Robert W. Corrigan (San Francisco: Chandler, 1965), pp. 123–24.

25. Bradbrook, "Dramatic Role," p. 145.

26. Elizabeth Janeway, *Man's World, Woman's Place* (New York: Delta, 1971), pp. 11–47.

27. Cf. Jayne, "The Dreaming of *The Shrew*," p. 55.

28. Cf. Mary Douglas, *Natural Symbols* (New York: Vintage, 1973), pp. 43–45.

29. Cf. Brooks, "Shakespeare's Romantic Shrews," p. 354.

30. Jacques Ehrmann, in "*Homo Ludens* Revisited," *Yale French Studies* 41, *Game, Play, Literature* (1968), p. 33, argues that the opposition that Huizinga and Caillois draw between play and reality represents "a fundamentally rationalist view" that fails to see that "there is no 'reality' (ordinary or extraordinary) outside of or prior to the manifestations of the culture that expresses it."

31. W. V. Hoskins, "The Rebuilding of Rural England, 1570–1640," *Past and Present* 4 (November 1953): 44–59. Hoskins suggests that the rebuilding occurred in cities as well, although subsequent replacement of buildings obscures evidence.

32. Berger and Kellner, "Marriage," p. 21; see Nona Glazer-Malbin and Helen Youngelson Waehrer, "Introduction: Sex and Social Roles," in *Woman in a Man-Made World*, ed. Nona Glazer-Malbin and Helen Youngelson Waehrer (Chicago: Rand McNally, 1972), p. 136.

33. Cf. West, "Petruchio's Wooing Dance," p. 69; Goldman, *The Actor's Freedom*, p. 132.

34. Barbu, *Historical Psychology*, pp. 154–55.

Chapter Four

1. See, for example, John Russell Brown, Introduction to *The Merchant of Venice*, ed. John Russell Brown, Arden ed. (Cambridge: Harvard University Press, 1955), pp. lvii–lviii; Barbara Lewalski, "Biblical Allusion and Allegory in *The Merchant of Venice*," *Shakespeare Quarterly* 13 (1962): 328–36, 339; Sylvan Barnet, Introduction to *Twentieth-Century Interpretations of "The Merchant of Venice,"* ed. Sylvan Barnet (Englewood Cliffs, N.J.: Prentice-Hall, 1970), pp. 3–6.

2. Cf. Robert Hapgood, "Portia and *The Merchant of Venice*: The Gentle Bond," *Modern Language Quarterly* 28 (1967): 29. Sigurd Burckhardt makes an analogous contrast of their attitudes toward the law in *Shakespearean Meanings* (Princeton: Princeton University Press, 1968), pp. 208–36.

3. Lawrence Hyman, "The Rival Lovers in *The Merchant of Venice*," *Shakespeare Quarterly* 21 (1970): 109–16.

4. W. H. Auden, "Brothers and Others," in *The Dyer's Hand* (New York: Random House, 1962), pp. 223–32; C. L. Barber, *Shakespeare's Festive Comedy* (New York: Meridian, 1963), pp. 167–68. For background, see L. C. Knights, *Drama and Society in the Age of Jonson* (New York: Barnes and Noble, 1937); R. H. Tawney, *Religion and the Rise of Capitalism* (New York: Harcourt, Brace, 1926).

5. *Summa Theologica* $2^a.2^{ae}.78:1$–2m, quoted in Benjamin Nelson, *The Idea of Usury* (Princeton: Princeton University Press, 1949), p. 14.

6. St. Raymond of Pennaforte, *Summa Casuum Conscientiae* (Verona, 1744), 2.7.2, quoted in John T. Noonan, Jr., *The Scholastic Analysis of Usury* (Cambridge, Mass.: Harvard University Press, 1957), p. 33.

7. Nelson, *The Idea of Usury*, pp. 83–85.

8. *On the Sentences* 4.33.1.3., quoted in John T. Noonan, Jr., *Contra-*

ception (Cambridge, Mass.: Harvard University Press, 1965), pp. 241–42. Another licit purpose of sexual intercourse was described as "paying the marriage debt"; the phrase suggests both other-centered motivation and the financial analogy. Noonan, *Contraception*, pp. 284–85.

9. Cf. Zevedei Barbu, *Problems in Historical Psychology* (London: Routledge and Kegan Paul, 1960), pp. 114–15; Richard P. Wheeler, "History, Character and Conscience in *Richard III*," *Comparative Drama* 5 (1971–72): 318–19.

10. G. K. Hunter, "Elizabethans and Foreigners," *Shakespeare Survey* 17 (1964): 46–47. On "devil" as a common anti-Semitic epithet, see Joshua Trachtenberg, *The Devil and the Jews* (New Haven: Yale University Press, 1943), pp. 18–31.

11. For discussion of Bassanio too as outsider, see Kirby Farrell, *Shakespeare's Creation* (Amherst: University of Massachusetts Press, 1975), pp. 146–47, 152–55.

12. See, for example, Ian Maclean, *The Renaissance Notion of Woman* (New York: Cambridge University Press, 1980), pp. 16–22; Rosemary Ruether, *Liberation Theology* (New York: Paulist Press, 1972), pp. 6, 16, 19–21; Rosemary Ruether, "Misogynism and Virginal Feminism in the Fathers of the Church," in *Religion and Sexism*, ed. Rosemary Ruether (New York: Simon and Schuster, 1974), pp. 156–69. See also Leslie Fiedler, *The Stranger in Shakespeare* (New York: Stein and Day, 1972), for a different view on Portia's relation to this tradition.

13. Burckhardt, *Shakespearean Meanings*, p. 208.

14. Noonan, *Usury*, p. 135.

15. Auden, "Brothers and Others," p. 232.

16. See Lewalski, "Biblical Allusion," pp. 328–36, 339; Nelson, *The Idea of Usury*, pp. 141–51. He is also aspiring to the Renaissance ideal of friendship, which involves elements from both classical and medieval traditions; see Laurens J. Mills, *One Soul in Bodies Twain* (Bloomington, Ind.: Principia Press, 1937). However, his relationship with Bassanio falls short of this ideal because of its inequality.

17. Martin Luther, *Von Kaufshandlung und Wucher*, quoted in Nelson, *The Idea of Usury*, p. 152.

18. See, for example, Graham Midgley, "*The Merchant of Venice*: A Reconsideration," *Essays in Criticism* 10 (1960): 125; Norman Holland, *Psychoanalysis and Shakespeare* (New York: McGraw-Hill, 1964), pp. 238–39.

19. Cf. Fiedler, *The Stranger in Shakespeare*, p. 89.

20. Anna Freud, *The Ego and the Mechanisms of Defence* (New York: International Universities Press, 1946), pp. 132–36.

21. Cf. J. D. Hurrell, "Love and Friendship in *The Merchant of Venice*," *Texas Studies in Literature and Language* 3 (1961): 339; Hapgood, "Portia," p. 26.

22. Cf. Auden, "Brothers and Others," p. 230, and Fiedler, *The Stranger in Shakespeare*, p. 90.

23. See Nathan W. Ackerman and Marie Jahoda, *Anti-Semitism and Emotional Disorder* (New York: Harper and Brothers, 1950), p. 26.

24. Cf. Auden, "Brothers and Others," p. 232.

25. Posthumous constraints on marriage were common in Elizabethan aristocratic families, but with the increasing concern for compatibility the trend was to loosen them; see Lawrence Stone, *The Crisis of the Aristocracy, 1558–1641* (Oxford: Clarendon Press, 1965), pp. 597–99.

26. For the view that the casket image defines woman as a sexual object, see Sigmund Freud, "The Theme of the Three Caskets," *Complete Psychological Works*, trans. James Strachey, 24 vols. (London: Hogarth Press, 1953–74), 12:292.

27. Noonan, *Usury*, p. 39.

28. Sigmund Freud, *The Ego and the Id*, trans. Joan Riviere, rev. ed. James Strachey (New York: Norton, 1962), p. 44; see also Holland, *Psychoanalysis and Shakespeare*, pp. 234–35.

29. A. Alvarez, *The Savage God* (New York: Bantam, 1973), pp. 105–6.

30. The conflict is a deadlock in an additional sense to that used by Harriett Hawkins in *Poetic Freedom and Poetic Truth* (Oxford: Clarendon Press, 1976), p. 71, of situations in which "opposed characters . . . each elicit both admiration and criticism." She discusses *Richard II*, to which I later compare *The Merchant of Venice*.

31. Antonio is self-controlled enough not to mock Shylock like Gratiano, and he does not take his share of the fine permanently, just on trust for Lorenzo during Shylock's lifetime. But however much the original audience preferred Lorenzo and Jessica to Shylock, honored Christianity, and condemned Judaism, they could see that the forced deed of gift and baptism punish Shylock, though ostensibly for his own good. Living in an age of religious persecution and of religious reform that stressed the individual conscience, many of them understood the difference between a free conversion and a forced one.

32. Cf. Midgley, "The Merchant of Venice," p. 203; Alvarez, The Savage God, p. 103.

33. See Burckhardt, Shakespearean Meanings, pp. 234–35.

34. Cf. Lewalski, "Biblical Allusion," p. 339.

35. Cf. E. M. W. Tillyard, Shakespeare's Early Comedies (New York: Barnes and Noble, 1965), p. 199.

36. Seneca, "De Beneficiis," in Moral Essays, trans. John W. Basore, 3 vols. (1928–32; reprint, Cambridge, Mass.: Harvard University Press, 1963–65), 3:13. The importance of this treatise in Renaissance doctrine of liberality is discussed by James Calderwood in Shakespearean Metadrama (Minneapolis: University of Minnesota Press, 1971), p. 75n. On this point as on many others, I find myself in agreement with Lawrence Danson's The Harmonies of "The Merchant of Venice" (New Haven: Yale University Press, 1978).

37. Edgar Wind, Pagan Mysteries in the Renaissance (New York: Norton, 1968), pp. 36–39.

38. Michael Goldman, The Actor's Freedom (New York: Viking, 1975), p. 133.

39. Cf. C. L. Barber, "An Essay on the Sonnets," reprinted from The Laurel Shakespeare, The Sonnets (Dell, 1960), in Elizabethan Poetry, ed. Paul Alpers (New York: Oxford University Press, 1967), p. 314; James Winny, The Master-Mistress (London: Chatto and Windus, 1968), pp. 170–96.

40. Recently, Linda Bamber, in Comic Women, Tragic Men: A Study of Gender and Genre in Shakespeare (Stanford: Stanford University Press, 1982), p. 28, has also argued that in Shakespeare's comedies women can be other without really being outsider and alien. In general, I find Shakespeare's female characters more psychologically developed than she does; at this point I believe Portia's otherness as a woman has become identified with the unmergeable selfhood of the individual, male or female—what Stanley Cavell calls, from another perspective, "the sadness within comedy. . . . Join hands here as we may, one of the hands is mine and the other is yours"; see Must We Mean What We Say? (New York: Charles Scribner's Sons, 1969), pp. 339–40.

Chapter Five

1. I use the term "actor" rather than "actress" throughout because "actor" is the generic term; see Casey Miller and Kate Swift, Words and Women (New York: Anchor, 1976), p. 50.

2. Norman Holland, *The Dynamics of Literary Response* (New York: Oxford University Press, 1968), pp. 75–79.

3. Robert Egan, "His Hour Upon the Stage: Role-Playing in *Macbeth*," *Centennial Review* 22 (1978): 327–45.

4. Jonas Barish, "The Anti-Theatrical Prejudice," *Critical Quarterly* 8 (1966): 343.

5. Stanley Cavell, "The Avoidance of Love," in *Must We Mean What We Say?* (New York: Charles Scribner's Sons, 1969), p. 332. See also Helene Keyssar, "I Love You. Who Are You? The Strategy of Drama in Recognition Scenes," *Publications of the Modern Language Association* 92 (1977): 297–306.

6. Janet Adelman, *The Common Liar: An Essay on "Antony and Cleopatra"* (New Haven: Yale University Press, 1973), pp. 105–13.

7. Michael Goldman, *The Actor's Freedom: Toward a Theory of Drama* (New York: Viking, 1975), p. 17 (hereafter cited in the text by page number).

8. Simone de Beauvoir, *The Second Sex*, trans. H. M. Parshley (New York: Bantam, 1961), p. xvi. Leslie Fiedler, *The Stranger in Shakespeare* (New York: Stein and Day, 1972), discusses woman as other, but he often identifies Shakespeare's attitude too closely with that of his male characters. Some affinities between women and the theater are noted in Juliet Dusinberre's *Shakespeare and the Nature of Women* (New York: Barnes and Noble, 1975), pp. 11, 247.

9. See Dorothy Dinnerstein, *The Mermaid and the Minotaur* (New York: Harper and Row, 1976); Louis B. Wright, *Middle-Class Culture in Elizabethan England* (1935; reprint, Ithaca: Cornell University Press, 1958), especially pp. 465–507; and Carroll Camden, "Iago on Women," *Journal of English and Germanic Philology* 48 (1949): 57–71.

10. Barish, "The Anti-Theatrical Prejudice," p. 330.

11. See Elizabeth Janeway, *Man's World, Woman's Place* (New York: Delta, 1971), pp. 112–13.

12. Philip Weissman, *Creativity in the Theater* (New York: Basic Books, 1965), p. 19.

13. Ibid., p. 14.

14. Nancy Chodorow, "Family Structure and Feminine Personality," in *Woman, Culture and Society*, ed. Michelle Z. Rosaldo and Louise Lamphere (Stanford: Stanford University Press, 1974), p. 44.

15. Weissman, *Creativity in the Theater*, pp. 11–13.

16. Barish, "The Anti-Theatrical Prejudice," p. 331.

17. Evidence supporting this appears in an interview with Dus-

tin Hoffman, whose acting in *Tootsie* is the closest contemporary equivalent I know to that of the Elizabethan boy who wanted his audience to imagine him as a woman: "In the film, Michael says he knows what it is to be a woman precisely because he is an actor. 'An actor waits by the phone,' he cries; 'he has no power when he gets a job.' . . . Hoffman thinks, too, that there is a lot of his late mother, who died a few months before filming began, in the nurturing side of Dorothy"; see "Tootsie on a Roll to the Top," *Time*, December 20, 1982, p. 77.

18. Barish, "The Anti-Theatrical Prejudice," p. 342.

19. See Lawrence Stone, "Walking Over Grandma," *New York Review of Books*, May 12, 1977, pp. 10–16.

Chapter Six

1. See Coppélia Kahn, *Man's Estate* (Berkeley: University of California Press, 1981), pp. 82–103.

2. See, especially, Raymond Southall, "*Troilus and Cressida* and the Spirit of Capitalism," in *Shakespeare in a Changing World*, ed. Arnold Kettle (New York: International Publishers, 1964), pp. 217–33.

3. See Gayle Greene, "Shakespeare's Cressida: 'A kind of self,'" in *The Woman's Part: Feminist Criticism of Shakespeare*, ed. Carolyn Ruth Swift Lenz, Gayle Greene, and Carol Thomas Neely (Urbana: University of Illinois Press, 1980), pp. 133–49.

4. See Madelon Gohlke, "'I wooed thee with my sword': Shakespeare's Tragic Paradigms," in Lenz, Greene, and Neely, eds., *The Woman's Part*, pp. 150–52, and cf. M. M. Mahood, *Shakespeare's Wordplay* (New York: Methuen, 1957), p. 60.

5. Cf. Kirby Farrell, *Shakespeare's Creation: The Language of Magic and Play* (Amherst: University of Massachusetts Press, 1975), p. 126.

6. See Harry Levin, "Form and Formality in *Romeo and Juliet*," *Shakespeare Quarterly* 11 (Winter 1960): 9; reprinted in *Modern Shakespearean Criticism*, ed. Alvin B. Kernan (New York: Harcourt, Brace, 1965), p. 287; and Roger Stilling, *Love and Death in Renaissance Tragedy* (Baton Rouge: Louisiana State University Press, 1976), pp. 77–78.

7. Cf. James Calderwood, *Shakespearean Metadrama* (Minneapolis: University of Minnesota Press, 1971), pp. 85–119; and Farrell, *Shakespeare's Creation*, pp. 125–26.

8. Cf. Farrell, *Shakespeare's Creation*, p. 128.

9. This contrast is emphasized by Stilling, *Love and Death*, p. 130.

10. See Lawrence Stone, *The Family, Sex, and Marriage in England, 1500–1800* (New York: Harper and Row, 1977), pp. 46–50; Peter Laslett, *The World We Have Lost*, 2d ed. (New York: Charles Scribner's Sons, 1973), pp. 85–86; and Ann Jennalie Cook, "The Mode of Marriage in Shakespeare's England," *Southern Humanities Review* 11 (1977): 126–32. On the age of the audience, see Alfred Harbage, *Shakespeare's Audience* (New York: Columbia University Press, 1941), pp. 79–80.

11. Cf. Robert Ornstein, *The Moral Vision of Jacobean Tragedy* (Madison: University of Wisconsin Press, 1960), p. 249.

12. In *Shakespeare and the Common Understanding* (New York: Free Press, 1967), p. 42, Norman Rabkin notes that both women "by one standard are worthless, and by another infinitely valuable." Critics who emphasize the play's treatment of men's attitudes to women include Ornstein, Stilling, Greene, and Janet Adelman, in a paper delivered at the 1979 MLA Special Session on Feminist Criticism of Shakespeare.

13. See Greene, "Shakespeare's Cressida," p. 137.

14. The uniqueness in Shakespeare of their lengthy kiss, and the disparity of their speeches, are noted by Robert Kimbrough, *Shakespeare's Troilus and Cressida and Its Setting* (Cambridge, Mass.: Harvard University Press, 1964), p. 82.

15. Comparisons between these scenes are also made by Stilling, who uses them as a critique of the "courtly love convention of the clandestine affair" (*Love and Death*, pp. 129–30); by Marjorie Garber, *Coming of Age in Shakespeare* (New York: Methuen, 1981), who sees the scene as Cressida's "sexual initiation . . . a moment of affirmation which not even her later faithlessness will entirely obscure" (p. 145); and by John Bayley, *Shakespeare and Tragedy* (Boston: Routledge and Kegan Paul, 1981), who notes, I believe more profoundly, that "*Troilus and Cressida* presents love, as it presents war, wholly in relation to activities and feelings that have no prospects or future but abolish themselves in expression" (p. 112).

16. Cf. Greene, "Shakespeare's Cressida," p. 143; and Kimbrough, "Troilus and Cressida," p. 84.

17. See Bayley, *Shakespeare and Tragedy*, p. 114.

18. Cf. Greene, "Shakespeare's Cressida," p. 142.

19. Ibid.

20. Contradictions between Hector's rhetoric here and his attitude to women elsewhere are noted by Rosalie Colie, *Shakespeare's*

Living Art (Princeton: Princeton University Press, 1974), p. 335; and Ornstein, *Jacobean Tragedy*, p. 245.

21. For the move from comic conventions to tragic, see, for example, Susan Snyder, *The Comic Matrix of Shakespeare's Tragedies* (Princeton: Princeton University Press, 1979), pp. 56–70.

22. See, for example, Harriett Hawkins, *Likenesses of Truth in Elizabethan and Restoration Drama* (Oxford: Clarendon Press, 1972), p. 52.

23. See D. A. Traversi, *An Approach to Shakespeare*, 3d ed., 2 vols. (Garden City, N.Y.: Doubleday Anchor, 1969), 2:3–21.

24. See Greene, "Shakespeare's Cressida," p. 136.

25. A similar contrast is made by John Bayley, *The Uses of Division* (New York: Viking, 1976), p. 206.

26. See, especially, Janet Adelman, *The Common Liar* (New Haven: Yale University Press, 1973).

27. See Peter Erickson, "*Antony and Cleopatra* as an Experiment in an Alternative Masculinity," in *Patriarchal Structures in Shakespeare's Drama*, forthcoming from University of California Press; and Carol Thomas Neely, "Gender and Genre in *Antony and Cleopatra*," presented at the International Shakespeare Congress, Stratford-upon-Avon, England, 1981. In these nicely complementary pieces, Erickson shows Antony's contributions to the relationship and Neely shows Cleopatra's.

Chapter Seven

1. Peter L. Berger and Hansfried Kellner, "Marriage and the Construction of Reality," *Diogenes* 46 (Summer 1964): 9.

2. Ibid., p. 13.

3. Ibid., p. 12.

4. Cf. John Bayley, *The Characters of Love* (New York: Basic Books, 1960), p. 159.

5. See Susan Snyder, *The Comic Matrix of Shakespearean Tragedy* (Princeton: Princeton University Press, 1980), p. 74.

6. On the Moor, see, for example, Eldred Jones, *Othello's Countrymen* (London: Oxford University Press, 1945), especially pp. 8, 22, 71.

7. Stanley Cavell, *The Claims of Reason* (New York: Oxford University Press, 1979), pp. 490–91. Since writing this, I have discovered that this interpretation is also argued by Arthur Kirsch, "The Po-

larization of Erotic Love in *Othello*," *Modern Language Review* 73 (1978): 721–40; and Stephen Greenblatt, *Renaissance Self-Fashioning* (Chicago: University of Chicago Press, 1980), pp. 232–54.

8. John T. Noonan, Jr., *Contraception* (Cambridge, Mass.: Harvard University Press, 1966), pp. 252–53, 319; C. S. Lewis, *The Allegory of Love* (New York: Oxford University Press, 1958), pp. 15–17; cf. Derrick Sherwin Bailey, *Sexual Relation in Christian Thought* (New York: Harper and Row, 1959), pp. 206–7.

9. C. L. Barber, "The Family in Shakespeare's Development: Tragedy and Sacredness," in *Representing Shakespeare: New Psychoanalytic Essays*, ed. Murray Schwartz and Coppélia Kahn (Baltimore: Johns Hopkins University Press, 1980), pp. 95–201.

10. Lynda Boose, "Othello's Handkerchief: 'The Recognizance and Pledge of Love,'" *English Literary Renaissance* 5 (Autumn 1975): 363–67. See also David Kaula, "Othello Possessed: Notes on Shakespeare's Use of Magic and Witchcraft," *Shakespeare Studies* 2 (1966): 126.

11. Greenblatt, *Renaissance Self-Fashioning*, p. 225, refers to Daniel Lerner's definition of empathy as "the capacity to see oneself in the other fellow's situation" in *The Passing of Traditional Society* (1958; rev. ed., New York: Free Press, 1964), p. 49.

12. W. H. Auden, "The Joker in the Pack," in *The Dyer's Hand* (New York: Random House, 1963), reprinted in *Othello: A Casebook*, ed. John Wain (London: MacMillan, 1971), p. 217.

13. Cf. Terence Hawkes, *Shakespeare's Talking Animals* (New York: Rowman and Littlefield, 1974), p. 135.

14. Cf. Jones, *Othello's Countrymen*, p. 97; Kaula, "Othello Possessed," p. 121.

15. Her continued strength is emphasized by Carol Thomas Neely, "Women and Men in *Othello*: what should such a fool / Do with so good a woman?," *Shakespeare Studies* 10 (1977): 133–58. I am much indebted to this article for its redress of critical disparagement of Desdemona, and my emphasis on her limitations is meant to be juxtaposed with Neely's lengthier discussion of her strengths.

16. Cf. William Empson, "Honest in Othello," *The Structure of Complex Words* (New York: New Directions, 1951), reprinted in Wain, ed., *Othello: A Casebook*, pp. 109–10.

17. Dorothy Dinnerstein, *The Mermaid and the Minotaur* (New York: Harper and Row, 1977) (hereafter cited in the text by page number).

Chapter Eight

1. See, for example, Alfred Harbage, Introduction to *King Lear*, ed. Alfred Harbage (Baltimore: Penguin, 1970), pp. 20–21; Maynard Mack, *King Lear in Our Time* (Berkeley: University of California Press, 1972), pp. 49–51.

2. Mack, *King Lear in Our Time*, pp. 100–113. He notes that the term was earlier applied to Lear's world by Enid Welsford in *The Fool: His Social and Literary History* (London: Faber and Faber, 1935), p. 258.

3. Alvin W. Gouldner, "The Norm of Reciprocity," *American Sociological Review* 25 (April 1960): 173–75.

4. Marvin Spevack, *A Complete and Systematic Concordance to the Works of Shakespeare*, 8 vols. (Hildesheim: Georg Olms, 1968–75), 4:984–88.

5. See, especially, Norman Holland, *Psychoanalysis and Shakespeare* (New York: McGraw-Hill, 1966), pp. 216–19.

6. Elizabeth Janeway, *Man's World, Woman's Place* (New York: Delta, 1971), pp. 37–47.

7. Peter Berger and Hansfried Kellner, "Marriage and the Construction of Reality," *Diogenes* 46 (Summer 1964): 17, 7.

8. See, for example, Simone de Beauvoir, *The Second Sex*, trans. H. M. Parshley (New York: Bantam, 1961), pp. 129–85.

9. Their attack on Lear draws on the role of the old as another stigmatized group, with another set of ready-made stereotypes overlapping with some of the negative images of women. For hostility toward the old in seventeenth-century England, see Lawrence Stone, "Walking Over Grandma," *New York Review of Books*, May 12, 1977, pp. 10–16, and Keith Thomas, "Age and Authority in Early Modern England," *Proceedings of the British Academy* 62 (1976): 205–48. As noted in Chapter 3, if patriarchy rests on male superiority in physical strength, it ceases to favor old men. In choosing Edmund, Goneril and Regan can be seen as following this form of patriarchy, which defines manhood by capacity for violence. The Elizabethan structure of institutional power did still favor old men, and Thomas suggests that this provoked much of the hostility.

10. See Marvin Rosenberg, *The Masks of King Lear* (Berkeley: University of California Press, 1972), p. 290, for the frequency of this gesture in recent performances.

11. Cf. Paul J. Alpers, "*King Lear* and the Theory of the 'Sight

Pattern,'" in *In Defense of Reading*, ed. Reuben Brower and Richard Poirier (New York: Dutton, 1962), p. 150.

12. Lawrence Stone, *The Crisis of the Aristocracy, 1558–1641* (Oxford: Clarendon Press, 1965), pp. 591–92.

13. Northrop Frye, "The Argument of Comedy," in *English Institute Essays, 1948*, ed. D. A. Robertson (New York: Columbia University Press, 1949), p. 62.

14. R. G. Hunter, *Shakespeare and the Comedy of Forgiveness* (New York: Columbia University Press, 1965). Hunter discusses the dependence of the forgiveness in Shakespeare's plays on a sense of common humanity that he identifies with the medieval idea of charity as distinguished from the modern one (p. 243).

15. Howard Felperin, *Shakespearean Romance* (Princeton: Princeton University Press, 1972), p. 87n.

16. Stanley Cavell, "The Avoidance of Love," in *Must We Mean What We Say?* (New York: Charles Scribner's Sons, 1969), pp. 310–53.

17. See Carolyn Heilbrun, *Toward a Recognition of Androgyny* (New York: Harper and Row, 1973), pp. 28–34, for a discussion of Shakespeare's "androgynous ideal" and its relationship to forgiveness and the father-daughter theme.

Chapter Nine

1. Cf. Madelon Gohlke, "'I wooed thee with my sword': Shakespeare's Tragic Paradigms," in *The Woman's Part: Feminist Criticism of Shakespeare*, ed. Carolyn Ruth Swift Lenz, Gayle Greene, and Carol Thomas Neely (Urbana: University of Illinois Press, 1980), pp. 150–70; Coppélia Kahn, *Man's Estate* (Berkeley: University of California Press, 1980).

2. This contrast has been well developed by Barbara Mowat, *The Dramaturgy of Shakespeare's Romances* (Athens: University of Georgia Press, 1976), pp. 8–25.

3. The importance of such qualifications was stressed by Toni McNaron in a critique of an earlier version of this chapter presented at the Midwest Modern Language Association, Minneapolis, 1980.

4. Meredith Skura, "Interpreting Posthumus' Dream from Above and Below: Families, Psychoanalysts, and Literary Critics," in *Representing Shakespeare: New Psychoanalytic Essays*, ed. Murray

Schwartz and Coppélia Kahn (Baltimore: Johns Hopkins University Press, 1980), p. 213.

5. Patricia Southard Gourlay, " 'O my most sacred lady': Female Metaphor in *The Winter's Tale*," *English Literary Renaissance* 5 (1975): 375–95. See also Carol Thomas Neely, "Women and Issue in *The Winter's Tale*," *Philological Quarterly* 57 (1978): 181–94.

6. Murray Schwartz, "*The Winter's Tale*: Loss and Transformation," *American Imago* 32 (1975): 150.

7. For an illuminating discussion, see Neely, "Women and Issue," pp. 189–90.

8. Mowat has noted that "neither cleverness, intellect, nor clear-sightedness avails to give the characters control over their lives" (*Dramaturgy*, p. 109). On the other hand, Howard Felperin suggests that, at least in *The Winter's Tale*, the pervasive metaphors from nature "endow the action of the play with something of the inevitability of the natural process itself," in *Shakespearean Romance* (Princeton: Princeton University Press, 1972), pp. 224–25.

9. See C. L. Barber, " 'Thou that beget'st him that did thee beget': Transformation in *Pericles* and *The Winter's Tale*," *Shakespeare Survey* 22 (1969): 61–62. Related ideas are developed by Peter Erickson in a chapter of *Patriarchal Structures in Shakespeare's Drama*, forthcoming from University of California Press.

10. Kahn, *Man's Estate*, p. 214.

11. Cf. Elizabeth Sacks, *Shakespeare's Images of Pregnancy* (New York: St. Martin's, 1980), p. 87.

12. Cf. Roger Stilling, *Love and Death in Renaissance Tragedy* (Baton Rouge: Louisiana State University Press, 1976), p. 291.

13. See Erickson, *Patriarchal Structures*, and also Janet Adelman, "The Marriage Plot and the Family Plot in *Cymbeline*," paper delivered at the 1980 MLA Special Session on Feminist Criticism of Shakespeare.

14. J. M. Nosworthy, ed., *Cymbeline* (1955; reprint, London: Methuen, 1969), p. 22n.

15. Cf. Murray Schwartz, "Between Fantasy and Imagination: A Psychological Exploration of *Cymbeline*," in *Psychoanalysis and Literary Process*, ed. Frederick Crews (Cambridge, Mass.: Winthrop, 1970), pp. 234–35.

16. Ibid., p. 279.

17. Cf. Barber, "*Pericles* and *The Winter's Tale*," p. 61, and Skura, "Interpreting Posthumus' Dream," p. 205.

Chapter Ten

1. See Phyllis Rackin, "Shakespeare's Boy Cleopatra, the Decorum of Nature, and the Golden World of Poetry," *Publications of the Modern Language Association* 87 (1972): 201–12.

2. Some general studies of the issues discussed here are Carolyn Heilbrun, *Toward a Recognition of Androgyny* (New York: Harper and Row, 1973); and Juliet Dusinberre, *Shakespeare and the Nature of Women* (New York: Barnes and Noble, 1975).

3. Sandra Gilbert, "Costumes of the Mind: Transvestism as Metaphor in Modern Literature," *Critical Inquiry* 7 (Winter 1980): 394.

4. See Michael Jamieson, "Shakespeare's Celibate Stage," in *The Seventeenth-Century Stage*, ed. G. E. Bentley (Chicago: University of Chicago Press, 1968), p. 86, reprinted from *Papers Mainly Shakespearian*, ed. G. I. Duthie (London: University of Aberdeen Press, 1964).

5. See Coppélia Kahn, *Man's Estate* (Berkeley: University of California Press, 1980), pp. 82–103.

6. See Gayle Greene, "Shakespeare's Cressida: 'A Kind of Self,'" in *The Woman's Part: Feminist Criticism of Shakespeare*, ed. Carolyn Ruth Swift Lenz, Gayle Greene, and Carol Thomas Neely (Urbana: University of Illinois Press, 1980), pp. 133–49.

7. However, characters from Holofernes to Iago imagine their brains as pregnant. See Elizabeth Sacks, *Shakespeare's Images of Pregnancy* (New York: St. Martin's, 1980).

8. See Robert Stoller, "Facts and Fancies: An Examination of Freud's Concept of Bisexuality," in *Women and Analysis*, ed. Jean Strouse (New York: Dell, 1975), pp. 403–11.

9. Philip Weissman, *Creativity in the Theater* (New York: Basic Books, 1965), pp. 13–14.

10. I am indebted to my colleague Mae Smethurst, who is working on a comparison between classical Greek and Japanese Noh drama, for information in this area.

11. John Keats, *Selected Poems and Letters*, ed. Douglas Bush (Boston: Houghton Mifflin, 1959), p. 284.

12. The fact that the King's Men bought the Blackfriars Theater in 1608 seems unlikely to account for this thematic aspect of the romances; coterie dramaturgy included few representations of childhood.

Index

Achilles, 120–21

Actor-audience relations: like gender relations, 19; mutuality of, 19, 41, 42, 161, 208 (n. 20)

Actors: compared to men, 19; otherness of, 19, 92–93, 96; compared to women, 19, 93–94, 199, 216 (n. 17); "ontological subversiveness" of, 94–95. *See also* Boy actors of women

Adam, 30

Adelman, Janet, 92, 181

Adriana, 24

African. *See* Moor as Renaissance stereotype

Aguecheek, Sir Andrew, 32, 34–35, 36

Alonso, 180

Alvarez, A., 74

Androgyny. *See* Gender crossing

Angelo, 15–16, 160, 199

Anteros, 23, 27

Antiochus, 185

Antipholus of Syracuse, 13–14

Antipholus family, 14, 178

Anti-Semitism, 64, 66, 70, 213 (n. 10), 214 (n. 31)

Antonio (*Merchant of Venice*): ideal of self-sacrifice, 63–64, 67–70, 72–80; anti-Semitism, 64, 70, 214 (n. 31); sexuality or asexuality of, 68–69, 73; self-criticism and depression, 73–74, 76; competition with Portia, 76–77

Antonio (*Tempest*), 160, 179–80, 184–85

Antonio (*Twelfth Night*), 34, 35–36, 37

Antony, 122–24; actor and audience, 91–92; definition of manhood, 196–97

Antony and Cleopatra, 91–92, 122–24; cross-gender imagery, 196–97

Aquinas, Saint Thomas, 64

Ariel, 184, 188

Arragon, Prince of, 71

Arviragus, 168, 169, 170, 179

As You Like It, 14, 22; mutuality in, 28–32, 42–43; gender relations compared with *Othello*, 144–45; male disguise, 188, 190, 192–93; definition of manhood, 191

Auden, W. H., 64, 135

Audience: composition of in Elizabethan England, 11, 109, 205 (n. 21); compared to women, 19

Audrey, 31, 43

Autolycus, 171

Bamber, Linda, 215 (n. 40)
Baptista, 55
Barber, C. L., 64, 132, 174
Barbu, Zevedei, 211 (n. 23)
Barish, Jonas, 88, 95
Barton, Anne, 41
Bassanio, 63; emotional distance, 15; relationship with Antonio, 68–69, 72, 74–75; attitude toward giving, 70, 72; ring episode, 77–80
Beatrice: combination of patriarchy and mutuality and, 7, 42–44; emotional distance, 15, 18, 23; lover and jester, 22, 27; ambivalent response to Benedick's wit, 25–26; love as recompense, 26–27; symmetrical mutuality, 27–28; definition of manhood, 191–92
Beauvoir, Simone de, 93
Belarius, 168, 169, 170, 179
Belch, Sir Toby, 32, 34, 35–36; advice on manhood, 191
Benedick: emotional distance, 15, 23; lover and jester, 22, 27; ambivalent response to Beatrice's wit, 26; love as recompense, 26–27; symmetrical mutuality, 27–28; combination of mutuality and patriarchy, 42–44; definition of manhood, 192
Benvolio, 100, 106
Berger, Peter, 46–47, 53, 61, 125–26, 152
Berowne, 15, 25, 105
Bertram, 16
Bianca (Taming of the Shrew), 52, 56, 57–58

Blackfriars Theater, 224 (n. 12)
Boose, Lynda, 133
Boy actors of women, 20, 188–89, 192–93, 199–200; in Two Gentlemen of Verona, 97; in As You Like It, 192–93
Brabantio, 17, 126, 127, 128
Bradbrook, Muriel, 41
Brook, Peter, 153
Brotherhood, 207 (n. 9)

Caillois, Roger, 47–48
Caliban, 184
Camillo, 8, 171, 180
Capulet, 17
Cassio, 130–32
Cavell, Stanley, 90, 132, 161, 215 (n. 40)
Celia, 30
Celibacy, ideal of, 69, 80
Childbirth, imagery of: Comedy of Errors, 14; Cymbeline, 18, 171–72, 176, 181, 198; Macbeth, 196. See also Pregnancy, imagery of
Child-rearing ideals: in Elizabethan England, 9–11; in Coriolanus, 11–12. See also Parent-child relations
Children. See Parent-child relations
Claudio (Measure for Measure), 17, 25
Claudio (Much Ado), 43, 178, 207 (n. 7); emotional distance, 15
Claudius, 16
Cleopatra, 122–23; actor and audience, 91–92; and boy actor, 189; cross-gender imagery, 196–97

Cloten, 168

Comedies: patriarchy and mutuality in, 6–7, 42–44; women in, 6–7, 83, 95, 97–98, 154, 190–93, 200–201, 215 (n. 40); emotion and control in, 13–15; men in, 83, 92, 191–93; sexual relations in, 144–45; genders less polarized in, 190–93; cross-gender imagery in, 190–94; male disguise in, 190–94, 200

Comedy of Errors, 13–14, 15, 18, 24, 178

Control: ideal for self-fashioning in Elizabethan England, 8–10; primarily masculine, 9; child-rearing and conflict with emotion, 9–11; and gender metaphors, 10, 16–18; in tragedies, 11–13; in comedies, 13–16; in romances, 16; and theatrical experience, 19–20. See also Manhood as control

Cook, Ann Jennalie, 205 (n. 21)

Cordelia, 7, 12, 152–54, 158–63; suspicion of pretense, 88; actor and audience, 89–90, 96–97

Coriolanus, 11–12

Coriolanus, 201

Cressida, 99–100, 111–19, 121–22; association of women with weakness, 194–95

Cross-gender imagery. See Gender crossing

Cymbeline: rejection of daughter, 17; imagery of childbirth, 18, 171–72; family

reunion and forgiveness, 168; fostering of Posthumus, 169; tears, 169; physicality of recognition, 179; love of wife versus love of daughter, 186

Cymbeline: childbirth imagery, 18, 171–72, 176, 181, 183, 198; suspicion of women, 165–67; repentance, 167; violence, 167–68, 184; tears, 169; relation of old and young, 169–70, 174; endurance in, 172–73; assertiveness of Imogen, 177; physicality of recognition scene, 179; jealousy and family experience, 181–83; private bonds as threats, 185; absence of mother, 186; masculine disguise, 188, 198

Davies, Kathleen, 5

Davis, Natalie Zemon, 42

Demetrius, 97

Desdemona, 13, 122, 125–49, 160; combination of mutuality and patriarchy, 7–8, 126–28, 130, 139, 144–45, 148; rejected by father, 17; actor and audience, 84–87, 95, 96–97; cross-gender imagery, 195–96

Diaries, Elizabethan: marriage in, 6; violence in, 9

Dinnerstein, Dorothy, 146–49

Dionyza, 185–86

Disguise: and mutuality, 6–7, 18, 83; and emotional distance, 11, 13, 14–15, 18, 23, 102

Disguise, female, 188–89, 199–
    200. *See also* Boy actors of
    women
Disguise, male, 200; and mu-
    tuality, 7, 18, 33, 42, 83; and
    patriarchy, 7, 42; and emo-
    tional distance, 14–15, 18,
    23; in *Merchant of Venice*, 74–
    75, 78; in *Two Gentlemen of
    Verona*, 97; in *Cymbeline*, 170,
    188, 198; gender symmetry,
    190–93; gender difference,
    192–93
Distance. *See* Control
Duke (*As You Like It*), 14, 30, 31,
    43
Duke (*Measure for Measure*), 25
Duncan, 87
Dusinberre, Juliet, 3

Edgar, 12–13
Edmund, 12–13, 153, 221 (n. 9)
Egan, Robert, 87
Eliot, George, 3
Elizabeth I (queen of England),
    204 (n. 14)
Emilia (*Comedy of Errors*), 14, 179
Emilia (*Othello*), 86, 141–43
Emotion, 3–4, 8–20. *See also*
    Control; Tears; Women: as-
    sociated with emotion
Erickson, Peter, 183
Erikson, Erik, 4, 148
Eros, 23, 27
Eros (*Antony and Cleopatra*), 197

Father-daughter relations: in
    Elizabethan England, 9; in
    Lear, 12, 150–59; in *As You Like
    It*, 14, 31, 43; rejections, 17;
    in romances, 171, 172, 174–
    75, 185–87

Father-son relations: in advice
    letters, 9, 10; in *King Lear*, 12–
    13; in romances, 169–71,
    174, 179
Felperin, Howard, 160–61
Ferdinand (*Tempest*), 177, 185
Feste, 22, 34; mutuality with
    audience, 40–41
Ficino, Marsilio, 39, 80
Food imagery, in gender rela-
    tions, 31, 207 (n. 10)
Fool. *See* Jester
Fool (*Lear*), 155
Forgiveness: in *Two Gentlemen of
    Verona*, 24; in *Antony and
    Cleopatra*, 91–92, 122–24; in
    Othello, 143, 160; in *Lear*, 159–
    61; in romances, 160, 177,
    178, 179–80; in problem
    comedies, 160–61; sense of
    common humanity, 186, 222
    (n. 14)
Freud, Anna, 69
Freud, Sigmund, 74, 214 (n. 26)
Friendship, idealized: in *Two
    Gentlemen of Verona*, 24; be-
    tween Sebastian and Anto-
    nio in *Twelfth Night*, 34; at-
    tempted by Antonio in
    Merchant of Venice, 68, 76, 213
    (n. 16); relationship to mar-
    riage in *Merchant of Venice*, 75,
    76–77, 79–80
Frye, Northrop, 159, 208
    (n. 20)

Gender, imagery of, 144, 190,
    198–99; and emotion/con-
    trol conflict, 3–4, 10, 16–18,
    144; in *Lear*, 16–18, 153, 156–
    58, 162–63, 195; in *Cymbeline*,
    18, 166, 171–72, 183; in *Mer*-

chant of Venice, 66; and woman/actor analogy, 93–97; in *Romeo and Juliet*, 100, 106–7, 194; in *Troilus and Cressida*, 111, 112, 119–21, 194–95; in *Othello*, 130, 136–37, 139, 144, 148, 195–96; in *Winter's Tale*, 171, 198; in *Pericles*, 172, 175; in romances, 174, 181, 186, 197–98, 199, 200; and boy actors, 189, 199; in comedies, 190–94, 200; in tragedies, 194–97, 200; in *Macbeth*, 195–96; in *Antony and Cleopatra*, 196–97. *See also* Childbirth, imagery of; Manhood as control; Manhood as violence; Pregnancy, imagery of; Tears; Women: associated with emotion; Women: associated with weakness

Gender as theatrical role, 20, 188, 191, 192–93, 198–200

Gender crossing, imagery of, 190, 199, 222 (n. 17), 224 (n. 7); and emotion/control conflict, 16–18; in *Cymbeline*, 18, 166, 170, 171–72, 181, 198; in *Othello*, 85, 130, 139, 148, 196; and "ontological subversiveness" of actors, 94–95; in *Romeo and Juliet*, 106–7, 194; in *Troilus and Cressida*, 111–12, 119–21, 194–95; in *Antony and Cleopatra*, 122, 196–97; in *Lear*, 153, 156–58, 162–63, 195; in romances, 164, 174, 181, 186, 198–99, 200–201; in *Winter's Tale*, 171, 198; in *Pericles*, 172, 175; in *Tempest*, 185; and boy

actors, 188–89, 199–200; in comedies, 190–94, 200, 201; in tragedies, 194–97; in *Macbeth*, 195–96. *See also* Boy actors of women; Disguise, female; Disguise, male

Gender polarization: in Roman comedy, 23; in *Romeo and Juliet*, 100, 106–8; in *Troilus and Cressida*, 121; in *Othello*, 144, 147–49; in *Lear*, 156, 162–63; diminishing in romances, 164, 166–77; limited in comedies, 190–94

Gender symmetry: in comedies, 23, 27–28, 39, 190–91; in *Antony and Cleopatra*, 91–92, 122–23; in *Romeo and Juliet*, 105; in *Troilus and Cressida*, 112

Gentleman (*Lear*), 89
Gertrude, 84, 95
Gilbert, Sandra, 192
Gloucester, 12–13, 153, 157
Gobbo, Lancelot, 70
Goldman, Michael, 80, 92, 93, 94, 209 (n. 2)
Gombrich, Ernst, 44
Goneril, 97, 152, 153, 156
Gouldner, Alvin, 150
Gourlay, Patricia Southard, 171
Graces, 80
Gratiano, 80, 214 (n. 31)
Greenblatt, Stephen, 9, 135
Greene, Gayle, 121
Grumio, 50
Guiderius, 168, 170, 179

Haller, Malleville, 5
Haller, William, 5
Hamlet, 93; suspicion of female pretense, 84; imagery of gender, 194

Hamlet: imagery of gender, 16, 194; boy actor of Player Queen in, 188

Hawkins, Harriett, 214 (n. 30)

Hawkins, Sherman, 15

Hector, 110, 119–21

Heilbrun, Carolyn, 7, 222 (n. 17)

Helen of Troy, 110–11

Helmer, Nora (*A Doll's House*), 151

Hermione, 8, 177; stone as metaphor for control, 16; mother-daughter relationship, 176; absence, 178; reunion with Leontes, 180–81

Hero, 17, 43

Hippolyta, 97

Hoffman, Dustin, 216 (n. 17)

Holinshed, Raphael, 87

Holland, Norman, 85

Homosexuality, 68–69, 73, 135–36

Hortensio, 56, 57

Huizinga, Johan, 46

Hunter, R. G., 160

Hymen, 31–32

Iago, 126, 129–41, 224 (n. 7); emotional detachment, 13; game-player, 145

Imogen, 8; relationship with Posthumus, 165, 177, 178, 181–83; disguise, 169, 170, 188, 198; pregnancy imagery, 176, 198

Isabella, 17, 160

Janeway, Elizabeth, 58, 152

Jaques, 29

Jester, 21, 22, 49. *See also* Lover as jester

Jews, attitudes to, 64, 65, 66, 70, 79, 213 (n. 10), 214 (n. 31)

Jonson, Ben (*Challenge at Tilt*), 23

Julia, 97

Juliet (*Measure for Measure*), 25

Juliet (*Romeo and Juliet*), 7–8, 17, 99–109, 122, 182, 194

Jupiter, 170

Kate: combination of patriarchy and mutuality, 6–7, 45–62; relation to social order, 46, 49, 52, 58–60; playfulness, 47, 48, 52–55, 60–62

Keats, John, 200

Kellner, Hansfried, 46–47, 53, 61, 125–26, 152

Kent, 199

King Lear, 150–63; conflicts about emotion, 12, 16–17, 18, 195; imagery of gender, 16–17, 195; imagery of cuckoldry, 17; resents female autonomy, 88; stereotypes of old, 96–97, 221 (n. 9)

King Lear, 88–90, 96–97, 150–63; father-child relations, 12–13, 150–59; mother-child imagery, 152–53; gender polarization and projection, 156–57; definition of manhood, 195

Lady Macbeth, 8, 153; actor and audience, 87–88; gender imagery, 195–96

Lady Macduff, 176

Laertes, 16

Laurence, Friar, 107, 194

Leonato, 17

Leontes: relation with Paulina, 8, 176–77; emotional control, 16, 186; behavior in jealousy, 165, 166–67; penance and tears, 169; attitude to children, 170–71, 183; patience, 173; reunion with Hermione, 180–81; cross-gender imagery, 198

Lord (*Taming of the Shrew*), 189

Love: as idealization of beloved, 28–29, 31–32; and food imagery, 31–32; unrequited, self-dramatized, 32–34; as reunion of two halves, 38–39; as resurrection and self-recognition in beloved, 39; as private world, 100, 103, 106, 108–9, 123, 185; as violence, 101, 107, 112, 116; financial imagery, 104–5, 112–13, 116. *See also* Friendship, idealized; Homosexuality; Marriage; Mutuality; Parent-child relations; Self-sacrifice; Sex

Lover as jester, 21–22, 25

Love's Labor's Lost, 24–25, 97

Lucentio, 46, 52, 55–56

Luther, Martin, 68

Lychorida, 179

Lysander, 97

Macbeth, 95; acting without Lady Macbeth, 87–88; definition of manhood, 195; childbirth imagery, 196

Macbeth, 87–88, 201

Macduff, 18

Macfarlane, Alan, 9, 10, 205 (n. 16)

Mack, Maynard, 150

Macmurray, John, 22

Male dominance. *See* Patriarchy

Malvolio, 32, 34; on jester's dependence, 22; reciprocity of revenge, 40; isolation from jokes and love, 41; on androgyny, 193–94

Mamillius, 171, 183

Manhood as control, 17; in Elizabethan England, 9–10; view criticized in plays, 18; *Romeo and Juliet*, 107, 194; *Othello*, 130–32, 136, 138, 144–45, 146, 148, 195; in romances, 180, 186–87; in *Hamlet*, 194; in *Lear*, 195. *See also* Gender, imagery of; Women: associated with emotion

Manhood as violence: in *Troilus and Cressida*, 100, 119–21, 194–95; in *Romeo and Juliet*, 100–101, 106–7, 194; in *Othello*, 136–37, 148; parodied or less glamorized in romances, 164, 166–68, 186; in *Macbeth*, 195; in *Lear*, 221 (n. 9)

Mariana, 15

Marina: reunion with Pericles, 172, 175, 184; reunion with Thaisa, 176, 179

Marriage: as friendship, partnership, 4; as play, 4, 46, 61; in puritan sermons, 4–5, 61, 80; in Anglican theology, 5; in Catholic theology, 5, 64, 212 (n. 8); in Roman comedy, 23; as private world, 46–47, 49, 54, 60–61, 125; animal imagery, 50–51, 57, 137

Marriage practices in Elizabethan England: disruption among aristocracy, 5; in diaries, 6; age, 11, 109, 205 (n. 21); household architecture, 61; posthumous constraints, 214 (n. 25)

Mary (mother of Jesus), 153; and post-Reformation religious need, 132; pietà allusions, 162, 170

Measure for Measure, 15–16, 25, 121

Menaechmi, 14

Men in Elizabethan England, 9–11

Merchant of Venice, 63–82; association of women and Jews with flesh, 64, 66; socioeconomic changes of Renaissance, 64–65, 67; relationship of marriage to male friendship, 75, 76–77, 79–80; male disguise, 74–75, 78, 188, 190–91; mutuality of lovers compared to *Romeo and Juliet*, 102

Mercutio, 101, 106–7

Merry Wives of Windsor, 176, 188

Midsummer Night's Dream, 97, 188

Miranda, 8, 177; relationship with Prospero, 174–75, 184–87

Montrose, Louis Adrian, 10–11, 207 (n. 9)

Moor as Renaissance stereotype, 13, 96–97, 130

Mother, sexuality attacked in family rejections, 17

Mother-child relationship: in *Coriolanus*, 11–12; imagery of in *Othello*, 129, 132–33, 140, 146–48; imagery of in *Lear*, 152–53; in romances, 176, 177, 179

Mother-daughter relationship, 128, 176, 179

Much Ado about Nothing, 25–28; plotters compared to Viola, 33; gender symmetry, 191; definitions of manhood, 191–92

Mutuality: tension with patriarchy in plays, 3, 6–8; defined, 4; in Elizabethan religious writing, 4–5; tension with patriarchy in Elizabethan ideals and practice, 4–6; in comedies, 6–7, 21–44, 83, 97–98, 102; in wit, 21–22, 25–28, 41; in *Much Ado*, 22–24, 25–28, 33, 42–44; in *As You Like It*, 22–24, 28–32, 42–44; iconology, 23; gender symmetry, 23, 27–28; absences of, 24–25; opposed to Petrarchism, 28–29; verbal rituals of, 30–31; image in *Masque of Hymen*, 31; emblematic mutuality in *Twelfth Night*, 34, 36–40; parodied in duel, 35; symmetry of, 39–40; requires audience imagination, 41; as private world of marriage, 46, 49, 61, 100; Portia's active capacity for, 66, 71, 72; need denied and expressed by Antonio, 68–69; emblematic in *Merchant of Venice*, 80; in *Romeo and Juliet*, 100, 101–5, 109; in *Othello*, 125, 126–28, 130, 139–40, 144, 148–49; pretense supplied by Iago, 134–35, 145;

comedy and tragedy compared, 150; in *Lear*, 151, 154, 155, 157, 160; in romances, 178, 181, 186; in medieval Catholic theory of marriage, 204 (n. 8). *See also* Pseudomutuality

Neely, Carol Thomas, 220 (n. 15)
Nelson, Benjamin, 68
Nurse, 100, 107

Old, the: stereotype of in Elizabethan England, 96–97, 221 (n. 9)
Old Shepherd, 169, 171
Oliver, 30, 192
Olivia, 36; emotional distance, 15; response to Feste, 22; self-dramatization in mourning, 32; response to Viola, 33, 193
Ophelia, 84, 95
Orlando: and emotional distance, 15; idealization of Rosalind as obstacle to mutuality, 28–29, 31–32; verbal rituals of mutuality, 30, 31; combination of mutuality and patriarchy, 42–44; definition of manhood, 191–92; response to Rosalind's androgyny, 193
Orsino, 36, 37, 40; and emotional distance, 15; self-dramatization as unrequited lover, 32–34; response to Viola's androgyny, 193
Othello, 8, 84–87, 125–49; stereotype of Moor, 13, 96–97, 130; conflict between emo-

tion and control, 13, 128–32, 136, 138, 140, 144–45, 148; suspicion of female pretense, 86; manhood as violence, 126, 136, 145, 146, 147–48, 195; as outsider, 133–34; animal and dirt imagery, 137–38; compared with romance heroes, 165–67, 180–81
Othello, 84–87, 125–49; mother-child imagery, 129, 132–33, 140, 146–48
Outsiders: in *Merchant of Venice*, 64–66, 74, 213 (n. 11); in *Othello*, 96–97, 133–34. *See also* Actors: otherness of; Jews, attitudes to; Moor as Renaissance stereotype; Old, the; Women: as other

Pandarus, 110, 111–12, 113, 116, 117
Parent-child relations: in *Coriolanus*, 8, 11–12; in Elizabethan England, 9–10, 159; in *Lear*, 12–13, 150–59; in *Comedy of Errors*, 13–14; in *As You Like It*, 14, 31, 43; in *Taming of the Shrew*, 55–56; in romances, 169–87 passim, 198, 200–201
Park, Clara Claiborne, 7
Patriarchy: tension with mutuality in plays, 3, 6–8, 19, 42–44, 104–5, 127–28, 130, 139, 181, 183–86; in *Taming of the Shrew*, 45, 46–47, 49, 50–51, 54–62; relation of young to old, 54–55, 62, 221 (n. 9); association of women with flesh, 66; control of women's marriage choice, 71; and

alliance against women's deception, 134; and images of women as object, animal, property, 137–38, 144; in *Lear*, 150–52, 154, 156, 160; in romances, 177

Patroclus, 121, 195

Paulina, 8, 166–67, 171; strength of, 176–77; cross-gender imagery, 198

Perdita, 8, 17, 171, 176

Pericles, 167, cross-gender imagery, 172, 175; passivity, 173, 186; importance of family ties, 175, 184; physicality of language in recognition scene, 178–79

Pericles, 167, 172, 173, 175, 178–79, 184, 186; mother-daughter relationship, 176–79; threat of private bonds, 185; absence of mother, 186

Petrarchan love poetry, 23, 25, 28, 29; and imagery in *Troilus*, 116

Petruchio, 6–7, 45–62; games of pretense, 47, 48, 49–50, 51; creates private language with Kate, 52–55, 60–61

Phebe, 15, 193

Pisanio, 166

Plato, 38

Playfulness: in comedies, 6–7; in *As You Like It*, 28–30; in *Taming of the Shrew*, 45–60; in *Merchant of Venice*, 77–80; and sexuality, 144–45

Polixenes, 170–71, 174, 180, 183

Portia, 7, 70–81 passim; and mutuality, 63, 66, 71–72; as outsider, 64, 66, 74–75, 79; casket scene, 71–72; male disguise, 74–75, 190–91; ring episode, 77–81; skepticism about hyperbole, 154

Posthumus: suspicion of women, 165–67; repentance, 167; as warrior, 167–68; dream vision, 169–70, 174, 182; endurance, 172–73; relationship with Imogen, 178, 181–83

Poyntz, Sir Nicholas, 21

Pregnancy, imagery of, 224 (n. 7); in *Troilus*, 120; in *Cymbeline*, 171–72, 174, 176, 181, 186, 198

Princess (*Love's Labor's Lost*), 97

Privacy in marriage: in modern nuclear family, 46–47, 125; in *Taming of the Shrew*, 49, 54, 60–61; architectural history, 61

Problem comedies: bed trick, 15; emotional distance, 16; mutuality, 25

Prospero: forgiveness, 160, 169, 179–80; tears, 169; non-violent power, 173, 184; relationship with Miranda, 174–75, 185–87

Proteus, 15, 24, 105

Pseudo-mutuality: *Twelfth Night*, 34–35; *Othello*, 134–35, 145

Puritanism: and ideals of marriage, 4–5, 61, 80; and theater, 204 (n. 7)

Queen (*Cymbeline*), 185, 186

Rabkin, Norman, 18, 44
Raymond, Saint, 64
Recognition scenes, 36–40,
    178–81
Regan, 17, 97, 152–54, 221
    (n. 9)
Richard II, 76
Rilke, Rainer Maria, 39
Romances, 6, 13; women in, 8,
    176–78; mutuality and patri-
    archy in, 8, 181, 183–86;
    transformation of emotion/
    control conflict, 16, 186–87;
    childbirth imagery, 18, 171–
    72, 176, 181, 198; genders
    less polarized in, 164, 166–
    77, 198; male violence paro-
    died or less glamorized in,
    164, 166–68, 186; men in,
    164–75, 178–87, 197–98;
    mistrust of women com-
    pared with *Othello*, 165–67;
    male interest in children,
    170–71, 173–75, 183; limita-
    tions on control, 173–74;
    mother-daughter relations,
    176, 179; physicality of rec-
    ognition scenes, 178–81;
    suspicion of women as
    childbearers, 181–83; pri-
    macy of generativity, 198–
    200
Roman comedy, 23
Romeo, 99–109, 194
Romeo and Juliet, 99–109, 122–23;
    mutual idealization in, 31;
    compared with *Taming of the
    Shrew*, 108–9; compared with
    Troilus, 109, 113, 115, 117;
    mother-daughter bond, 176;
    gender polarization, 194

Rosalind: combination of patri-
    archy and mutuality in, 7,
    42–44; disguise, 14–15, 18,
    23, 190, 192–93; draws Or-
    lando into mutuality, 18, 28–
    32; lover and jester, 22; com-
    pared with Viola's technique
    in disguise, 33–34; links boys
    and women, 199
Rosaline (*Love's Labor's Lost*), 25
Rosaline (*Romeo and Juliet*), 100–
    101

Saint-Exupéry, Antoine de, 51
Sebastian (*Twelfth Night*), 35; as-
    sociates tears with women,
    16, 191; idealized friendship
    as mutuality, 34; recognition
    scene with Viola, 36–40;
    gender symmetry, 191
Self-sacrifice, 63–65, 68, 74
Seneca, 80
Sex: and medieval Catholic
    theology, 64, 132, 212 (n. 8);
    in ring scene of *Merchant of
    Venice*, 77–79; as violence,
    100, 112; as mutuality, male
    dominance, and male sub-
    mission to passion, 144–45
Sex roles. *See* Gender, imagery
    of; Gender as theatrical role;
    Gender crossing, imagery of;
    Gender polarization; Gender
    symmetry; Manhood as con-
    trol; Manhood as violence;
    Women
Shakespeare, William, life of,
    200–201
Shaw, George Bernard, 56, 211
    (n. 23)
Shylock: as outsider, 64, 65–67,

79, 153, 214 (n. 31); in trial scene, 72–73, 74–76, 80–81

Skura, Meredith, 170

Sly, Christopher, 45–46, 51

Sonnets, 16, 28, 69

Stone, Lawrence: on disruption in Elizabethan marriage, 5; on emotional control, 8–10, 12, 186; on kneeling to parents, 159; reviews of, 205 (n. 16); on hostility to the old, 221 (n. 9)

Symposium, 38

Taming of the Shrew, 6–7, 45–62; contrast with Merchant of Venice, 79–80; contrast with Lear in treatment of female pretense, 152; disguise of page, 188–89; genders not polarized, 191

Tears: associated with women, 16–17, 96, 157–58; associated with theater, 96; in Othello, 145–46; "holy" and "fellowly" in romances, 169; and boy actor, 189; men in comedies, 191

Tempest: forgiveness in, 160, 179–80; power in, 173, 184; old regenerated by young, 174–75; assertiveness of Miranda, 177; physicality of recognition scene, 179–80; relinquishment of private bonds in, 185–87; female disguise of Ariel, 188

Thaisa, 176, 178–79

Theseus, 97

Thomas, Keith, 221 (n. 9)

Touchstone, 22, 31, 43

Tragedies: women in, 7–8, 83–84, 92, 95–96; emotion and control in, 11–13; men (tragic heroes) in, 83, 84, 92, 95, 164, 186–87; concern about manhood, 194–97, 200

Tranio, 46, 51, 56–57

Troilus, 99–100, 110–19, 194–95

Troilus and Cressida, 99–100, 110–19; compared with Romeo and Juliet, 112, 113, 115, 117, 121; compared to problem comedies, 115, 121; suspicion of women, 117; imagery of gender and gender crossing, 111–12, 119, 120, 195; women associated with weakness, 194–95

Trumbach, Randolph, 9, 205 (n. 16)

Turner, Victor, 42

Twelfth Night: emotion and control in, 15; mutuality in, 22–24, 32–44; male disguise in, 188

Two Gentlemen of Verona, 97; absence of mutuality, 24; male disguise, 188

Usury, 64, 67, 72

Valentine, 24

Vincentio (Measure for Measure), 25

Vincentio (Taming of the Shrew), 51, 54–55

Viola: combination of patriarchy and mutuality, 7, 42; disguise, 15, 23; lover and jester, 22; draws Orsino and Olivia into verbal mutuality, 33–34; parodic mutuality of duel, 35; recognition scene, 36–40, 178; kinship with Feste, 93; described as androgynous, 193–94

Volumnia, 8, 11, 12

Weissman, Philip, 94

Whitefield, Ann (*Man and Superman*), 56, 211 (n. 23)

Widow (*Taming of the Shrew*), 57–58

Winter's Tale, 165; emotion and control in, 16, 186; suspicion of women in, 166–67; penance and tears, 169; relation between old and young, 169–71, 174; cross-gender imagery, 171; patience in, 173; women in, 176–78; physicality of reunion, 180–81; male envy of childbearing, 183–84

"Woman": polarized image of, 111, 153, 177, 218 (n. 12); associations of, 198–99

Women: in Elizabethan England, 4–6, 9, 204 (n. 12); controversial literature about, 6; associated with child-rearing, 10, 146–47, 152; associated with emotion (passion, flesh), 10, 66, 93, 95–97, 199; suspicion of female sexuality, 17, 93, 155–56; as other, 66, 93, 96, 215 (n. 40), 216 (n. 8); suspicion of female pretense, 83, 84, 86, 92, 95; compared to actors, 83, 92–98, 99; compared to audience, 83–92, 96–98; kinship with fool, 93; dependent on pleasing others, 93–94, 95, 121–22; suspicion of, 99, 115, 117, 164–66; associated with weakness, 100, 107, 111; as property, object, 104–5, 110, 112, 117–18, 121, 137–39, 214 (n. 26). *See also* Gender, imagery of; Gender crossing, imagery of; Gender polarization; Gender symmetry

Wrightson, Keith, 6

Young, Richard, 28